BOY

BOY

A Woman Listening to Men and Boys

Hathaway Barry

Cover photo: Wynn Bullock, *Child on a Forest Road*
Interior photos: page xi, unknown; page 8, Olivier Follmi; page 18, Michelle Feileacan; pages 40 and 308, Wazari Wazir; page 72, ©Ana Stewart 2007, "Mutum," Gloria Films; page 86, Skip O'Donnell; pages 132 and 230, Heather Frandsen; page 256, Mara Blom Schantz; page 276, Miranda Medina; page 346, Ina Von; page 359, Sandro Michahelles

ISBN 978-0-692-59254-0

To order copies of this book:
www.listeningtomen.com

9 8 7 6 5 4 3 2
FIRST PRINTING

12/2018

To boys and men everywhere
and to everyone
who cares about them

∼

Contents

"I did not come here to solve things, but to sing
and have you sing with me."

—PABLO NERUDA

Introduction

Everywhere I go now, I see men differently.

In the middle of putting together this book, I began to feel overwhelmed by all the stories I'd heard listening to so many men and boys. I wanted to go to the desert, where there is less of everything. I wanted to plunk my body down in the quiet of a Utah wilderness canyon. I got in my old Subaru and drove for two days on Highway 50, "the loneliest highway in America." I had been living with these guys for several years and I was tired. I wanted to be held by the space and stillness of wild beauty. I needed to sleep out where the stars go all the way down to the ground.

As it happened, I pulled in late to a motel in a tiny town in Nevada. The parking lot was filled with pickup trucks. In the night I was awakened by cries of anguish from down the hall. I sat up in bed and listened through the thin walls. At the "continental" breakfast the next morning I was the only female.

The next day, after a particularly long open stretch of two-lane highway, my car died. I coasted down the hill into Milford, Utah. A couple of men stopped to see if they could help. One called the nearest auto shop. Several more came along and joined forces to push my poor, tired car around the corner and down the street to Mike's Tire & Oil. While Mike had a look, I was given donuts and kindness and a t-shirt. Mike phoned another man who then towed it an hour and a half to the nearest big town. And there, again, it was men who were eventually able to put it back together so I could be on my way. I drove off with my refurbished engine and my souvenir t-shirt, a gift from Mike's featuring, on the back, a scantily clad babe riding a spark plug and the slogan, "Let us service you."

When I at last arrived in the wilderness I roamed about, following one dirt road after another, searching for a place to rest. I was lost. I didn't know what to do with all the stories I'd been told. I kept driving deeper and deeper into the desert. Well over 90 degrees, no shade. On one long road to nowhere, I got stuck trying to turn around. Wearily, I climbed out and squatted down next to the front wheel, now deep in red sand, leaned back against the hubcap, defeated, and chugged water. Lots and lots of water.

Listening to all of these boys' and men's voices, I had lost my own. What was I doing out here, alone, trying to get comfortable in the middle of nowhere?

Chased from one potential campsite to another by no-see-ums, mosquitoes, a five-foot snake, and wind that tossed my papers and post-its about, I finally settled down in the shade of a desert-varnished sandstone wall.

I had carried with me a brown paper bag full of brightly colored files. Transcripts, edits, scribbled notes—the distilled voices of the men and boys. I began to go through the bag. First, I pulled out the list of names of all the boys and men I had interviewed. Slowly, I made my way through, one by one, from youngest to oldest, stopping a long while to remember. I wish I could find a way to bring alive for you how it was to sit with each of them. Their faces, their voices, their unique ways of expressing themselves, their body language and gestures. The joy it was to have the chance to just listen, as best I could, without agenda. How the light was, the time of day, where we met, what we ate, how lovely it was to look into their eyes and feel what was alive in them. It was one of the more wonderful things I've had a chance to do.

Seeing their faces in my mind's eye, a wave of feeling and affection overcame me—their openness, their trust, their willingness to participate in the continuing education of a curious woman and whatever this project might turn out to be.

Their generosity of time and spirit, in many cases to a total stranger. As I made my way through the list, tears began to roll down my cheeks with the growing awareness in my body of how things are for them. Or maybe, too, my sadness at not having let it in sooner. Being a man is a role, but this role it seems they're not allowed to take off.

In the vast stillness of that canyon, in the company of unconcerned wild desert creatures, as I got quieter and quieter, what I heard, underneath all the pressure of having to "be a man" was vulnerability—tender feelings of fear and sadness. *Human* feelings, not particular to males. The plain fact of being a human being, and the courage and dignity it is, for all of us, finding our way from birth to death.

~

I have loved and appreciated and felt exasperated by men in many ways—father, brothers, relatives, playmates, friends, lovers, mentors, colleagues, husband, ex-husband, son, long-term partners. I know the goodness of men. And yet, after more than a half century of living with them, I realize I am still mystified by much of their behavior.

There have been moments when I might have been tempted to give up on men all together. Having a son keeps me hostage to the world of men. It's a kind of hostage I want to be. We're here such a brief time. I don't want to miss anything.

Here's how it began.

In my later fifties I fell in love again. I felt an inexplicable depth of connection with this man. He was the most open and vulnerable man I'd loved *and* the most elaborately defended. So tenderly close and then . . . unreachable. My heart was scrambled. He didn't seem to be aware of his behavior or how hard it was to be on the other end. And it would recur. It was the most confounding experience I'd had. I'd wake up in the middle of the night, pierced with anguish. What do I not understand here? In the midst of heartache and confusion, stillness found me, and the word "BOY" appeared in my mind's eye. I had no idea what that was about, but I trusted it.

Writing is one of my ways of letting things sort themselves out. So I went to the wilderness to listen for poems. Not much luck. It dawned on me I needed to listen to *actual* men. To see what I could learn about some of the puzzling ways of relating I'd experienced. What's at the heart of it? And what's my part in it?

What if no one's "wrong"?   Or "right"?

I am a woman living in a culture primarily thought up by men. I have carried a boy child inside me. He was part of my body. I get it that it's *human* being first. And yet, because of his gender, my son has had to navigate a whole other world than that of his sister. I wanted to know more about this world. I wanted to know what happens to boys growing up? Maybe I would need to listen differently if I wanted to find out.

I didn't want to close my heart. To me, at this time on this earth, it seems essential to stay open and embrace what I don't know and don't understand.

So I came closer and listened more deeply.

Not knowing how to reach the disappearing man, I started asking questions of other men. I began with trusted friends. And their friends. I interviewed many men I did not know, but almost no one who was unknown to either me or to someone I know. The interviews all came from circles of trust. I felt passed along from one warm hand to another. In this way, a quality of openness and candor was created that perhaps might not have been otherwise possible. If there was *any* hesitation on the part of the interviewee, I did not proceed. Complete confidentiality and anonymity were assured. I've identified the boys and men only by their age (at the time of the interview) in years or decades and have sometimes changed specific identifying details. Some men chose to keep their names. The interviews lasted at least two hours and often much longer (even up to six hours!). The only exception was the pre-teens, who said what they had to say in about an hour and went out to play.

With each interview I adapted the fledgling questions and learned from my mistakes. If I heard a word or theme over and over I would create an additional question—sometimes at the suggestion of one of the interviewees. When women friends heard what I was doing, they had questions of their own—some of which I added to the list. The questions refined and reshaped themselves. I wasn't listening for anything in particular. I was just listening, as best I could. The more than two dozen varying questions were entry points, not a questionnaire.

I've listened a lot in my life—working with kids, especially in the outdoors and, for many years, as a mediator. But I am not a social scientist or an anthropologist. I am not a journalist. I didn't set out to write a book, and this is not a survey or representative sample. I just wanted to listen without blame or judgment to how it is for men, a whole half of the human species I knew less about. I wanted to hear their honest human stories, without gloss or performance.

I had a freedom as an interviewer. I was no one in particular in relation to these boys and men. Not wife or lover, colleague, boss or employee. I was just curious.

Sometimes, in the midst of an interview, I was aware how rare this kind of time with another human being is. Like when we first fall in love or when a child is born or a loved one is dying. Clear, uninterrupted time to simply listen.

We usually met wherever the interviewee lived. Sometimes we met in my home and, a few times, in a quiet corner of a public place. Several interviews occurred on the phone, but this was usually only with men I already knew or a follow up to an in-person interview. We often laughed; sometimes cried. We had a good time. One man in his late sixties told me, "Boys want to be outside running around. Not in a classroom." So we had our interview walking. He said it felt more comfortable.

The more than eighty men and boys I interviewed (and dozens of mini-interviews wherever I'd go—people I'd never met on airplanes, on trains, in restaurants, waiting rooms, in a tow truck, at the gym etc.) range in age from 9 to 94 years. They are men of color, white men, gay and transgendered men, straight men, married men, bachelors, brothers and fathers. They are all Americans—African Americans, Asian Americans, Latino Americans, Caucasian Americans, Native Americans. Most now live on the west or east coasts. There's one Canadian. They are Jewish, Christian, Buddhist, Muslim, atheist, agnostic, and come from a variety of educational backgrounds. Men who have fathers and men who don't. Men who have lots of money and men who have very little. And these are some of the kinds of work they have been engaged in:

Special Ed teacher, painter, investigative journalist, spy, boat builder, magazine publisher, emergency room nurse, electrician, community organizer, small business owner, activist, surfer, sculptor, student, EMT paramedic, tile setter, fireman, real estate developer, Zen teacher, athlete, university CFO, musician, Marine, mortuary pilot, computer programmer, chiropractor, psychotherapist, writer, filmmaker, environmentalist, bookstore manager, editor, engineer, contractor, tow truck operator, psychologist, baseball player, broker, actor, air traffic controller, vision quest leader, doctor, university president, environmental studies professor, English professor, pool cleaner, children's theater director, construction worker, tech company CEO, waiter, musician, magazine publisher, sailor, playwright, Iraq vet, Vietnam vet, WWII vet, violence prevention coordinator, high school teacher, gang member, wildfire fighter, farrier, global hedge fund CEO, medical school professor, plumber, parent, poet, medic, attorney, artist, author, sound engineer, stage hand, choral director, immigration judge, Air Force technician, FBI agent, substance abuse counselor, handyman, prosecutor, naturalist, stone mason, landscape architect, foundation program officer, international tour guide, tantra educator, IT consultant and organizational consultant.

I started interviewing men who were in midlife and then I began to be curious about younger men and boys. Later, I interviewed much older men, trying to listen to men from each decade, though the 50- and 60-year-olds have a bit more than their share of pages here. I purposely did not ask the men directly about their work lives, since this is traditionally how men have self-identified. Nor did I ask directly about their sex lives, though this, too, naturally sometimes came up.

Occasionally, I would catch myself wondering—what am I doing listening to all these males when I was someone who had muttered, more than once, about being tired of always listening to men, and men not listening in return? I really didn't know. I just knew I had to do it.

~

Tucked into a canyon, this time in Arizona in the guest house of friends, I spread out my heaps of papers in a circle around me. I had no idea what to do with them. They covered the floor and the furniture. My friend brought another six-foot fold out table. That too filled. I sat down in the middle. What now? Okay, guys—What are you saying? And after a while I found myself moving about putting pages together. So many piles. So many voices. They stayed with me for years, wherever I went.

I wanted to share with you the privilege I had listening to these boys and men, so I kept sorting and sifting and put together this book.

There is a slant to the stories I've selected. Although I asked a variety of questions, I've mostly chosen to share the more vulnerable responses, those perhaps less easily spoken about publicly. Or, the ones that touched me most or just felt true. Sometimes I arranged them around a question and sometimes around a theme that emerged. A chorus of voices. And I've included some longer stories.

With a deep bow of gratitude to boys and men everywhere, especially the ones who so generously shared their stories, here is some of what I heard.

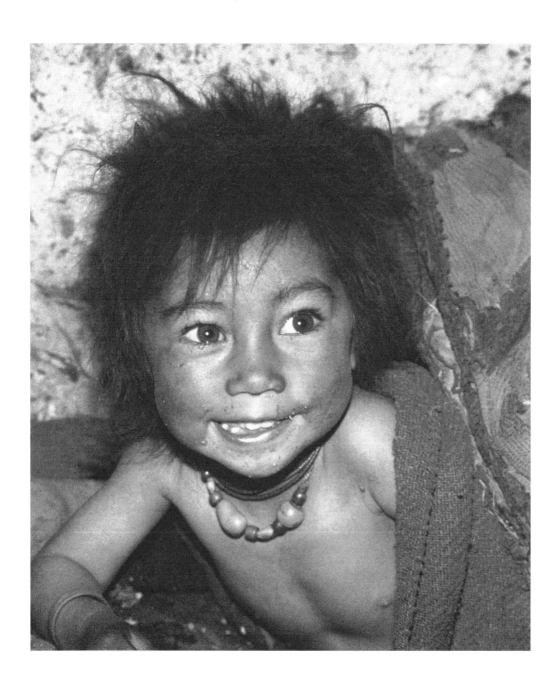

The Joy of Being a Boy

If we're not supposed to dance,
Why all this music?

— GREGORY ORR

When I was a girl growing up in the Midwest, I loved playing with boys. I was a so-called "tomboy" simply because I didn't buy into the culture's idea of "girl." I wasn't waiting for a Prince Charming to kiss me awake. Boys were my friends. Fellow human beings. We liked each other. We were pals. Equals. And then, something changed. I wanted to know about this something.

As I was setting out on this inquiry, my grown son said to me, "I challenge you to find any man who doesn't wish he had more of his 'boy' alive in him." I remember him as a boy, a child of six or so, asking, "How about I skip school and we spend the *whole day* and just talk questions? Maybe we could even do 48 hours!" And when he was eight years old, so aware of the play of life in everything, he admonished us — "I feel like everything's living but it seems like you and [his dad] don't feel that way. Grown-ups can't really feel it as much as kids. Because if you did, you'd touch the floor and [makes pushing gesture] it'd go in — 'cause it's alive, too."

My question, and one of my great pleasures, was asking these men of all ages, including a few boys as well, "What is the joy of being a boy?" Almost without exception, the men's faces lit up — their eyes brightened, their tone and body posture changed — as if a fresh breeze had suddenly slipped into the room. It was contagious. And there we were — kids together — in a kind of timeless moment. I felt allowed briefly into their boy world in a way I perhaps never had been before.

So what is the joy of being a boy?

≈

My friend Javier and I, we go down to the train track. We like to walk down the tracks. There's a big stream, so we have to put a wooden board to get across. There's this metal thing over there with tons of snakes under it. The fun part about snakes is just watching them, seeing what they do, how they eat crickets and stuff. The garden snakes we find they like to eat goldfish — live ones. I don't know how they do that, but they do.

(9 yr.)

If you take anything back far enough, it turns to mystery. Like a truck. A tree. You know?

(10 yr.)

Peeing outdoors was a favorite of mine. Shoot, I must've been like five or six, and we were at Disneyland. I had to pee bad, and my dad said just pee on this bush. Ever since then, I've been, like, yes! Peeing outside is so much better. Back to nature.

(20s)

Hiking up to the waterfalls, hanging out there, getting away with certain things — causing mischief, being a bit of a handful, rambunctious and a bit loud. There's a kind of exuberance, a jubilant excitement at every little thing. Pretending pine-cones are hand grenades, playing swords with sticks and twigs.

(20s)

Break dancing. We'd clear back all the furniture and just bump. Michael Jackson and the Beat Street soundtrack. We'd start out on top of the chair, jump up and do a little split in the air. We thought we had the coolest moves. I was eight. My brother was five.

(20s)

Playing with Tonka trucks, I had dreams of being a big machinery operator, dig-ging holes, building things, driving over things. I was fascinated by the tire tracks that a bulldozer or a tractor makes. When I had to go inside, I was a Lego fanatic.

(20s)

In the summers on my dad's land, I'd stack up dead trees and build little cabins. I made moccasins and a loincloth. That's all I'd wear. And the bow and arrows I'd made. I got to be completely free in the moment, in the mountains. Just be who I was and take off running in the field.

(30s)

Just knowing that you can make anything happen that you want to make happen — that's how I felt as a boy. Everything's good, everything's rockin' and rollin', all the planets are aligned. I was turned loose to ride up into the woods — "Get outside and go do something." I got carried back to the house several times, and helped carry other kids back — broken bones and stuff like that. But nobody ever got killed. The parents didn't have to fight the Nintendo or the computer, because none of that stuff existed. They just flat didn't want us in the house. I'd leave after lunch and not be expected back until supper. That to me was the joy of being a boy, that limitlessness.

(30s)

You can be anything, say anything, do anything without worry of repercussion. No restrictions. You can just be. Joy is kind of like one of those plants that will survive under even the most arid circumstances. No matter what.

(30s)

I remember this feeling of softness with Lucy — in her sweater or her hair or whatever. Like floating and being head over heels in love with her throughout that whole week of day camp. Then to hold her hand that night at the campfire was just like beyond. It was so amazing to be close to her. And she liked me. I was eight years old.

(40s)

I used to do it regularly as a kid — cut vines and swing from them. It's just — go for it. Something special about swinging from a grapevine rather than a rope, because it has its own little tricks. It can move in unpredictable ways. It has a life of its own.

(50s)

Pushing out into the world with bravery. You feel you can finally handle this power that you have connection to as a boy—almost a birthright. You shoot a gun for the first time, or you drive a car for the first time, or fall in love or flirt for the first time. All those things are terrifying, but you're learning how, and learning what your power is.

(50s)

My only escape from what was going on at home was the physical. Running about, finding a new swimming hole, a new river, a new creek. Everything's fun, every rock, every stone, every tree, every canyon. The freedom, the carefree-ness, a sense of no time. Anything can happen. Holding your breath is magic. Everything is magic.

(50s)

Bikes, bikes, bikes! Riding with no hands, and being gone all day and no one knowing where I was. The feel of the wind on my face.

(60s)

It's just like . . . you can do everything.

(60s)

Running, that was my secret. No matter what else happened, I could run like the wind. It's pure and running fast is like flying. When I got older, I wanted to write like the wind and love like the wind.

(60s)

Where I grew up, if you had a baseball glove and a bike, you were fully equipped for life. During the summer, you knew you're playing baseball from nine to one. You knew you were swimming at the Winfield Corporation swimming pool from one to four. After dinner you were playing baseball again from six to nine. That was your day. I wish I'd known what a gift that was.

(60s)

Part of the joy of boys is that you get to play together. It was uncensoringly okay to be close. Then adolescence shows up. Game changer.

(60s)

No pressure and no expectation to be anything other than who we were. We'd be down in the swamps before the sun came up, drinking coffee and smoking rum-soaked Crook cigars, just being part of the group. That early morning beauty was incredible.

(70s)

I had asthma as a child, so I was not up to the competitive thing. Hank, my buddy for ninety years, he and I—we hid in our basement. We'd build up forts together. In the back of our property, there was land and we dug caves—secret caves, torture chambers and all that. We had tree houses and coasters with wheels way out the sides. We'd go down a road, jump and crash.

(90s)

One of the great things I remember is climbing into bed with my dad and mom on Sunday morning. He would read the funny papers to me, and also subject himself to an incessant question-and-answer period. I was most anxious to learn a lot of things, and he would take the pains to tell me how things worked. I was an only child until I got to be thirteen and my little sister was born.

(90s)

More of the joys I heard:

Getting *really* dirty, a bath maybe once a week, jumping off roofs, peeing in the gutter to see how big the arc went, having so much energy, wild, out of control, yelling from the tops of trees and scaring my mother half to death, sleeping on the roof and counting shooting stars, not having to worry about being stupid, feeling comfortable around girls, whimsy, softness and lovingness, taking clocks and watches apart and not being scolded for it, being forgiven, becoming stronger, discovering sexuality, hanging out, being goofy, naughty, nutty, playful, spontaneous, spunky, sensitive, silly, playing pranks, no problems, no sense of time, having a grandfather who taught me to fish and was a real pal, getting into trouble, making spectacular mistakes, not worrying what people are thinking, not so much thinking, planning, seriousness — just alive!

~

After they shared their stories, I would often sense wistfulness. A look out the window. A long pause. A clearing of the throat. As if to savor . . . and then, shake it off.

What happens to the aliveness of these boys?

I sensed that it isn't only that they get older and have more responsibilities and have to make a living and find their way in the world. None of the men I spoke with wanted to be a boy again. They *liked* being men. They just wanted to have more of that spontaneity, spirited delight and open-hearted joy in their present daily lives, whatever their age.

When I would talk with other moms about this, a common sadness came up. How hard it is to entrust this vulnerable aliveness, this openness, to the dominant male culture. We all remembered the private trembly feeling the first time we had to let our sons (at maybe 5 or 6 years old) go to the public restroom alone.

Looking out on the horizon of what "being a man" seemed to be all about, I wondered about my young son — how will he keep his tender heart alive? The vulnerability so essential for feeling what what we're feeling and feeling what someone else is feeling, too. For caring and connection. Well-being. How will he keep his joy?

I

Some Challenges of "Being a Man"

"Do not believe in anything simply because
it is spoken about and revered by many."

— BUDDHA

Shaping Ourselves to Fit the World

"Nobody really knows what it is to be a man."

Giving birth to my son blew my mind. It was my first time. Who *is* this?

I asked our midwife what she saw in common at all births. "If no interference—two things: complete openness of the woman giving birth and complete openness of the newborn's face." This is how we all start, yet somehow we get lost in the plot of becoming somebody, longing all the while to simply be who we are—open.

Boys (like girls) arrive in the world whole and unfettered human beings, and then they are asked to be something. To "be a man." What is this something? What does it *take*? I was curious about the traditional concept of "being a man" and how it plays out in the world.

I realized I haven't really thought about "being a woman." It seemed to just happen naturally. A bodily experience. The old assumption was every woman wants to get married, be a mother and raise children. The Feminist movement gave us permission to tell the truth, explore more of who we are and experiment with some "male" traits. But what about guys?

As these boys, wide open to a world they know nothing about, set out on the adventure of life, what is the message they're receiving about this world and their place in it? How are they welcomed? What stories are they told to lighten or burden their way?

I wanted to know about that journey, so the next question I asked these guys was—What were the stories you were told, explicitly or not, by your fathers, your mothers, by your culture—about what it is to "be a man"? Who were, or are, you *supposed to be*?

∼

A more responsible person who has a job and shaves and stuff. Also, you can't, like, have seven girlfriends. You have to have one. And you have to know—you don't *have* to, but we should—know how to drive.

(10 yr.)

Exhausting!

In a satisfying way. Like when we go to the airport, my dad is carrying all the bags and he looks so strong. Even though it might be tiring and hard work, I think if I do that one day, I will enjoy helping others, and being, I guess, the man of the house. I don't want to say no, because it's our job. And it's so cool to be the one who knows everything and can help someone in a down situation or with their homework or when a girl likes them or something.

There's a lot of expectations on guys as you get older. There's an expectation to be close to perfect.

(11 yr.)

My dad says how to be a true man is having to do work without being told, and being tough about everything, and to forget playtime or going outside with friends if you have to do something like schoolwork. My mom says to be a man is to respect women and their needs, and to put them in front, like if you have a woman in the car, you open their door and let her go in first.

(12 yr.)

Well, I'm supposed to grow up to be responsible for people. You're kind of the stronger sex. You're the one who, like, takes charge.

(13 yr.)

One of the messages from society about being a man is not just that we're allowed but we're expected to be violent. Men should have it in them if need be.

(20s)

My dad's example was, generally, that of providing. But also, interestingly, lots of expression of affection and love and encouragement. Positive emotion was readily expressed. Negative or difficult emotions were more swept under the rug.

What society taught me about being a man was totally different — men definitely shouldn't show weakness, shouldn't cry. Men are tough, men get the job done, men are superior, and not just to a woman. Coming from white middle class America, you could say white middle class men are superior, period. Men should strive for success and the measure of success comes through wealth and material things. You know, beautiful wife and a big house and the whole thing.

I grew up with the archetype of the masculine as mysterious, strong, muscular, slightly frightening but intriguing, handsome, dark, dangerous and powerful. Powerful meaning that the man by himself is physically powerful and can get what he needs to get done, even by force if needed. Or he is capable of making things happen, creating something out of nothing, or even that he's dangerous. Also powerful in the sense of being able to accomplish things and have influence in the world.

From my mom the message was maybe what it is to be a *good* man. And that, perhaps, good men are not easy to find. Something I got from both of my mom and my dad was kindness — that it's totally good and right for a male to be kind to others, which is total polar opposite of what I think society taught.

(20s)

In my generation there's a crisis of manhood. The old model doesn't work. Most of the guys I know feel like they're still boys, or at least act like it. People in their twenties now are sort of in extended adolescence. Even most people well into their thirties, when I interact with them, I don't feel the solidity I used to associate with manhood. It's like there's not a center of gravity. When I was five or so, somebody my dad's age, which is almost the age I am now, was in a completely different category.

My mom and my sister both go for hard, manly men. When I was in my early twenties I remember not understanding, because it was like they had a double standard. When they were talking to me about my qualities, talking about women, they'd be yeah, you should be able to get any women you want because you're so great. Because they're my sister and my mother! And my mom was in this really shitty marriage with this guy who's a total asshole — but from an external point of view he was very much a man's man. I was trying to line up those two versions of the truth.

(20s)

If you step outside of the man box, one of the challenges you face is being ridiculed or chastised, and having to face the other men that are challenged by you stepping out of the man box. The other thing is being responsible for things that you don't do. So if I walk down the street and a guy says, "You stupid ass bitch" and slaps a lady, I feel like by not stepping in, I'm giving him an okay.

(20s)

I wasn't told a story about being a man. There were very, very few role models in my life. One of my grandfathers, a businessman, tried to instill in me that I had to be what he wanted me to be in order to be a success. I couldn't play; I couldn't be frivolous. When I was seven, he took me into a stockbroker, cashed in a couple of savings bonds and I picked two stocks. Oh, and he gave me like a 300-page book on how to invest.

My dad wasn't an absentee father; it was just he worked all the time. And he had a lot of emotional challenges himself. My parents were not a very healthy couple, at all. I remember seeing them kiss once in my entire life — when I was sixteen years old and they went into couples counseling. I had to run out of the house because I thought I was going to vomit — it was so nauseatingly upsetting because it was so outside of the norm for me. I was used to them screaming, hating each other.

There was very little adult instruction from anyone in what being a boy or a man was about. There was one kid in my neighborhood who went to a Catholic school who would talk about the first time he had sex-ed class. I remember the story he told, and I realize now he was totally making it up. But at least he was talking. It was so gripping to me. I was ten or eleven years old.

The first time my dad ever said anything to me about sex, I was seventeen or eighteen. I already had a girlfriend. He just looked at me and said, "Don't do it in the house." "Shit, Dad, you should have told me that like a month ago." I was starving for information.

(30s)

My parents divorced when I was four years old. I learned about my dad through my mom. The message was—"Don't be your dad." It was confusing. I had a lot of shame and guilt. Had to join a men's group of older men to learn about being a man.

(30s)

I guess the story I've heard and understood is the male has to be an all-around perfect being—infallible in every way. Like you have to be emotionally totally sensitive and accommodating and a good listener and all that, and then you also have to be rigid and hard and a good moneymaker. You can't be angry ever. That does feel like a fraud. I attempt to live up to that and it's totally impossible. I can't do it! So I find myself sometimes being untrue or being a level of falseness in trying to maintain that face, that image of trying to not be angry ever. I guess I've just felt that there's never an opportunity to really release or be upset.

It's overwhelming. Even in my dad's generation that sense of being a man was kind of lost. Like what was the role? My dad was totally into doing the household work and building our house and providing for all those needs, but he didn't provide very well financially. My mom felt like he really didn't live up to his part of the bargain.

She was the main breadwinner and would have liked more equal participation. My dad was essentially my mom. My mom would have liked to have been the parent to stay home with me more. It didn't work out that way. They split up.

(30s)

I feel like I was raised more like a woman. I don't know how to be an alpha male. I feel like I need to learn to be more of an asshole—tromp over people and not care—if I want to be successful.

(30s)

My dad was the classic male. Stubborn, spoke in absolutes, always thought he was right, wasn't willing to compromise or listen very often. He accepted me fairly easily for some weird reason. Maybe because it was San Francisco, and he knew gay people didn't have three heads and weren't crazy.

(40s)

The idea of what it is to be a man just felt very limiting to me. It was sort of jostling for power and who could be the alpha male at any given time and I didn't like that. I thought it was a lot of work. I found theater in high school. It was great 'cause that's where the sort of more fluid boys went. They weren't as concerned about or interested in being confined by what America thinks of as male.

(40s)

My mom had a broader definition of what was okay to be as a man. She gave me a little baby doll to play with and take care of. I had a chest of drawers next to my bed and kept the baby in the bottom drawer.

(40s)

I was taught you can do almost anything you want, but make sure you do what you say you're going to do.

(40s)

There was no older guy around. Once, I had to wear a tie, and I was too old to get away with a clip-on. I had to go down to our downstairs neighbor. "Teach me how to tie a tie." Embarrassing. As I was going into puberty, I didn't have an uncle or a friend of the family or anybody I could talk with about being a guy, or about hormonal things and girls. I felt like, "Wow, I have to navigate this all on my own."

(40s)

Take care of business. Take care of family. Go to work. Do what's right by your country. All my family are vets. If my country says, "You go," you don't ask questions. You go. It was not okay to get food stamps or not do what you needed to do.

(50s)

Being a man was about work. I grew up on a farm so there was plenty of it. I had a lot of freedom. My dad's way of teaching about sex was brief, simple, direct. He took me to watch the stallion mount one of the mares. His rules were equally brief, simple, direct: Don't hurt yourself. Don't hurt anyone else. And go have fun. The door is locked at midnight, so don't bother coming home.

He told me "I don't care what you do in life as long as it makes you happy and you do your best." He asked his sons *not* to be farmers. My mother was English and wanted me to be a gentleman with proper manners, treating people with respect.

One of my grandfathers was one of the sweetest, kindest, most compassionate people I've ever known. He had a hunched back from working, and missing fingers. The worst thing he ever said was, "Well, ain't that a corker!"

(50s)

The story is, get good grades, go to college, be financially successful. End of story. The only story.

(50s)

Men are given the message that we need to know and it's not okay to be vulnerable and ask for help. So we develop strategies for faking it. Fake it till you make it, you know? Then, we need to perpetuate the lie and the myth. We become our myth and story and are afraid to open up—to be honest and real. It's a house of cards

(50s)

I didn't know faggot meant gay until I moved to California in my 20s. I thought it meant un-cool, weak. I had no idea. I called my brother. "Did you know faggot meant gay?" "Well, yeah." And so, right over my head.

I think it's about vulnerability.

So what is the derogatory connotation? And why are men so afraid of it? Honestly, down to the core, I don't understand it. The best I could offer is—if I'm gay, then I'm not a man. It's a black and white zone. If you don't fuck women frequently, you're not a man. And to not be a man means—it's not just a social contract—it means you don't have a right to exist or belong.

The word has to be derogatory because it's the only way to keep it away from you. Because if it's me, then I'm not this other thing—"being a man"—wherein I find all my safety.

A lot of my feminine was pummeled out of me from the way I grew up.

(50s)

There was such a lack of father models. No father map. That's why I sought out a guru. There was a hole.

(50s)

One of the things that fascinated me as a kid growing up was the smell of my dad. He had an upper dresser drawer that he had arranged in a certain way with his belt, his cufflinks, his handkerchiefs, and all that stuff. I used to love to look at that. As a boy, I wanted to know, how does the guy do this?

(50s)

From my dad, I learned that men are ignorant, pushy, emotional infants. They have one emotion—anger. I learned he was a jerk, and then he died. I was with him on his deathbed. I didn't try to guide him, or help him transition. I didn't buy into any of that crap, and he didn't have to take care of me. We were just two souls in this incarnation, and one of us was passing. We just sat with each other. It was such a blessing. He let me be with him. Extraordinary. I learned something about being a man then—that the man is just a patina, and underneath that is the soul.

(50s)

My family wasn't Quaker, but I went to Quaker schools. Quakers have very simple principles, which is why I think they worked for me because it's not complicated.

Just two things. There's a spark of good in all mankind. They actually say "mankind." So everyone is good, not just the people you like. The other thing is that no one can teach anyone else. There's no preaching. Everyone finds their own truth. You are not given the right to tell other people what's good or bad or what they should or shouldn't do, or that you're better or they're worse. Not only can you not do it, but you're disallowed for doing it. If a kid is beating up another kid, that violates the two principles right there so extremely you don't have to go into anything else.

(50s)

My father was a very abrupt, gruff guy. And very capable of whatever it is that he did. The words were, "Do the best you can." But the real truth was, that was never good enough. But he also had a very soft side, which was not shown very much to the world. So one of the messages I got was that you need to be tough on the outside, but it was okay to be soft on the inside.

(60s)

After getting an MBA and a law degree and working in those fields, when I had a change of heart and opened a deli, my mom was horrified. My dad communicated more about being content, feeling good about yourself in relation to people you care about. Mom was always dissatisfied, showed no affection. Only my dad did.

(60s)

For both my mother and father, it was always about service. These are people who know how to love. The message was, take your gifts and dedicate them to making the world better.

With my dad, there's this wonderful roguish twinkle space — "I'm alive. I do jazz. I have this twinkle in my eyes, and people love me. Women love me, and I'm totally committed to your mother. Be alive. Don't dampen that down. Don't lose it, son." First, you have to learn your instrument well. Then, get out of the way, go into the gap and listen. Let the jazz come through you. If you've got that kind of light, playful space, you can bring it to anything. He said the only real failure in life was not going for what you really wanted to do.

The story from my mother about being a man? The first thing is to love God, and the way you do that is by loving the person in front of you. The second thing is to listen to the back side of your being, your sixth sense.

(60s)

You have to have sex as much as you can. The more you have, the more of a man you are. There are certain things you are supposed to accomplish. Because I didn't own a house, I felt emasculated—a total failure.

(60s)

Being a man is about being able to beat the pee out of other men, or kill them when you need to. That is the essence: being strong, being tough. There used to be a ditty that my physically abusive brother-in-law used to say: "First your money, then your clothes. First your wife, and then your life." That's the world men live in.

(60s)

We're not taught about being a man. We're not only unguided missiles, we're misguided missiles!

(60s)

There was one neighbor, my friend's dad, who lived on the corner. We'd always go to his house. There was something about his presence that was so genuine and soft. He wasn't hard. I remember seeing this guy and thinking, "Wow, it's just . . . something different." I guess I was taken by him because he reminded me of me. Kids are like animals. They can read people. They just know.

(60s)

My father was an athlete and a terrible sexist. That was the age when all men were, pretty much. We didn't believe that women could accomplish much outside of the kitchen. So I got that message about women, but I didn't get many positive messages from him about the way men were supposed to be.

My mom taught all her children to be kind. It had to do with being honest. It had to do with being compassionate and considerate. She was all of these things. She never ever said, "Be a man."

(70s)

My dad always found time for us, and we did things as a family a lot. He was a good dad. All my life, I've felt a sense of well-being. Just being myself. It's just natural to me. I see myself not as male or female, but human. I am what I am.

(70s)

My father taught me to be a man by dropping me off the back of the boat and yelling, "Swim!"

(70s)

Noble (20s)

"As a man in today's world you just need
to have a softer, feminine side. Otherwise,
I don't think you're going to make it."

I was five years old when we left the reservation. After that, I didn't see much of my father. Unfortunately, due to his addiction to alcohol, he wasn't necessarily able to see me with an unclouded state of mind. Sometimes things got out of hand. The scariest thing was wondering if something's going to happen and not being able to prevent it. Sort of a helpless feeling. A pot falling could set him off. I felt like I had to try to protect my mom and siblings because that would be anybody's instinct. I just wasn't sure of how to do it. I was five years old. It's a very hard job, you know.

I heard about his good side, but I didn't experience it. I was eleven or twelve when he died. In my heart, I wished he could have stayed sober and made things work. Later on in life, I realized how incredibly devastating that was. It really hurt. At one point, I had high hopes of being a fireman and a policeman—both! Maybe vicariously, even back in that early age, I was thinking I could be around somebody who could guide me, much like a father would.

I always tell people flat-out I am Tewa Pueblo, and on my mother's side I'm Swedish. When I worked in the museum at the Pueblo, the visitors would peg me as everything from Japanese to Pakistani—almost an identity crisis, but on their part, not mine.

After my father died, we moved away and I couldn't fulfill my tribal obligations or duties. A couple years later, we did return, and I went for my initiation, but I always felt like an outsider looking in. My dad and grandparents spoke a lot of our native language, but I didn't get that. Not being able to speak fluently is probably what held me back from more participation in my tribe. I'm still trying to find a way to connect with my family members by learning the language. It's one of the most quickly disappearing things for indigenous people, so I need to get that in order. I'm tempted to contact Rosetta Stone and say, hey, when are you going to have a Tewa edition?

I still go to certain ceremonial feast days at the Pueblo that I've been attending ever since I was a little baby, and I sometimes wonder, almost like a paranoia, who will accept me? I don't want to be the elephant in the room. On the other hand, I know this is my Pueblo, know in all my heart and in all my soul that I would do anything for my people and the land. Anything. But I wonder, would the favor be returned?

After my dad died, we moved back and lived next door to my grandparents. My dad's passing was definitely like 99% of what got my grandpa to stop drinking. That, and contracting diabetes. My grandpa was the most important man to me, my ultimate benchmark, my hero. We would take care of him and my grandma. Sometimes, I would chop two or three wheelbarrows full of wood a day for them. Likewise, when I went on my initiation, my granddad packed for me—the traditional meals and everything. He had seen so many things, been to many places. I would like to live a life as cultured and interesting as his. He used to be an alcoholic too, but he came out of it with a level of honesty and integrity. He wanted to change, and he did. That's what made him so great. Having lived through it, he was less apt to be judgmental. Maybe just the admittance that you're not perfect can make you perfect.

My grandfather was a healer person. He would work on people physically and energetically—a so-called "bone-setter." He would mend everything from structure to the whole person if they felt they'd been witched or whatever. They came from all over the world to visit my granddad. On average, I would say we had about twelve visitors on a daily basis. I never knew how they found the house, way back down that rutted road. My granddad kept everything he needed right there by the front door: eagle talons, hawk fans, peyote buttons. It was spiritual medicine, of course. He was something else—once in a lifetime kind of stuff. If you missed him, you missed out.

My mom has been both mom and dad for us. Losing her is my deepest fear because I've had so little family support or people I have truly felt the connection with. She's always the last to sit down to eat. When it comes to being unavailable emotionally, it's refreshing because my family doesn't do that. My mom and my sister are all about breaking cycles. Not talking about things? That's out the window. Abuse of alcohol and drugs? That's out the window. You just try to get a healthy perspective, figure out what you want, and break certain cycles, whether it be with yourself or with family issues.

Growing up, I think it was necessary to keep my feminine side alive. My mom, she has been such a mix of both male and female. Not in a weird way or anything, but to see how well both sides of her blended, it made sense. As a man, not to have a feminine side in today's world is just something I don't think you can do. Being male, you want to be seen as perfect, the alpha, the ultimate, but wearing a mask or emotional camouflage is not a great way to live. You need to have a softer side. You need to express your feelings or do whatever it is that feminine is for you.

There are a lot of pressures on a guy, to be a provider, for example. I always like to keep certain things going, whether that be firewood or meals or whatever. The place I feel safest is when I'm busy. Whether that means I'm running with my dogs or hauling water or chopping wood, it doesn't matter as long I'm focusing on something that can be my meditation for the day. It keeps me from thinking too much. At a certain point, you are going to need to make a fire, you're going to need to drink water, so you might as well get those things done.

Another pressure on guys is to have it all together. It's an unfortunate stereotype that's difficult to avoid, and isn't going to lose steam anytime soon.

I also feel a lot of pressure when it comes to substances—another stereotype. You are male, so you have your hard liquor, your this, your that. It's strange being pressured into something that won't even give you benefit. I've been around twenty-two years, and I'm not going to start ruining my life now. I see so many people going down that self-destructive path. It helps to see it from the third-person perspective. When you're locked in, you can't understand what's happening. But looking from the outside, you can say, "Okay, well, I don't want to go through that." It's always harder to see our own self—that level of honesty.

≈

As a Native American, when you meet somebody who's rude or says disparaging things about your culture, you have to take the high road and find an eloquent and levelheaded way of telling them that that's not the case. You almost have to be a representative for all of us, like a dignitary or a diplomat. You don't want to set a bad example, be it for your family or the tribe. There's a lot of pressure, because everybody's so quick to dismiss anything Native American. People are so quick to say, oh, I'm this percentage Native American, and be so happy about it. Then in the next breath they say something disparaging about another tribal affiliation, almost like they want to be seen as Native American, but don't want to actually live that lifestyle. The idea that my culture would be an afterthought, something that people could grow out of—that's kind of alarming.

≈

I always put my views or opinions straightforward. By not being passive, I'm making a stand. It's a good preventive measure as well, just saying I don't want to be involved in this or that. Well, sometimes it works and sometimes it doesn't. People will try to get you to do something you don't want to do, just to bring you down to their same level. That's what I've seen.

I have a very giving personality, and when I can't help somebody, I feel vulnerable and rotten. Sometimes, what I'll do is write things down to see them from a different perspective. That letting-go helps me move through it. As for physical pain, I just keep trying to be stronger or have a higher pain threshold.

When I started out at the manufacturing plant where I currently work, there was a guy who came up to me, and said, "You're the reason this country's so messed up. We shouldn't be spending all of our money on grants so you people can come across the border and take advantage of all of our programs, and then just go back to Mexico when you're done." I was shocked. I didn't have anything to say to him. I wondered, "How long has he been watching me?" What he said was one of the silliest things I've ever been told in my life, but what intrigued me the most was, he'd never spoken a word to me. He just assumed. That was his agenda, I guess.

With something like that, to a certain degree you internalize it. It's almost like a moment of inspiration. I tell myself, "I know I'm not these ignorant things, and I'm just going to try to live my life the best that I can, and leave it at that. "So I've learned not to take it personally.

When you're angry, you want to make noise about it. That tool has been great for me, because sometimes I feel the hot sensation welling up inside, and at a certain point it just boils over. So I do scream therapy. Never *at* anybody, so they don't become an emotional punching bag. Sometimes you just need to scream at the top of your lungs. You're angry, you're going to get through it, you're going to be fine, but you don't need to make it somebody else's problem. That's why I have been doing more secluded sessions lately. I wouldn't want my yelling or screaming to set someone off, and perpetuate another machine of anger.

If you have peace of mind, you pretty much have everything. Too many people are trying to live life by somebody else's definition. You just need to be comfortable with who you are, where you're at, what you're doing, and make the most of it.

≈

I had to deal with bullies all the time. Not just being teased. I was beaten up a lot, for apparently no reason. Certain people, from their first day of school they're shut down. It's like you're stalled in neutral, and you can't get into any other emotion. Or else you have extremes — extremely happy, extremely sad, extremely mad. From 8am to 3pm, you can't be yourself. Call it survival mode. You switch that part on, then, when the school day is over, you switch it off. It's hard to go through.

I would miss a couple of days of school. If I was super sick, I'd miss a week. Then I'd go into the counselor's office, and he would yell full-blast in my face, even though I'd brought an excuse. He was like, "Your mom's going to jail because you missed so many days of school!" That was almost constant. My body was probably trying to stay home sick just so I could get a break from all that. Having people yell at you — bullies, school officials, people at home — that was hard. At that point in my life, my only solace was sleep.

The boys were always competing. The most insecure boys were always the toughest, biggest bullies, the meanest guys. In third grade, I was simply walking down the hallway, carrying my books and hurrying to class because the bell was about to ring. All of a sudden, I dropped my books on someone's shoe. Not on purpose, but he took it personal. He was maybe a grade up. He pushes me around, and we end up getting into a fight. The bully was completely doing it for show. The teacher's assistant was there, somebody I thought I could put my trust in, but he does nothing. Not even trying to help. I think for most bully situations, that's what happens. People turn a blind eye until there's some sort of situation where it's a big problem for everyone — like Columbine.

So there I was, being pushed around, and I took a couple of punches to my chin or my neck before it got broken up. To resolve such things, it's always the same. They command you to say you're sorry, even if you're not — a show-type apology. How are you going to say you're sorry for something that just *happened*? And whatever happened to open discussion? Whatever happened to mediation? I felt betrayed by the people in power. I realized, well, they are just here to babysit, not to do any type of real conflict mediation.

They gave that boy a slap on the wrist. I saw him once more, and it's odd how after an altercation like that, the person can be okay to you. There was no anger. I guess for him it was either a bad day, or some type of initiation. We didn't hold bad feelings toward each other. In the big picture, both of us were being betrayed by the adults in our lives. When I had a really crappy day at school because of bullying, teasing, hazing, totally not feeling like I fit in, I'd go home and it was my safety. I don't know what I did to get through it. Survival of the fittest, for sure.

In this culture, what are the skills that would help young boys know, first of all, that it's safe to feel afraid? Then, to be able to talk about it and work with it so it doesn't go to anger? Maybe some sort of anonymous suggestion box would help, to say what you're feeling. Then you could work toward actually getting people with names and faces involved. Personally, I was glad I was able to deal with it early on. A blessing and a curse, just because you see what you don't want to be. I made a really committed decision to not be what I've seen in the past. For me now, success is just to be true to myself.

Regarding sex, no matter what people tell you, you don't have to take things so fast. Ultimately, you're going to be hurting yourself and whoever you hook up with. You don't need to be pressured into doing anything. It doesn't matter what other people have to say about it. Honestly, I'm still a virgin, and people ride on me for that all the time. It's something that I don't want to give up just for anybody, I guess. In general, what I would say to young men and boys would be, don't take everybody's advice. You need to find really good places to gather your information from. You need to experience things first-hand.

~

I used to see my grandpa cleaning out a household or a structure of its negative energy. Or he would just bring, I don't even know what you'd call it, a bad energy or spirit out of somebody. I never want to say one way or another if I have those gifts, because I don't want to let people down. There wasn't a pressure to follow in his footsteps, just a general sense that it's something to keep an eye on and be aware of. Currently, there's somebody actually quite close to the Pueblo that I'm meant to apprentice under. We've never met, but she knows who I am. Nobody's ever given her any information about me, but she knows. And, yeah, I think my granddad has a lot to do with that.

What Do They Want of Me?

"We're not who we are because we think
the world needs us to be somebody else."

I've often felt, in the voice and body language of many men, a weight—as if they were carrying something cumbersome. I remember noticing my own son, at a young age, drawing pictures with crayons of men with very big shoulders. As if this were a model of what he was supposed to be (or, perhaps would *need* to be to survive). From what I was hearing, so much of "being a man" is a performance. At work, at home, even in the bedroom. Not a lot of places to let down and just be themselves, however that might be. You have to be this, you have to be that, you have to provide, protect, pretend. A whole lot of "supposed-tos"! A man in his 30s told me, "There's really nowhere for a man to rest." And a 66-year-old said, "Men generally don't raise children to be themselves. We raise children to be 'men,' as we are men." I know a mother who put a headband with a pink bow on her baby boy so people would treat him nicer. They did.

Listening to these men and boys, I began to feel a lot of sorrow. A man in his 50s said, "You're always *proving* you are." I've never felt I had to *prove* that I am a woman. No one's ever told me to "Be a woman!" or to "Woman up!"

Men are supposed to know how to do everything, really. It's part of the job description of "being a man." Their words: how to fix a carburetor, pleasure a woman, tie a knot, fix the dryer, change a tire, dig a hole, fix anything that's broken, light the pilot light, chop wood, start a fire, strap a boat onto the car, what to do with a dead animal, not get squeamish when I have to deal with the snake in the garage, and, even when I'm new in town, know which restaurant to choose, where to park, be able to reassure everyone that yes, everything will be okay, the car will not get towed, etc. How many times have I received incorrect directions from a man who, apparently, simply couldn't say, "I don't know"?

With all the pressure and expectation on men to already know, to be the expert, be "on top," have it all together, it would be pretty hard to find your way back to the wide open, endlessly curious and awake quality—the integrity and authenticity of that boy. The light heart we started with.

I was learning that the joy of being a boy is *not* knowing. That's the fun. You're open, inquisitive, exploring, learning. *Alive!* You have all the grace and room to not know how, to follow your curiosity and make glorious mistakes, to get hurt and get back up. You can ask, you can fail. And out of that relaxed openness and vulnerability comes creativity, imagination, and all possibility.

A man in his 60s spoke wistfully of his boyhood, "There's not a lot of cherishing of our sweetness, spontaneity and our sensitivity." And from a 72-year-old, "If we can't be vulnerable, how can we connect and see the world and each other as sacred?"

These boys are filled with dreams, and then they are told to *be* somebody. The light in children's eyes. What is *that*? And where does it go?

"Being a man" is a heap of ideas. A story that needs to be constantly created, told, and defended. Who made this up? A man in his 50s distilled it for me: "It's the 'should,' and then the shame on top of it." Who might these boys be if they didn't have to "be a man"?

When I asked, "What are the pressures you feel being a man?" the responses poured out.

∽

There's pressure from each other. Boys want to impress girls in a way that doesn't make the girls give up on them or make them feel not welcomed to the world.

(11 yr.)

You're supposed to be part of the team. But then there's this big pressure to be an individual. It's confusing.

(12 yr.)

Sometimes I just get so angry I have to punch my pillow. A lot. [The sound of] a toilet flush calms me down. My parents would *definitely* be nicer to me if I was a girl, like my sister. They're much easier on her.

(12 yr.)

There's a pressure. The more girls you can sleep with, the more you're really a guy. So it's a pressure rather than a pleasure, like a performance.

(16 yr.)

They make fun of you and, for sure, I'm not going to wear a pink t-shirt again.

(17 yr.)

They said, "Go get your brother," and brought me in to mediate. I'm twelve fucking years old. I was like, "What do you want me to fucking do about it?" This is one of the big pressures. Being the only guy in the family, everyone's looking to you to solve it, solve it, solve it.

(20s)

I've always struggled with the fact that because my dad was a musician and an artist, he never taught me how to build things or any of that handy guy stuff which I'm expected to do, and I feel really embarrassed about it. I'm really insecure. I'm sure I can do it if someone would take the time to teach me.

Recently, I drove with a friend to visit her family in upstate New York. We took her car, which is a stick. I never learned to drive a stick shift. There was some discussion between her and her dad about driving back. She was really tired, so he said, "Just have Steve drive." She said, "He can't drive a stick." Her dad turned to me and said, "Are you a man, or what?"

(20s)

There's pressure on a man to have it all together. To somehow *already know.* You're supposed to have it up, no matter what. It's ruthless, almost like it'd be nice to be sent away as a teenager somewhere where there isn't so much pressure, no TV or movies or internet, and learn how to live on the land or grow food or something practical. Postpone it, because you don't have the consciousness to go with the hormones yet.

(20s)

You have to be strong and unfazed by everything. I was a sensitive kid. I got good at presenting what people wanted to hear. My goal was to not let anyone see what was going on inside me. I was still in just as much pain, even if I traded addictions—methamphetamines for riding my motorcycle at dangerously high speeds.

(20s)

A lot of times guys will respect you for being good at something they're not good at. Like a lot of guys aren't that good with girls. They don't have a game, or whatever it's called. You just have to be yourself. But there are a lot of pitfalls along the way because you start not being yourself because you want to impress the guys, or to get the girl—to impress the guys. Guys are measuring each other a lot. You're always staying aware of what the other guys think. One-upping—the clothes you wear, the language you speak. Respect is everything.

(20s)

Women call on the guys, like, "Hey, how do I figure this out?" without even trying themselves. If a guy friend called me about something not working on the computer, it would be a very different conversation. "I'm doing this thing and this thing and I think it goes like this, but does it go like this?" And I'd say, "Well, no, it goes like this," and then he'd say, "Okay, great." That feels like it's an exchange, whereas with a woman it tends to be more, "Save me!"

(30s)

Someone recently said, "I'm gonna give you a man hug!" We grip hands and then the kind of one-arm thing where our chests are sort of bumping. I was wondering why does it have to be a man hug? Why can't it be just be a hug? I guess we're taught that it's less acceptable for men to show affection. When women are physically intimate in public it's perceived as sisterhood or camaraderie. But for men to be vulnerable to each other, it's somehow become more loaded, dangerously so.

(30s)

There's this tube you're allowed to be in as a guy and if you don't fit into that tube, you catch hell for it. I've had guys shake my hand, and they either pull me toward them or push me away *with force*.

(30s)

My wife doesn't give out any helpless vibes but, yeah, there is protector/provider pressure. To me, it manifests itself more profoundly as a success pressure. To be somebody. Be financially successful and be the protector. Wherever we stay, I'll always choose the side of the bed that's closest to the door. It feels biological, not a learned behavior.

(30s)

Looking after the family is the biggest "supposed-to" that's ingrained, that I never questioned because, to me, it just seems right. That's the kind of stuff that I think is absolutely in line because that's why men evolved with testosterone and women evolved with estrogen.

Now that I'm in the caregiver role more, from time to time I feel conflicted because I'm not making the money right now. But I do 98% of the shopping, and 98% of the preparation, so I can justify it with myself by saying that I'm still providing and taking care of the family because I'm still doing that stuff.

I've always been a physical worker — on ranches or, even as an EMT you sit around a lot, but when you work it's physical work, and you have to exert. And this is physically so much easier, but it's such a mentally straining and fatiguing thing. I used to come home with my body just absolutely exhausted, but my mind was refreshed and awake and I wanted to read or watch a good movie. Now, when my day's over I'm just — I'm zonked. I don't want any more stimulation, you know. I'm overwhelmed. It's — oh, my god, that's gonna make me cry.

I'm aware of the fact that people probably would judge me differently because I'm a man doing the traditional woman's role. But that doesn't make me feel conflicted. The conflict comes in when I question myself. I think — Well, you know, when I had a real job I didn't feel like this. Men can't get women's roles and women can't get men's until you do it. So nobody quite gets what you're dealing with.

I never really understood how deep the woman's work was until I was the stay-at-home parent. It's one thing to provide the cupboard, another thing to actually empty it and put it into your family.

(30s)

You know, nobody questions my perseverance at work. But I think that there's always kind of an unspoken sense, especially in the skilled labor end of the spectrum, of: "Well, you know, who's gonna step up? Who's gonna do the thing that needs to get done right now? Who's the one who's most capable of figuring out this puzzle? Who's the person that's gonna rise to the challenge?" And if I'm not doing that, I feel pressure.

(30s)

I would like to have known earlier, as a boy, how fun sex was, because it felt like a test. And a performance. Because your masculinity is tied to virility. You're proving. And that anxiety persists. Are you good at having sex?

(30s)

There are pressures to be strong physically and emotionally meaning to be reserved and not very expressive, to be that space where other people can express their doubts and insecurities but you are the rock that says, "It's going to be okay. We'll get through it."

(40s)

You're supposed to go for the money. Fight hard for your kids. Work hard so they get a leg up. I think that dynamic of sacrificing for your children is deeply resented by a lot of men. There is a great sadness around that as you become conscious of it.

(40s)

There's pressure to have all the answers, to be able to figure anything out. If there are six people in a room and we're trying to make a decision, more often than not, they will look to me to give the reason why we should do something. I pretend that I know what I want at all times. But I don't. I guess they know that I'm gonna make the decision that will work best for the group. They have confidence in me, but it's just because that's a role I learned to play early from my dad.

(40s)

If you take time to actually understand what you're feeling, you get scorned — can't come to a decision, aren't strong. As though reflection, in and of itself, is just a bad thing.

(40s)

I think a lot of young guys feel like they have to be totally in charge and confident and not have sex be a mutual exploration. Like there's not room for how it can be playful and doesn't have to be a certain way. There's someone you're supposed to be, and it's an act. You have to perform this thing and not admit that you don't know what you're doing.

(40s)

The pleasure is that when you're doing the thing, playing that part, this role that's very important and valued in society, and when you're able to do it successfully, it's very satisfying. And there's a lot of pressure and fear of failure because that's always looming over and you can't refuse. To me, it explains a lot of the behaviors.

(40s)

The pressure is to be independent, alone. It's habitual, not natural. Actually, men are starving for connection.

(40s)

I'm embarrassed to say that I don't remember anybody expecting me to know things, but I do think I actually participated in handing it down to other men and boys. For instance, I've said to my son sometimes, "Well, you've got to know how to drive a stick. That's just part of the deal. You've got to know how to use an electric drill, a Skil saw. That's just part of what you need to know." Oftentimes, he'd say, "Well, why Dad?" "Well, you're with a girl. She lives in an apartment. She's got something broken and you fix it. Then she likes you more." But the stick shift I was definitely like, "You just got to know that."

More than anything for me, it's that state of expectation that you should always be on your toes ready to respond immediately with some action. It's the "should," and then the shame on top of it.

(50s)

By teenage it was pretty well nailed down. I had the awareness that I was acting out this thing I was supposed to be doing. It's kind of a default or shadow that's always present. Men are just trapped in an image of something that they don't want to be and it's not very good to be anyway. Kind of a strong, if not dominant at least commanding, forceful, assured, competent being. And underneath that there's just an emotional, blubbering mess of weakness and vulnerability. The only real kind of role models or powerful models of men I've ever seen are men that embrace that rather than try to cover it over.

The point where you know nobody else is gonna do it for you and it's a hard thing to do and you have to do it. That's a pretty cool statement of taking responsibility to the deep level.

(50s)

The message is: "If it's not hard, you're not doing anything." I love to cook. I can do it without too much thinking. I also love set design. My father said, "You can do that *after* you become a doctor." After he died, I was able to help the mortician by sewing up the cuts on his body. I was glad to do it for him, but I had stopped being a doctor by then. And he was going to be cremated anyway so, come on. Now I'm doing set design.

(50s)

The pressure is really about how to make a place for oneself as a man in the culture by showing utility. And that's to prove my dick is bigger than yours—in a very blunt way. It's a power deal.

(50s)

You've got to *do* something—you've got to *be a man.* I can't just receive something you're saying, think about it, and then say something to you, which you'll then take in, receive and reflect on. Which is the dance and the play. That's the fun!

I never got that because one or the other of us has an idea of how the other person should behave, right? That's the "supposed-to."

(50s)

To be willing to not know—that is absolutely not in the curriculum. The patriarchal masculinity thing. If something's broken, I want to fix it, like—now, everything's okay. This is a huge part about men. Absolutely conditioned. Being right makes me feel safe. Being in control.

(60s)

There is a certain caché about having a pretty girl on your arm. Maybe even a smugness. Men are highly competitive. And so we compete for access to females, probably not so much at my age but we definitely have some one-upmanship that we want to express and to demonstrate our fitness. To get biological about it, the fact that we're good partners, that maybe we're good sex partners, that we're successful. As we get older it's less about physicality and more about success culturally, in terms of recognition. People see you, they know who you are, you've got money, you've got a successful job, people look up to you or you have a pretty girl on your arm. So all of those things are part of the whole package of making yourself more dominant in the male society that we all exist in.

(60s)

The pressure is to be better than, so I was always comparing. The performing is for other guys—athletics, business, sex. A team at least softens it some. My step-grandfather, an old communist my father hated, was the only one who saw me and was always encouraging.

(60s)

In this culture, the hallmark of a "real man" and a "real boy" is that you demonstrate the capacity to be in control at all times. The ultimate way to control is to kill. Patriarchal society offers many rewards to the men who master this game. Rewards that, in this culture, are *defined* as what's great. You get to have money, stature, respect. You get to have people be afraid of you, and there are many payoffs to that.

Every man has to figure out a way to present himself to other men as someone they don't want to mess with.

I was at Barnes & Noble recently, and I saw a magazine called *Personal and Home Defense.* It had an article called "Bedroom Guns" — the guns you have in your bedroom so when an intruder enters, which do you shoot him with?

(60s)

When my kids were in high school, my daughter would refer to me as Captain Control. For Thanksgiving, there were times we had twenty-some people here, and I would get very tight. I thought I had to be sure everything went okay, and I knew I couldn't. Finally, I confronted it. "Oh, shit, I don't want to live this way."

(60's)

You've got to be out there slaying dragons. It's frightening because you fear failure.

Sometimes, the thought of dying and not having to compete . . . I love the game, the hunt. You get addicted to the score. It's a rush doing what you do well. But I wouldn't miss the pressure of being a man. I wouldn't miss the pressure of having to succeed, to look good, to be clever and witty and all the things that get dumped on guys.

(60s)

If you're a man and you're even the least bit depressed, you're a complete failure. You've got to be on top of things. What's wrong with you that you're letting things get to you like that? Why aren't you just dealing with it and moving on?

(60s)

Depression is perceived as weakness. To be a man is to be able. With physical disability at least you can display strength. But you can't muscle your way out of emotional disability. It requires a different kind of courage. A courage of vulnerability and willingness to feel uncomfortable feelings like despair, regret, grief. We don't want to feel these shunned emotions, fearing we will become stuck in them, or that they will define who we are. It's hard to trust that, if we abide, stay with these feelings, they will open and change. There's not a lot of support for this. There are two things that are the most off limits, even in my men's groups: perceived failure and sexual incapacity

(60s)

If you're responsible for 350 people, you're never not on—imagine if it's 3,000 or 30,000. It weighs on you. Maybe that's why these guys who run corporations are so out of touch.

I have to guard against this. It really is addictive to have people defer to you and they laugh at jokes you make that aren't funny and they bring you whatever you want. You want your lunch brought to you today? Do you want this? Do you want that? So it's kind of nice at that level, right?

You just get addicted to it. And the price you pay is your own authenticity. Because you know you're a phony. I mean we all know we're faking it.

(60s)

You have to "Make your mark," goddammit! After the accident, laying there in the hospital, you see all these people who have been doing service. All their lives. It gets you thinking.

(60s)

A woman's sexual organs are on the inside, and she opens her legs and receives, and she feels things more internally. A man's organs are on the outside, and he has to perform and act upon the world, and the appearance of things can substitute for things felt and received. He is measured by that outside performance. A man has to perform to survive. It is mandatory. That is why the men you're interviewing don't feel entitled, they feel embattled.

(60s)

Do your duty. Behave well. Live up to expectation. I experienced it as a push from behind, not a weight.

(70s)

All through graduate school, what's gonna happen if I don't get my Ph.D. and then, getting the Ph.D., well am I gonna get a job? And then, once I get the job, well am I gonna get tenure? It just goes on and on.

As a boy, I loved animals — bugs and snakes and turtles. That child is so squashed, so frightened now — too frightened of the world to come out.

(70s)

Pressures to defend. I've never been in any rough neighborhoods or situations where I felt that I would have to defend my family, my children, wife or woman. But I know that I would have. I know that I would have fought to the death to defend anyone I loved. Fists, rocks, whatever I could get my hands on. And that, I think, is instinctual and primitive and very deep.

(80s)

When I was coming into manhood, it seemed quite simple. The man was the breadwinner, and he was supposed to be responsible for, well, in a way, everything. Including responsibility for his wife's happiness. Oh, God. That makes me laugh. That's a tall order.

(80s)

Patrick (40s)

"I had no idea what it was going to cost."

I make a million dollars a year, apart from my stock options and benefits and bonuses. Sixty or seventy percent of the time, I'm on the road. The thing I would like my wife to understand, and women in general, is how hard it is to do what I do. I'm a Senior Vice President of a very successful company. The go-to guy. Everybody trusts me. A deal can be in process, not be going well, and then I come into the room. Because I pride myself on integrity, even though my company may not at times, people trust me. I am wanted. I'm all over the planet for these deals. Hardly ever at home. My wife says I complain too much. The truth is, I'm lonely.

I was raised in a big working-class Catholic family on the East Coast with nine brothers and sisters. I'm a middle kid, and there was never enough attention or money to go around, but there was a lot of love. We played baseball and soccer in the streets. Now here I am in a life where I hardly ever get to play ball with my kids. I don't even drive them to school most of the time. They're chauffeured.

We were sports guys in my family. My brothers pounded on me, but I always thought of them as helping me. They pounded on me to make me stronger, to be able to take on the bully. That's a key thing—being able to face the playground bullies. It's the only time you get free of them.

There's terror there. Still is, too, because even though you're bringing in a big income and you've got a lot of whatever, you're still not in charge of your life. There are still bullies in my life, real jerks who are above me. Real assholes. Oh, boy, you talk about violence or the desire to punch somebody, that's when I feel it. When someone comes at me in that way, even if they're my superior, I rankle at it. But I can't lose my job. So what do I do? I cave. Then I go out and close a few deals to make myself invaluable, and if there's a way to take this guy on, I do.

In our family, if you got beat up by somebody who bloodied your nose, you'd better get it together and go knock him down. We're tough guys and we're good guys, and we win at sports. If I was on a sports team in high school, I was the captain. People looked to me to come through. When I was in the Air Force, I was always the go-to guy. It's the same energy I have now.

My dad comes from the generation of men where you work very hard and sacrifice. Dad worked long hours in an aircraft factory, and he made pretty good money. The good news was, he never brought his work home like I do. I'm never off duty. People call me night and day, from all over the world, whereas Dad would come out and play with us. The best memories I have of my father are him playing softball or basketball with us—just running around with us kids. He was tired, and we knew he worked hard. That was just what men did.

I learned growing up that shame was the worst thing you could experience. There was shaming in our family, but it's also in the whole culture. The older brothers would shame the younger brothers in terms of athletic skills until we got it right. We would haze, and get hazed—toughen up, buck up, be a man. Mom lets you get away with going, "I don't want to do that," or, "I'm scared of this," but as soon as the teenage boy culture takes over, especially if you want to do sports, you friggin' better show up, or you get shamed.

None of my high school buddies have gone on to be as successful as I am. I'm in touch with my old friends, but I have to be careful. They're trying to pay a mortgage on a house that's worth a tenth of what ours is. I love these guys. They are my good buddies, and I don't want to lose their friendships, so I never put on airs. They're making $40,000 a year, I'm making a million. So I can't really talk to them about the full dilemma I'm in. They'd say, "Well, why do you send your kids to private schools that cost $50,000 each? That's absurd. Send them to public schools." They can't understand the world we live in, so when I go to see my family, my brothers and my friends, I just drop back into sports.

From the neighborhood where I grew up, I took a big jump. I went to an Ivy League school. My family—at best a few of them went to community college, right? I ended up going to Yale. That was huge. It was like coming out of one world, and going up to another. During my first year there, I thought they were going to find out that I was a pretender. I know guys who feel this way a lot. It's so in us.

I had a good mom. She didn't have enough time for us with so many kids. She's very tuned to the fact that I'm not so happy now. She never told me I had to jump into this other realm. I felt loved by her just like I was.

One of my dreams, even now, is to be a high school history teacher and baseball coach. That's what I really want to be, and when I say it to my mom, she gets it, "That sounds great, honey." But when I say it to my wife, whom I love, she looks at me like I've lost my mind.

My extended family doesn't have much money. Everybody is on my shoulders, and not to carry that is shameful. I'm a simple guy. I want my wife to acknowledge me. I want to have some loving, affectionate, romantic, sexual time with her. I want my kids to love me. I feel if I don't come through for my family, not only my nuclear family, but my extended family, then there is shame. So I have to keep it together. I live in a world where, if you don't cut those deals, you don't have the status.

Our Paleolithic forbearers who were going out to hunt wooly mammoths and wooly rhinoceroses, I would be willing to guess the guys who went out had a shame-based setup in terms of succeeding and not succeeding. I feel like I'm part of that same culture. It's better to avoid shame, and seek honor. If you have to die, you die.

~

I'm an employee. I just make a lot of money. People trust me because I really am this working-class, blue-collar guy below the surface—the real thing. I've leveraged that, plus an MBA from Harvard, to where I now live in a fancy neighborhood in Westchester County. Our neighborhood friends are successful driven people and most of them have more wealth than we do. Real wealth. Relative to them, we're just the kids on the block who have to scramble. My kids have all kinds of amazing things. Live-in nannies, gardeners, somebody who drives them to school—you name it. In the neighborhood where we live, if you don't have those things, it's not okay.

My wife is hooked on what I'm providing. Our three kids are all in school at $50,000 a year apiece. Anything less than that would be socially unacceptable. I'm in this gray flannel suit, and I want to be in my jeans playing baseball with my kids. I could become somebody else, a simpler person who could no more support our lifestyle than the man in the moon. I tell her, "Look, I could get a job for $200,000 a year." She says, "I gave up my career and the business I was starting for this. Now you're successful and you're doing it, and you want to quit? No way you're going to back out of this, buddy. You got me into this."

Look, I know how this story is going to strike people who can't get work, or have been laid off and are working part-time. I'm not ungrateful. I am from a poor working-class family. I *am* grateful. I'm just trying to explain that it's not as simple as it looks. There is a price—a very large price. Once you get on this system of reference, there are certain pre-schools you send your kid to, certain high schools, certain colleges. My wife and I share a certain sense of insecurity, because we're both from the same working-class background, but I don't like where we've gotten to. For me, it's eighty hours a week, nose to the grindstone.

I talk to my wife about it all the time. I don't have any sense of liking the social world we're in. I don't fit in, while she fits perfectly. She's charming and lovely and attractive and smart—a star, and she drags me along. When I come in from Singapore or Hong Kong, I just want to have a simple picnic and a softball game on my weekends. She has six events set up, and they're socially important. She's a good person, and I'm the one who got her into this. It's complicated. When we got married, I was on this trajectory. I just had no idea what it was going to cost.

We got married young. She was finishing her MBA at Columbia, and I was finishing mine at Harvard. We recognized each other as being from similar neighborhoods, with a similar kind of energy. She was fun and sparkling and gorgeous. I just loved her, and she could really take me on in this way that I loved because I was a natural leader. I love that part of my life. What I fear is that I am not modeling for my children the kind of authentic leadership that comes out of who you are as a person rather than your title. That's what I really want to communicate to them. I learned it on the sports field. I learned it in my working class life where you just show up. I want them to have that, and I fear I'm not spending enough time with them so they get that's who I really am.

I want my wife to adore me. I'm a loyal guy, too. I do not mess around on the road. My wife is impressive. She is an incredible organizer—very acknowledging of people. She uses the kind of empathy she learned in our class background, and people adore her. She knows how to win without becoming shark-like or harsh. Yet she's always trying too hard, because she doesn't have "real" money. She can get really pissed-off that she needs me to make this amount of money, and more. Unless you have the money and power to start with, you're still working for somebody, still paying a price. You're in there making your way up the ladder to get access to these opportunities. Every deal that I close, there's a bonus. So, that's me.

≈

For a while, I had bad physical pain. Back pain and shoulder pain. I did a lot of work on becoming aware of how emotional pain and frustration can go into the physical body. The pain was so bad, it got to the point where I had a reason to say, "I can't play any more." A part of me was celebrating, but my wife looked at me like "Get it together." She leaned in and said, "Fix it. Fix the pain." We're supposed to go out and sacrifice for the tribe, you know, the family. That's who I am.

I don't know, the pills help. They give me a little more Teflon. I've always avoided opiates or anything like that. I avoid misusing alcohol, too, because there's an alcoholic gene in our family. I just take your basic anti-depressant that lets me deal with things a little better. It helps with the pain, too, a little bit. I don't know, I don't have a solution. It just grinds on from year to year.

My kids love me. They love me, and they miss me. I check in with them. I try to call them every night, no matter where I am. The worry is, they're growing up in a more entitled, less generous, less sharing world than I did. They don't have access to the things that really helped to shape me. I love my kids, and I'm a heart guy. That's why people trust me in these big deals. But that also makes it harder to be me in this world. There are so many sharks. It's a predator's space. I'm not a predator personally at all.

I feel like I jumped into a stream, and the falls are coming up. It feels out of control, and there is nobody in that world I can talk to. I've got no empathy for myself. I beat up on myself. I'm really stressed-out and my worst fear is that nothing will change. The stress will continue to accumulate in my body, and I'll have a heart attack at fifty or fifty-five. Just die in the trenches.

Sometimes my wife and I have deep talks. It helps, because she softens, and I feel she hears my pain, and she doesn't roll her eyes. But she just sort of says, "Well, I get it, but I don't see any way for us to realistically make a change until we put our kids through college." We have three. Our youngest is seven. That would mean waiting until fifteen years from now. We can only stand to have this conversation occasionally because it's so upsetting.

I don't believe in divorce, and I love my wife. I think she's amazing. But I don't want to be dead from a heart attack during the next year either. I don't see a way out. I feel if I were to get off my white horse, I'd let everybody down. Not just my family, my immediate family, but all those folks who I represent from the working class. And I would feel shame.

Does my wife love me? I believe so. You know that spark thing? We used to have that. If I could go back and change the past, boy, would I lean in differently. The real truth is, she's way more of a powerhouse than I am. I'm usually the smartest person in the room, in terms of deals. But I'm not driven at that level. I just want to do well so everyone's provided for. But my wife, had she gone on to be a business woman, I think a lot of this pressure in our marriage wouldn't be there. She wouldn't be depending on me, and putting so much pressure on me. So I regret that. It isn't good modeling that we're giving for our daughters.

My wife and I have both been aspiring to what the culture tells us we should want.

~

What keeps me going? I'm Catholic. I believe in a life being used for a good purpose that is very fulfilling. When I dream about a simpler life, I think about reaching out to the community, about being a high school teacher and coach. A real member of the community. I thought that was going to be my life, but it's not.

I don't have a sense of meaningful purpose that is connected to the life of my children within a community. I'm this highly paid guy who goes around and makes stuff happen. That's part of the pain. Not only am I cut off from my kids, I have no belief whatsoever that what I'm doing is helping the planet, or other people, and that goes against my religion.

I would like to have a job with that kind of value, at a level of the economy that my wife would love me at. I would drop the gray flannel suit in a flash, if I could just get her to sign up for that. But I have a deep fear that if I stumble on the trail and don't bring back the wooly mammoth, I fear she's more wedded to her life-style than to me. If we took more time to be a family, I think she would be happier.

God, what I really want is for my wife to love the me that I want to be, that I know is in me, that local community guy. From my point of view, he is a much bigger guy. I'd love my wife to be in love with the guy who I think I really am.

~

A lot of what we men do—not everything, because male friendship certainly matters—but a lot of it is to please and be acknowledged by women. I wanted to be the guy on the white horse. I don't fault anybody. I wanted to be somebody. The message I got was, if you're that guy, you get to have a special wife. You get to be with somebody who is amazing and live in an amazing place and have kids.

I thought getting into this other world was going to make life better for my kids, right? In fact, it might be a handicap. Growing up, I didn't have access to anybody who lived in this world, so I never got that this is a big tradeoff. I had no idea. I regret I never got to have this kind of conversation with my dad before he died. I would've loved to have a beer with him, and explain that I understand how stretched he was.

In my own way, I'm stretched like that, too. I feel sad, because I don't get to run around with my kids. I'm hardly with them. I try. Trust me, when I come in—I might have flown in from Dubai all night—but I get up and I play with my kids. I love it. It's the thing I look forward to the most, even though it might be only two or three times a month now. Not almost every night, the way it was with my dad.

You Don't Even Know You Don't Know

> "I played the game. I won! I won!
> And I feel depressed as shit."

Having a name like mine — "Hathaway Barry," I have frequently been mistaken for a man. Before people meet me, that is. Or they reverse the names to "Barry Hathaway," which is even more masculine sounding, and put a "Mr." before my name. I could tell by the tone of letters I would receive or when I booked rooms or tickets online — just the slightest sense of being taken more seriously. It bugged me.

When I was a girl and first heard of the Equal Rights Amendment, I was in disbelief. Why would such a thing be necessary? Doesn't everyone have equal rights? A child mind puzzling over the way "grown-ups" treat people of different colors and shapes and backgrounds, before it becomes "normal." When the notion of "rape" dawned, I was beyond baffled. How could it be that so many women are still treated like fossil fuels? I couldn't make sense of these things. How would any man who loved any woman not be doing everything in his power to insure that inequality and rape were not tolerated? Why weren't they as horrified and astonished as I was? What way of seeing the world allowed this to be okay?

Maybe these men haven't seen that the Equal Rights Amendment is for them, too.

I had grown up with privilege myself. And yet, it became increasingly apparent that the males in my life were even more privileged, simply because they were men. In "training" as a girl, I remember making sandwiches, or treats like cinnamon buns from a pop-open cylinder, frosting them, and bringing them to my brothers and father as they were watching sports in front of the TV. I enjoyed serving them, and this, of course, was appreciated. But I don't remember them ever doing the same. I wondered about this.

Male privilege is often silent. It is preferential treatment that goes unnoticed. "Privilege," one young man told me, "is things that people take for granted." Men are looked at and listened to first.

I also wondered where guys in their upbringing often get the idea of being *superior*? At times I have felt a sense of permission, an old belief that women are actually here *for* men—to serve them, feed them, have sex with them, take care of them. Perhaps, because we all originally come from mothers?

I wanted to know: Were they aware of their own privilege? How did they feel about that privilege? Did they feel entitled to it? And if so, why?

So I asked about privilege.

~

There are privileges just being a male—whatever your color. When you talk, people listen; you're given a lot more respect in a lot of settings; you have a lot more power and control.

(20s)

Appearance doesn't matter as much—not to the degree that it does to women. Women have more insecurities about this because the way women in Western culture are so driven around their looks—if you're attractive or have nice features or a nice body, you'll make it further in life, which is real fucked up. A lot of men like younger women 'cause it's easier to have power and control over them. Gives you the illusion of safety.

What you know, no matter what kind of background you have as a man, is that you're above women.

(20s)

Yes, men are privileged. But that same privilege is what causes conflict in men. You know men are ultimately more vulnerable than women because of that privilege.

We don't have to face these emotions and these issues. But at the same time they eventually catch up with you. Eventually all negative things are going to go through that grinder. The universe tends to balance things out, whether you want to or not.

(30s)

It's lonely in privileged land. You lose connectivity. I have a fear of loss of privilege.

(30s)

One of the interesting things of transitioning [from female to male] and being perceived as male is that I'm not automatically allowed to be a feminist the way I was when people thought I was a woman. I sort of have to prove my credentials. One of the other complex things is that I do have this male privilege now. And that is something that is really problematic that I have to stay aware of all the time. Just very little things, like people will hand me the check. I get treated with more deference on the phone. There are so many things I just hadn't really thought of. I guess that's what privilege is. You don't even know you don't know.

(30s)

The freedom I have to feel safe physically, like walking around at night, is something I take for granted. Certainly if I didn't have that, it would be a big loss.

(40s)

Something that I often hear women say, particularly feminists, is that it would be different if women were in charge—if we had a woman president, if we had women CEOs, etc. Then I'll say, "Well, what about Margaret Thatcher? What about so and so?" And they will always say the same thing. "Well, those women are behaving like men because they had to in order to get into their positions of power."

My response to that is always, "Did it ever occur to you that those men who are in power had to behave that way in order to get in their positions of power?"

(40s)

As any privileged person knows, one of the signs of privilege is that you don't recognize the privilege. So I can't say a lot about male privilege except for what I've learned by hanging out and traveling with colleagues, particularly women of color. They are appalled at how I'm treated. I basically skate through life and I never realized it until I had these other experiences. Traveling with an African-American friend, he'll get asked for his ID, and I won't. The reality is, I get treated with due respect, and I expect everybody to be treated that way.

(50s)

The people who, in our culture, are considered the top of the heap, privileged white males, who are tall, strong, handsome, smart, athletic — who have all the gifts, in a way — the disadvantage is that they haven't had to look at it. Enough of the illusion works for them that they don't set themselves free. Some of these men are the least aware of their privilege and least aware of their suffering.

Men with a lot of power and privilege are often isolated and insulated from the truth because people who depend on them often don't tell them the truth. The "rewards" of the castle — titles, fame, money, sex, prestige, power, etc. — upon deeper reflection, become imprisoning.

(60s)

It has been dawning on my cloudy mind that the only way to look at male entitlement is through the experience of a woman's loss of entitlement. Just as white people don't realize they're entitled until you look at blacks' lack of entitlement.

(60s)

As well as the difficulties, the stresses, the discomfort, and so forth of existing as a man, there is a good deal of fundamental security locked up in being a man. First of all, and it goes without saying, men know that they are "on top." Western society — come to think of it, all societies — gives privileges to men, and this is no small thing amid the stress, vacuity, and awkwardness of being a man. I should think that few men to whom you have talked would trade their identity and become women. Some form of residual safety is there for every man to have. And that, day in and day out, is a kind of pleasure.

(70s)

Amir (20s)

"Down under, we are all bonobo monkeys."

My mom is from Fiji and was raised by her Sikh Indian mother, my grandmother, who currently lives in the States. My grandmother is eighty-nine years old now. Of her thirteen kids, three passed away. My grandfather wasn't really around, as far as I know. The boys in the family kind of stuck to him, because of the culture. Like, Dad is dad, he can do whatever he wants.

A story I heard about my grandfather was about one time when he brought another woman to the house. My grandma opened the door with a knife, and said in Fijian, "Should you ever bring her back here again, I'll chop her up and send her back to her family." For the most part, I was raised by my grandma because my mom was working full time.

From my dad, I never really got a "Don't ever be afraid of nobody" attitude. But I heard from my uncles that my dad used to be like that when he was younger. He's an inch or two shorter than me, and he will fight anybody. I got that attitude from people on the streets, like when you show fear you're showing that you're vulnerable, and vulnerability is a weakness.

My parents were both raised overseas. My dad, who is Pakistani, was a lot more lax, I think because of his gambling problem. I can't be mad about it, because it made him so vulnerable at times. It was like he knew he was wrong. He never put his hand on my mother, but he would do other physically abusive things like intimidation, or like, "Well, you're lucky I don't hit women, 'cause look at all these dishes I just broke." My mom loved dishes, and we have no money. She'd buy boxes of them, and stack them in the fucking garage. She just loved dishes, and if tensions got high, he would break them.

I wanted to play the piano when I was younger because my best friend played the piano. It's such a tight talent. When I find my queen, it'd be something nice. Like looking at the stars, go play a song on the piano, right? But my dad said—I think it might have been because we were broke, but the way he put it was, "Why do you wanna play the piano? Playing the piano is for faggots." And I was like "Oh, I guess I won't be playing the piano then, right?" Another time, I think I was five, my dad was eating dinner, and I just ran over and put my hand on his knee, and he's like, "You don't touch a man on his knee."

Some things about me might be masculine, and some things about me might be feminine. I don't think they necessarily have to be associated with male and female, like crying is a feminine thing. Okay, well, I'll cry. It's like learning to be in a relationship with yourself. Just trying to understand, "Why do I feel sad right now?" And answer some questions and get to the bottom. Lately, I tell myself, "Don't force yourself into a relationship just to have a relationship. Because then you're going to settle for less, or you're going to end up hurting somebody." There's a poem, I forgot the guy's name, that says, "Walk like a king, and your queen will come to you."

Some people would be like, "I haven't learned shit from my daddy. He didn't teach me how to tie a tie. He didn't teach me how to be a man. He didn't teach me how to treat a woman. He didn't teach me shit." But I've always looked at it like, I saw the stuff my dad did that I liked, then I saw the stuff I didn't like. I avoid gambling as much as I can. I don't get addicted to stuff. I have a lot of strong will power, and part of that comes from my father. Because he's Muslim, we fast every year for Ramadan, though we were never really strong in our faith, like praying five times a day or stuff like that.

I won Class Clown in high school. I remember one day, I was literally just walking in the house, not thinking funny or anything like that, and my dad said, "Hey! Stand up straight. Stop walking like a fucking clown." I'm like, "Oh, okay. Yes, sir." This is the stuff I got from my dad. It forced me to mature faster, which I think ended up being a good thing.

My mom was the reason why the household stayed together. My father gambled a lot, like a lot a lot, so he was never really the provider. I saw my mom put up with a lot of stuff.

Growing up in a house full of women does one of two things to you. Either you have such a respect for women that you clash with the male-dominant society a lot, like I feel I'm doing. Or you use the power you have from overhearing their conversations to manipulate women to get whatever you want, meaning you can get money, have them chauffeur you around, break you off cash and stuff like that. Which I started to do a little bit, but I was never able to do it too comfortably. I grew up in a black neighborhood. The shit I would get from black people is the same shit I get from white people. I get shit like, "Arab, Ice cream truck, 7-11, go back to—!" Especially after 9/11. That's why I have so many scars on my hands. I wouldn't put up with that shit. I was taught if you let them do that, then they win and they'll keep doing it.

You have to be your own equalizer. Right now there are more black people in this neighborhood, and no white people. So immediately and directly, they're running things here. As a minority, where do you fit in? It becomes like a power clash, like a war. You got the Samoans fighting blacks, or you have blacks from one neighborhood fighting blacks from another neighborhood. Everyone is trying to gain power any way they know how, even if at the end of the day it doesn't really mean shit.

The way people are raised out here, we develop an array of superiority complexes and inferiority complexes. "I'm superior to blacks." "I'm inferior to whites." "I'm superior to women." Not literally, but within the American social hierarchy, you know what I'm saying? So you find your place in the world. Then you start to say, "Okay, these people are inferior to me. So what better way to maintain my dominance than to do what is done to me?" I think people do it subconsciously. Everybody loses in the end, because it's all based on hate and pain, and we just perpetuate it.

Right now, I'm the head of some violence prevention programs in our city. Once I started doing this type of work, I started thinking about the different leaders I have looked up to, people who really stood for what they believed in. Martin,

Malcolm, Tupak. They didn't live to be that old. I don't want to say I'm some kind of radical revolutionary, but this shit is fucked-up.

Privileged white men are the definition of masculinity. They never want to talk about the past. Always want to put everything behind them, act like nothing's wrong and the past doesn't affect the present—like no accountability is needed. In a white man's world, those who advance the highest are those who act most like the white man. Be you a black woman, a white woman, me, whoever you are, the more you can be like an aggressive white male, the higher and faster up you're going to move.

One very Amero/European/Western thing is always feeling like your problems are bigger than everybody else's. For most white people, or white men especially, that's how it comes off. Like, "I just want everything to be equal, and I hate being labeled a white male." Okay, I see, but be happy that you're labeled a white man, and figure out what are the perks and the benefits and the privileges that come along with that. Then figure out how you can flip them, and help the people that have been labeled black and brown and useless and ignorant and fat and slow and retarded.

If you're white, you understand you're privileged. You didn't ask to be privileged, but you sure benefitted from it. Come down and invest in our businesses. That would be a way to help. There isn't even a grocery store on this side of town. There's no financial literacy, no economic development. That's why these residential areas are all drug turf. That's the only way to make money.

I feel that white people are victims of their circumstances, too. Like if you were raised in a place where you're taught that you're economically, politically, socially and culturally superior to everybody else, chances are you're going to believe it. It's not like it's their fault. I don't think they're inherently evil, or anything like that.

~

I feel like in our society, the way it's built, men are usually raised by women. They don't have any strong males in their household, so they're not taught how to disrespect women at home. They learn that from how the system treats women, and because everybody is so cutthroat, they end up getting their throats cut too. And end up becoming assholes. It's a cycle. It's like, "I'm an asshole. I just want to fuck her, so I'll take her virginity, whatever." Now, what happens to her? She'll be like, "There's no good guys out there."

Women have a harder time when their appearance clashes with society's notions of what beauty is. I got teased about my nose and my height. Still do sometimes. But I feel most men are like, "Okay, I can't do nothing about it. I'm going to find a female anyways."

Sex is like a drug to me. I stopped for a while to gain understanding, because I felt like I can't understand it when I'm still engaging in it. I see how many people use it to numb pain or fill voids in their lives. People think you can just go and have sex and you'll feel better. You're depressed, go take some shots, you'll feel better. Go smoke some weed, whatever. When you come back down to reality, your problems will be the same.

Down under, we are all bonobo monkeys. They fuck other monkeys. They suck dick, they eat pussies, they masturbate, they have homosexual sex, heterosexual sex. If you take away our buildings and our jobs, that's us—bonobo monkeys. Other than work and wearing clothes, that's pretty much what we do, just fuck and clean, and some of us don't even do both. Others of us have to find time to raise our kids, too.

If you ever noticed, lots of women like older guys. They say it's because the women mature faster, but I don't think that's necessarily true. I feel like a lot of my early relationships, I was boyfriend *and* protector/father, because a lot of women never had a strong male figure growing up. Nobody really knows what it means to be a man. It's not clear.

I hate when, say, I'm messing with a girl for three months, and she's like, "We need to talk," and I'll be like, "Shit!" I'm afraid she's going to bring up something I don't really want to deal with, or maybe don't know *how* to deal with.

The fear is, I don't feel it as deep as they do. Like, "She's in love with me. I'm not in love with her. Fuck, I'm going to hurt her. Damn!"

To me, it's like true power comes through control and humility. Like, why is it that I hear a woman's voice and I can get aroused? Where's my control? Sometimes I just feel like I need a girlfriend, or I need to cuddle up at night. It's hard, because you just get so used to that. You love that affection. In society, it's almost like you're nobody without somebody.

~

I live in the hood. I do everything the hood people do, only I don't drink or smoke. I didn't realize how important that was until I was thinking about drinking again. The people who knew me started crying when I told them. They said, "Don't drink, because that means a lot to me that you don't drink." That touched me so much that I was like, "Fuck it, I'm not drinking no more." What I get out of not drinking is giving them hope that they could be who they are, they can be from where they're from, and they can do better things than just get high and be drunk all the time.

In college, I had my red pill, blue pill moment. I was like, "Wow, all these people who fought for change were murdered." Malcolm X, Martin Luther King, Jr., Mahatma Gandhi. No matter how they fought for change, they got killed.

At that time, I closed my eyes, and pictured my future—myself living in the suburbs somewhere, working a desk job, doing some stupid-ass shit like advertising or being a clinical psychologist—no offense to them—or some cool shit like being an actor or a rapper or whatever. And I'd be saying, "I'm living good, eating good, I've got a beautiful wife, I've got three kids, I ain't worried about shit."

The thing was, I felt like if I got to that point in my life, I wouldn't really be happy. In that lifestyle, I would turn my back on everybody that died for me, everybody that struggled, every person that was tortured for me to have opportunities and be able to fight for the same struggle they fought for. Most of all, I'd be turning my back on my kids and my future generations, because if I don't do anything about it, they could fall victim and be manipulated and become perpetrators of the same shit that's killing everybody.

So I'm going to give people the one thing that America can't. That is, loving them. I'm real, and I love people. I love the fuck out of people, and you can see motherfuckers who have never been hugged before, people that never felt no love before. It's disgusting.

The path is not always clear, but I know what direction I'm going in. I have faith in my spirituality that whoever the Creator is, molecules mixing in the air, butterfly flapping his wings on the other side of the world—that if I go in this direction, I can just close my eyes and see where I'm supposed to go.

This Big Ball of Boy Energy

"You can't quite be vulnerable, even with close friends."

Testosterone and competition weren't topics I asked about directly, but the words came up so often I decided to include some of what I heard. A number of men referred to "the burden of testosterone" and learning to "manage their maleness." I hadn't fully appreciated what a challenging energy this magnificent life force might be and how little I really know about it. Measuring and comparing and competing—they seem to be inextricably woven into the notion of "being a man." In many tribal cultures men compete, but they are also responsible for the welfare of their opponent. That piece seems to be often missing in our culture.

Another missing piece was real and useful education about sexuality from an early age. I heard a longing for help and guidance with how to work with the energy of this powerful hormone.

I thought about how different the energy of female hormones is. My experience with estrogen has been, for the most part, one of attuning with life, with the flow of tides and cycles of the moon. I was fortunate not to suffer from terrible menstrual cramps. On the first day when I'd get my period I'd try to do very little and spend time in nature if possible. I declared it my "woman's day," and as I got quieter, tears came. Usually, they'd seem to be about something specific in my life. But quickly, they'd shift to a much larger field, softening me to the tenderness of life. Opening me to the sorrows of the world. I loved the monthly tug and bodily ache and the feeling of connection with everyone and everything. The world regained its sparkle.

What would it be like to have an injection and have that *testosterone* flow of energy in my body?

Watch little boys, they'll pick up a stick and they'll start beating a tree. There's just this energy, right? That's the force. It's almost like it builds up and you have to disperse it. There are so many men who are angry, because they don't know how to do it different. You're not taught healthy ways to express it and to drain it out or to work with it. There's no way that I know, besides sports, to actually work with it constructively.

My son, Tyler, who was the sweetest, gentlest, most sensitive kid ever. When he was fourteen, I was his lacrosse coach. One day some kid knocked him down from behind, a vicious hit, and Tyler, this gentle kid, got up, turned around and dove into this guy, screaming. He was ready to punch the kid's lights out. Cute little Tyler, right? He came off the field and looked at me with these wide eyes. "Dad, what just happened? What was that?" "That's adrenaline and testosterone, Ty. Get used to it." It's a Molotov cocktail.

(50s)

I have this big ball of boy energy to wrestle with and not a whole lot of guidance.

(20s)

I was scanning all the time for a mate. Like, all the time. I was lonely. I could never relax and just be okay. Part of it was sex, part was companionship, and part of it was this impulsive thing — like addiction or something. Just feeling agitated all the time. It's crazy. It's really intense, and it's not like it's dissipated since I've been in a relationship. By any means.

I still have to attract within the relationship, but I don't have to get a new woman to notice me. I'm not performing. Probably I still am on certain levels, but it takes a huge level of that off the table immediately. I was able to relax into myself in ways that I haven't been able to, probably ever. Also, I think that relaxation has lulled certain parts of my being into some less active, less creative state. I haven't figured out where to find the other energy, because I feel way less ambitious than I used to. Which may be the years passing, I don't know. Maybe part of ambition is a kind of restless uncomfortableness.

(20s)

Testosterone, I think, is the main reinforcer of "us" versus "them." Look what happens to boys at puberty.

(30s)

Between the ages of twelve and eighteen, I had these strong instinctual urges. I had an extreme desire to hunt food. It wasn't just to experience killing something. I wanted to provide my own food. I'm not saying that a man has to be violent, but I think that it's part of our biology. Not that we have to be abusive or destructive, but it's part of our evolution. To cut that off in one or two generations and say that's no longer appropriate under any circumstances is really challenging to deal with.

(30s)

Fathers and sons yelling at each other—that's testosterone right there, that feeling of, "I don't have to take orders from you." Absolutely consumes a young man's brain.

(40s)

My wife and I were standing on the corner waiting for the light to change. A car came by with a number of men—boys—in the car. Someone pounded the side of the car with their arm, making a loud noise, just as they were in front of us. Then there was a lot of screaming banter, catcalls at my wife, and I was . . . I was off of the sidewalk ready to kill! It was just pure aggression—scary as hell—this defensive thing that came out. It's such a powerful thing. It's what men do. That's the male animals' side of the balance. It happens incredibly rarely, but it's in there, available.

I've experienced this before. I feel like I'm a warrior. When there's a situation where I'm challenged, it scares me; and if someone scares me, I'm like a bear. I will attack. It's terrible. In the moment, it's primal. I am absolutely focused on who violated my . . . territory, I suppose. It's challenge to my territory and dominance. When I realize what's happened, then I'm back in the body that I live in. It absolutely shocks me.

My wife says she thinks that I'm somehow disappointed in myself for having that surge of male violence come up because I feel like I shouldn't do that. Well, it's just so foreign. It's the fight-or-flight response. I feel one way and then in an instant I feel like a monster. I felt like I became the giant Hulk, one of those stupid super heroes, like I could reach out forty feet with my arm and stop the car, fly through the air, pick up the car and throw it. This huge surge of power I felt inside. Hopefully, if the car had stopped, I would have just taken a deep breath and turned around and walked away. If a weapon came from the other side, then I would sacrifice myself to protect my loved ones. There would be no question. I wouldn't be able to think it through. It would just happen. At least, that's the sense I have.

I know that the animal, the male animal, is in there and it's very powerful. So I don't have anything to prove. I just want to keep it at bay.

(50s)

I never had to manage sexual drive. I don't know any men like me. In a monogamous relationship, I tend to be very sensual and sexual, but that's about connection. I mean, I think about sex, but mostly in relation to that person. Believe me, I have read where men have sexual thoughts every thirty seconds. Really? Who the hell are they talking to? It certainly wasn't applicable to me.

And yet, if someone wrongs me? "I'm gonna kick your ass." So that impulse is still there.

(50s)

If people want to go fuck, that's their business. It's aggression—"I'm gonna get me some." But what I get from men, when they're actually inside a woman—there can still be a lot of aggression and all, but that's when the mind finally quiets. They're in. Even if they can't quite articulate it, there's a sense of quiet. Of, "Oh, my God, I'm wanted," or, "She's here with me." I don't want to put down aggressive sex. It has its place, but I think it's a perversion of a spiritual longing. The man is engulfed. He can rest.

(50s)

I mean, testosterone just really affects behavior. I want to go back to the biology, chemistry of being a male, because it's very clear that the presence of testosterone results in behavior that is more aggressive, which doesn't necessarily lend itself to having compassion, but to anger or striking out. If you inject females with testosterone, they start behaving the same way. So there is this biological imperative, if you will, to fuck it up, because that may give you access to more females. There is a way in which testosterone does serve men.

(60s)

Men feel incredibly both weak and angry with women, but not for the standard reasons. I think it's because, at the end of the day, women get to decide who has sex. If you push against that, then it's rape. And men basically want to do it with everybody, right? There's very little training from elders about sexual energy. That is a void in this culture.

(60s)

I'm not comfortable sitting eyeball to eyeball and talking to somebody. Especially guys. Women, I can do. It is sad. I'm sure some of it's competition. If you're vulnerable, that could put you one down. Somebody might use that against you. And you have to keep your place, your position.

There's a lot of comparing myself and measuring against that goes on in my psyche. And if I start comparing I can feel really lost. It's a recurring thing in my life, feeling competitive. It has such a down side. You can't take true joy in someone else's accomplishments because you're making them somebody else. It's a constant battle. I know it's not cool, not healthy. I think it's terrible. And yet, sometimes I find myself doing that, you know. I'm just getting over it. I'm done with it. I'm done. I'm too old to keep doing that. I'm almost seventy!

(60s)

Adrian (30s)

"I'm still learning about the man code."

When I started to transition, I was so concerned with being perceived as male that I didn't realize the complications that would come with that. Which is that now people were tending to perceive me as an effeminate man, or as a gay man. Which is fine except that it subjects me to a different kind of threat of violence than being perceived as a masculine woman does.

I didn't even really know what a trans person was until college. I didn't know people could do that. I was really naïve. I thought I was destined to be miserable and hate my body. When I was little, I thought I was a boy, until I was disabused of that notion. They forced me to wear dresses, and I was like, why should I wear this thing? I wanted to dress in boy's clothes. When I was referred to as a girl, it traumatized me. I was experiencing dysphoric injury without even knowing what it was. I had no language for it.

I ran away from home when I was sixteen because my parents weren't okay with me being queer. They waxed all fundamentalist, like I was going to hell and all of these things. Some of my relatives said things like, "You'll always be my little girl," and I'm like, "Well, actually, no. If you want to know me as a person, you need to realize that's not who I am. Not only have you feminized me, you've infantilized me." Ultimately, they accepted my being queer, and ultimately they'll be able to wrap their head around my transition, but they still often refer to me as "she." It's sometimes hard for people who knew me before I transitioned to use male pronouns for me. Your gender is the first thing that people register about you. Once they've clicked you into a category, it's extremely hard for them to change that. People I meet now, they just see me as a guy, and they use male pronouns.

I lived the first twenty-five years of my life passing as a woman, so I have that experience. I have a certain knowledge that cis-men [men born biologically male] don't have. But how society inculcates boys with the knowledge of how they're supposed to act, I don't have that. So now I'm learning how men are with each other. I'm still learning about the man hug and the man code.

I know of at least two people who would like to transition but can't, either because of family or job. I didn't have a choice. It was sort of like, if I want to live and be happy, this is what I need to do. Otherwise, I wanted to die. I actually did. No, I never tried to commit suicide, but I felt I didn't want to live if I had to live this way. It was a very pre-lingual feeling.

My grandmother is Native American, so I learned a little about that culture growing up. As with the Japanese, there's a certain way that men speak and a certain way that women speak. On the reservation, there is a person who's seen as a seer or prophet and who can speak both ways. I don't know exactly what that person's conception of their gender is, but I'm thinking that maybe my being in the world, or other transpeople being in the world — that binaristic ways of being can be bridged. Hopefully it's something healing for humanity just to realize that there doesn't need to be these two ways. There can be a third way or a multitude of ways.

I would like people to realize there is a range of masculinity, like Kinsey's concept of the spectrum for sexuality. My sense is that the same is true for gender. It's not always something people think about. There can be an extreme femininity and extreme masculinity that we tend to idealize as a culture, but the reality is that most people fall somewhere in between. People like to divide things into binaries, because that's easy. Right and wrong, black and white. With gender, as I was saying, once people think they have figured out what you are, it's very difficult for them to change that perspective. Or conversely, if they can't figure out what you are, there is a potential for violence. First, uncomfortability, then violence.

∿

Towards the beginning of my transition, there was a period where I was passing both ways. "Passing" is kind of a fraught term, but I'll use it as a placeholder.

Sometimes people would see me as a woman, sometimes as a man. And dating a woman who is lesbian has its own complications. We were both worried about being perceived as a heterosexual couple.

If it's dangerous to be perceived as a masculine woman or a feminine man, it's even more dangerous when people can't figure out your gender. I had this experience on the subway in New York City. There was a group of teenagers—and they couldn't figure out my gender. One of them was like, "Dude, are you a girl, son?" They followed me out the subway and up the street saying shit to me and I tried to play it cool because there were eight of them, and I wouldn't have stood a chance. Eventually, they gave up following me.

And a couple months ago, this man just started attacking me out of nowhere. My partner Elaine and I were coming out of a restaurant, and he just grabbed me by the throat and slammed my head against the wall. He said, "I'm gonna kill you, faggot!" In that moment, I realized, oh, wow, people are made so uncomfortable by feminine men that there's a threat of, you know, having your ass kicked or getting murdered. The man had a girlfriend, a person with him who started screaming for him to stop. I didn't even think of doing the standard things, like kick him in the balls and whatever. I just wanted to get out of there. I was shocked. I was shaken. I was really freaked out.

Elaine and I got into a cab. Then I realized I should've called the police, so I did. They categorized it as a hate crime because the guy called me a faggot. I have to say the hate crime detectives were pretty sensitive, but when I went into the police precinct, the regular police were just joking with each other. I can't tell you how many times I heard the word "faggot." One of them was teasing another that he had gone to the tanning salon, and how gay that was. Another one suggested maybe getting a pedicure, and the first one was like, "that's for faggots. I'd rather have my feet amputated."

⁓

The stereotype or clichéd response would be, the attacker's uncertain of his own sexuality. Obviously, he was threatened by me. He has a hatred of, you know, feminine men or people he perceives to be gay. So why is that? Is it because the thought of two men together is disgusting to him? Is it because he's afraid he might be attracted? I don't know, but it's really sad for that person, you know?

I actually didn't feel angry. I mean, I did immediately afterward, but after talking to the police, I felt sad. Sad for him, and sad for myself. Sad that this situation exists. Anger would have been easier somehow.

I've been trying to figure out ways, if this happens to me in the future, ways that I could diffuse the situation. Like, the concept behind Aikido where you take the person's energy and redirect that violence into something else. Maybe this is idealistic, but I would like to sit down face-to-face with this guy and members of our community and ask him why. Talk to him. Let him know that I'm a person.

I think there should be some fall-out. He shouldn't be able to get away with it. I think a lot of the violence towards transpeople stems from other people feeling they're being tricked. They think the person is one thing, and then they realize that "actually" they're something else — and that's where the uncomfortability comes from. People make that instant categorization. Then when they discover someone is trans, they're like, "Oh, you tricked me." No, I am what I present, and you don't need to know anything more.

Being a trans person I worry because I don't feel like I am aggressive, nor do I want to access that, nor am I interested in perpetrating violence or responding to violence with violence. How do I walk the line in order to be safe, in order to be seen clearly? I don't think I'm there. I'm getting there, but I'm not there.

One of the interesting things about being perceived as male is that I'm not automatically allowed to be a feminist the way I was when people thought I was a woman. I have to prove my credentials, and rightfully so, because I now enjoy male privilege. I mean, I identify with feminists, and I am a feminist, but it's sort of like when fags are allowed to call each other fags, but someone from the outside isn't allowed to do that. I can't just throw around the word "bitch" or whatever.

People would ask me, "Oh, are you transitioning?" The question sort of threw me off-guard, because I didn't see it as a change. I saw it as lining up language with how I already felt myself to be. So I said, "Well yes and no. I've always been transitioning, or trying to."

The first feeling I remember after starting hormone replacement therapy was an enormous sense of well-being and happiness. For the first two weeks, I wasn't passing yet, people were still calling me lady—but I was just smiling. I didn't even care anymore. There was an ebbing of the turmoil and anxiety. I didn't even realize I was missing that profound sense of peace. I was beginning my process, and the hormone itself felt incredibly good. I wasn't crying, anymore. I actually just didn't feel the need to cry at all for a year after I started. It wasn't like I wasn't feeling the same depth of emotion, but I just wasn't as quick to tears. I don't know if that's because I was feeling happier myself, or if it had something to do with the chemical effect of testosterone. I still feel that same sadness, I still feel the same emotion that I had before, but I just don't cry as much.

I kind of do miss being able to cry. I miss the camaraderie of women. Women feel very easy being intimate. And I have to say, at this point, I have more close female friends than I have men friends, so I haven't actually figured out how men are intimate with each other.

As to the long-term effects of testosterone, there's no science, just anecdotal evidence. I'm subject to the same things men are subject to, like losing my hair and a higher risk for heart attack—anything that a biological man is subject to. I was more driven after taking testosterone. It's difficult to learn how to mange these two impulses: sex and violence.

Men who knew me before I transitioned sometimes don't know where to put me. They treat me as a guy, but occasionally I have been wary of that. I wonder, are you really treating me like how you would treat another man? Early in my transition, there was this internal querying that can, if you're not careful, verge on paranoia. It's like, what does that person think of me? Do they hate me? Do they think I'm a freak? You have to quiet down those fears, because there's almost this obsession with whether you're passing. It gets in the way of living your life.

~

I've been transitioning for a year and a half, if you count the start of my transition with the taking of testosterone. I'd say I'm perceived as a man 95% of the time now, but I still don't feel safe enough to outfit myself in feminine articles. Masculinity is the unmarked mode. Like I can be in a tux, and all I would have to do is put on a barrette or some lipstick. That would mark me as feminine.

One thing trans people go through is having to deal with the law. For example, Adrian is not my birth name. I changed my name legally because I felt I had to line myself up with the language. That was my first conscious step towards transition. It's very difficult, if not impossible, to have a gender on your birth certificate changed. I have been able to change the gender on my driver's license, but not my birth certificate. Luckily, that went without a hitch, even though it was kind of complex to do. Right now I'm working on the gender of my passport.

For a while before I started HRT, when Elaine and I would go out to dinner, and when the server would say, "What can I get you ladies?" I'd burst into tears. It was that traumatizing for me to be perceived as a woman. Yet there wasn't any other way people could have been expected to perceive me. Now, if people do say "you ladies," I can just laugh, or I can correct them. It's fine.

It's a bizarre thing, male privilege. I have to stay aware of even little things, like people handing me the check at a restaurant, treating me with more deference on the phone. I had a funny experience talking to a loan officer on the phone. He was like, "Oh, I'd be happy to help you with that, Mr. Caballero. Uh-oh, I see it says Miss Caballero here. So sorry, I'll change that right away." I was like, "It's not a big deal, but if you could change it, that'd be great." And he was all, "Oh, wow, I would be so upset if I saw that someone had put my name as *Miss* Anthony, blah blah blah." Yeah, the man code. There are so many things I hadn't thought of. I guess that's what privilege is. You don't even know you don't know.

My body is more autonomous, not as immediately subject to being sexualized. That's great in a way, but it makes me more of a feminist because I am realizing how terrible it can be for women to be under this gaze and be subject to it. If they talk back, they're a bitch. If they respond, they're a slut.

I am of the opinion that chivalry is just sexism cloaked in a pretty dress. I try to be chivalrous to people of both genders, open doors for people, older people, regardless of their gender. You know, giving up your seat on the train. But this is just kindness.

I think regard is a really good word because it comes from the French word *regarder,* which means "to see." To have regard for someone is literally to see them clearly. We're often not seeing each other clearly and that's why these dynamics persist.

≈

As a poet, my life's work is to try to expand the language, and through that expand people's thinking around gender. Ha! Like you have to learn the language of the oppressor in order to use it against them. Use it against *him.* In reality, the oppressor is the system itself. I want to get people to break down the gender binary in some way. Like using gender-neutral pronouns, even invented pronouns like "xe" and "sie." There are two issues. One is, how do we use gender neutrality? I think we already do with "they." Just as challenging are people's assumptions. You hear even little kids say, "Oh! Look at that dog. He's really sad." The masculine is the generic.

I sometimes worry about getting respect or being accepted because I'm not interested in the man code. How do I toe the line? In the end, I think if you just tell the truth, it's irresistible.

There's A Shyness About It

"Men are starving for connection."

When I get together with women, there's usually laughter and food, and out come the stories of our lives. I hadn't often observed this kind of thing with the men I knew. And yet, I know men feel affection and camaraderie with one another. So I wondered—do men define friendship differently than women do? What does it mean to them? How do they experience it? Not being a man, I couldn't possibly know.

"Well, Bob and I get together and go to the Giants games on a regular basis. He's my friend. What's the matter with that?" "I don't think that, initially, men are very curious about each other," another man in his 60s told me. But many of the guys were also saying they miss having close friends. They're wanting something more than doing things together without much conversation, or really confiding in each other. I was curious about what they do with their feelings if there's no place to share them?

If you don't know about your own feelings, if you don't have the habit of paying attention to what goes on inside of you, how can you possibly share that? Maybe friendship means something else to men.

I was already well into the interviewing process when several women asked me, "How come so many of the men I know don't seem to have close male friends? Did they have to give up having real friends to 'be a man'?" Sometimes women spoke of experiencing this as a burden, an added pressure. So I began to ask the guys. The answers ranged from, "I don't have any friends, no real ones." to "My wife is amazed at how many friends I have."

Guys say mean things to try to act cool, because if they don't act like fifth graders, then their friends will think they're sissies and won't be their friends. I don't act all tough. I just be myself. That's why I only have a few friends.

(9 yr.)

[After hearing the story of the man with a ninety-year friendship.]

Men don't have more friends because they're busy all the time. They work and they get a life and pay the bills and stuff. They don't have time to just sit and chat. I have lots of friends now. I think someday my friend, my first friend, even if we part, someday we'll meet again when I grow up.

(9 yr.)

I wish I could tell everyone my secrets, not just keep them inside. Everyone would tease me and talk about it and keep it for a long time. If I tell all my friends, they'll be like—what are you doing? And then they won't be my friend any more.

(9 yr.)

I feel I can be honest mostly with Sam. I'm just really myself. Jacob and Ryan I can be honest with, but sometimes I put on a different personality with them. Boys have to put on that cover to act like you're tough. You just adapt to having to be somebody you're not, and say, "All right, it's the game I have to play." With Sam, we might both be doing that at school, but when we're by ourselves we don't do it.

(11 yr.)

What makes a good friend is someone who stands up for a guy who's being put down, or who can laugh around sadness, doesn't turn his back on others, and is respectful.

Kenny welcomed me when I moved to a new town and a new school. At first I felt like I wasn't really appreciated, like I had to do something, be somebody else around my friends, but I could just be myself with him.

It may sound silly, but I think its fate. You're destined to be friends.

My dad's like Kenny, my best friend, but an older guy who has more experience. He always says, "You have someone you can talk to. I'm right here." I can talk to him about anything. If I didn't have him I don't think I would have made it through all the moving and divorce and stuff.

(11 yr.)

With good friends you wanna be sure you pull the honesty out. If you're living a lie, the older you get the farther you get away for yourself.

(20s)

I've had so many times where a woman's come up and just congratulated me and another guy friend for how affectionate we are with each other — the big hugs and the not being afraid to be really close to each other. I can't believe it so surprising 'cause, to me, it's not.

(20s)

I think it is the competition thing. It's at the root of most men's lives with other men. Because if we are vulnerable and show vulnerability, which is a lot of what friendship is, then we might lose our place in the hierarchy. Might use it against them. It's hard to find a man that you can trust as a man. I think because men are subject to testosterone and testosterone will sometimes leave a man unreliable. Since we all have it, we know that about ourselves and about other men, too.

(30s)

There is an unspoken rule that guys need to man up and be strong. Even brothers, like my siblings and I, despite being very close in every kind of way, we'll often not be close in discussing women for some reason. Very few men will get into serious, open, honest discussion about insecurities they feel in these relationships. Occasionally, you'll break through that when somebody has broken up with a girlfriend and they're being open and exposed. But even in those situations, the guy who has lost his girlfriend will still try to keep people at arm's length to whatever extent possible.

(30s)

In this country, the extent of physical touch between men is maybe a high-five, and that's it. My natural reaction is to touch. With my friends in Mexico, if people are sitting around a table and I arrive, I'll put my hands on my friends' shoulders — like, "What's up?" Here, even something as innocuous as that can be completely misinterpreted. It doesn't even have to be, "Oh, he's homosexual." It would be felt as an invasion of space, or it just feels alien to the other person — awkward.

If men aren't allowed to be vulnerable and affectionate with each other it's a vicious circle, because it perpetuates this behavior amongst men that we aren't emotional beings. It affects your health. Or maybe even, if you do it long enough, you lose access to those feelings.

(30s)

I've spent so much time just healing and surviving I haven't, for a very long time, had much time for friendships. Even though there were people in my life who said and would think that they were my friends — because I couldn't feel like I trusted anybody, I didn't realize how distant I'd made myself to them in my own heart.

(30s)

When I was in college, I had a really close friend. We were roommates, super close. Did almost everything together. After he graduated, I got to be close with another guy. At one point, referring to my former roommate, he said, "Oh, I thought you and he were gay." I was like, "You did?" It was a shock to me, because after that he wasn't willing to have any kind of friendship or be open. Whereas with my wife and her women friends hanging out, nobody assumes they are gay. It's not fair for guys.

(30s)

There's certainly a lot of stuff that goes on in guy culture that makes things scary, even connection. There's always a sense of hierarchy. You can't quite be vulnerable, even with close friends.

(40s)

Friendships can feel like they're taking me away from my wife and kids.

Something I do is, I reach out on my birthday. My friends and I get together, and first do an obscure sport none of us is good at. Then we drink some beer — it's silly, physical, fun and friendly. We have a nice meal, and end up with serious talk, sharing ideas about what's possible in the world and what we aspire to and what's holding us back. We're really just delighted to be together.

My best friends are the most free and the most interested in talking about some kind of soul aspiration. The conversation is revealing, vulnerable — but in a nuts and bolts way. For instance, one of my friends is a screenwriter and he wants to express stories to the world. Another friend is more political and tends to come from "Where's the outrage?" They're fun, exciting people who have humanity. They have an interest in service or a desire to make positive ripples if not waves. In some ways, all of the men I consider good friends are "drop outs," making a positive choice and not playing the game — because that's freeing. The writer chooses to live in a tiny town across the country from Hollywood. Another friend is in a collective. Two others are teachers. They all value freedom and creativity.

I see good friendships happening when men claim a territory where they can be freer — they may still have some success, but mostly they're enjoying themselves. For me, part of it might be getting my role from smaller scale cultures — from real people instead of people I was reading about. Male role models are generally all about powerful, grand achievement — tangible, kick ass, being The Best.

Contentment, for a man, isn't really touted that much. It's how much can you do, just how good can you be? A lot of men are attached to their achievements, and not so much to their liberation. Self-respect rather than confidence is freeing.

One of my friends is competitive in sports, but he lets his light side into his stories, his failure and insecurity. It's why I can come to him with my story. As he listens, I'm more ready to laugh at it all. There's that other, different, miserable thing where men look for a scapegoat group to laugh at. Playful humor works when you're all laughing at yourselves. You feel good, but it took some humility.

(40s)

Friends? Not a hoard. Maybe six or so people on the planet. That is a lot. But they're all over the place. It's not like I see them every week. It's hard to maintain. I mean, I don't think I'm a private person. Sometimes I'm very much like a woman. I'll feel, "Oh my God, Jeff was annoying me so much the other day." We all want to be the heroes of our own life, especially guys. If we complain about what's going on in our life, it means that we're not very heroic at the moment. And I don't think guys really want to show that we're failing very often.

(40s)

A lot of the asshole-ness and distancing of males is because we don't have real intimacy. With a good friend, you know the backstory. You know why they're being such assholes. Makes it hard to judge.

(40s)

I fell in love and I knew—I guess I was gay. I didn't know the word "gay" at that time. But I think I was 12, 13 something in that age. He was two years older than me, like an older brother. And when Sammy died of leukemia, I went into this very odd years of limbo. There was nothing physical, but I adored this person so much. I just liked being close to him. He was 17 and I was 15 when he died, but it was long enough to know that.

I think kids are aware of people that they can trust and want to be around. I might say that it was because I must have been gay or something now, but that's not really true. I think you just love to love and be loved. It's so mysterious and wonderful.

(50s)

In the male culture, there's a premium put on competence and performance. I had a lot of friends growing up in school, especially on the athletic field. I mean, we would go drinking together. There wasn't a learning about how to relate to men, outside of a sports environment or a work team environment where it's all male. I learned all my skills for relating, in terms of friendship and trying to share, from women. So I can talk to any woman about my feelings.

With men, it's a different story. You've got this segregated thing. You're no longer relating to men, because you're not playing on an athletic field. You get married or you have a girlfriend and you've got a job, so that's what you do. You go to work to make the money to provide for your family, you go home, you relate to your wife, that's it. Why does one need friends? Especially if one doesn't know how to do it. It takes you out of your comfort zone. That's the idea I had.

When your marriage starts to fall apart and you're no longer able to talk with your wife about certain things, then you start to talk to men, and you talk to them like you learned through women.

(50s)

You know, I don't think any man really wants to know what the other man feels. When it does happen, it's extraordinary. It happens because there's already a bond. When a man shares with another man that he is in love with a woman, that shows a kind of vulnerability. It's a big deal. It's only happened a few times to me. When it has, I feel so honored.

(50s)

Have there been men? Yes, I'm not going to lie, and that's the first time I've ever said that. When you don't have someone, don't get a hug, nobody says, "You look nice," there is a thirst. I hired a personal trainer for that reason. When he spots me and his hands touch my elbow, do I feel that warmth? That's what I do it for. Quite honestly, I envy gay men. They hug each other on the street, for Christ's sake!

(50s)

I don't have many friends. It's one of my current kinds of sadness. It's really. . . I don't like it. I started trying to cultivate male friends, but haven't been too successful. Maybe I'm not doing enough, or maybe everybody is just so busy they don't have time. It's not the biggest priority, plus there's a shyness about it.

(60s)

It's a difficult thing. I have one friend in this world that I call on a regular basis. And we actually talk. I feel very comfortable on the phone because I don't have to worry about how my face is or how I'm coming across. In person, I feel he might be measuring me. That's what guys do. We judge each other.

Men don't have more friends because they don't have time. That's the sad part. They haven't valued it. You have to give up competition to have friends, too. You have to be vulnerable.

(60s)

I have a friend who's very open, very malleable. He's more like a river, a flowing person. I can have a conversation with him, and it can duck and dive, which makes it fascinating. He's not constantly asserting himself. Often, older men are like that. It's a capacity not to have too strong an opinion about who you are—deconstructing that. The idea of who I should be and what I should be feeling. As men, we're always defending the part that makes us miserable. At some point you've got to feel an extreme sense of loneliness, because the thing you're trying to get rid of is the part that feels the loneliness.

(60s)

You've got to trust your friends, and you can't trust other men. You just can't. If you have closer friends it takes away from your ego. If a man can manage to make friends with another man it's a miracle.

(60s)

To have friends, I have to be willing to talk and be self-revealing about my life. If there's a mutuality in doing this, that gives me permission to be myself. The critical question is—can I be vulnerable?

From my chaotic upbringing, God knows I had no idea what people were about. I figured out very early that doing therapy was a place where I could get close to people without having to risk very much. I could finally figure out what people were about and learn how to relate intimately. That's why I became a therapist. I had the protective shell of my role. My work for the last ten or fifteen years has been to let go of it.

You don't know what you don't know. You can't miss what you don't know you've lost. Every now and then you meet someone who knows what he knows. He's unfiltered. He's just himself. There's a kind of innocence.

(60s)

I'm blessed with friends. I can't say I was unloved as a child. But I was not demonstrably loved as a child. So I sought out love wherever I could find it. I was sent off to boarding school when I was eight. Probably the earliest loves in my life were my buddies, my male friends. Going to an all male school and all male camps I learned to establish close, emotional relationships with men—boys—when I was growing up. 'Cause I had no alternative.

(60s)

It's hard for a university president to develop genuine friendships on and off the campus. One always suspects that the friendship is actually masking some other deal, or something else is going on below the surface, or they want something—a favor or for me to put in a good word for them here and there.

I think it's very hard for men to develop friendships. Particularly, I would think it's hard for everybody as you grow older. So I go on an annual fishing trip with three other fellows. We can't talk much during the day, just chitchat, because we're fishing. At the end of the day, we always have a lot to drink—too much—and tell dirty stories. Maybe there's something wrong with me. Maybe it's our culture. For my take on it, friendship between men—it's tough. A lot of us have forgotten how to play now and be fully expressive. To break down the armoring, we use alcohol instead.

(70s)

Hank Katz is my buddy for the ages, my oldest best buddy. Known him for more than ninety years. When Hank was born, he was in a crib on the neighbors' front walk and I was standing in my crib, at two years old, looking down at Hank. I remember that. We grew up like brothers. Never had a fight or a disagreement. We built caves and tree houses and coasters and wagons and cars and everything together. Hank has been there for me, and I'm there for him, for all our lives.

(90s)

Michael (20s)

"Gays are a bridge between masculine and feminine."

I was the first person ever to be openly gay in our school district. Once I got into high school, and everyone knew that I was the gay guy, four other guys finally came out. All of them were way more out than me, so everyone in school put their attention on them. Now I was just the weird gay guy who had a bunch of weird girl friends. Just the side gay dude.

It was hard coming out. I was pretty suicidal for a while—not tendencies of actually wanting to kill myself. I was just like, "Please someone, kill me." If I saw a dangerous opportunity, I was like, "Oh, my God, please, please, please let it happen. Get me out of this."

My parents didn't really know this was going on. My mom, forced it out of my friend Jayle. She saw a note I had written to Jayle, confiding in her about what was happening to me at the time. I guess my mom freaked out. "Why doesn't he talk to me about it?" There was never a moment where my mom was like, "Why are you gay? Why are you doing that?" She wasn't angry. She was hurt for a while, but she completely accepted it, even though she was afraid for me, telling me I couldn't act in certain ways. For her generation, being gay equals death.

My mom would just try and be a mom. When I lashed out, she didn't see it as, "Oh, he's in pain." She saw it as, "You're being a brat, a total asshole, and I'm going to discipline you." And I would be like, "No, I'm doing bad things because I'm hurting. I'm lashing out because I don't know what else to do." It was a strange period. Between ages thirteen and seventeen, I had some very hardcore moments with her.

My mom has a lot of strength. She knows what she wants, and she's not afraid to tell people how it is. But she also believes you have to sacrifice your personal goals in life to have a family.

My mom is Hispanic but it's Spaniard basically, and my father is Mexican. They've been married about thirty years now. They were raised in this country. My mom was an army brat. My dad grew up in Texas, and I was born in San Antonio, a very conservative town. I'm the youngest of three.

My father's a very good man. He has a lot of strength and knowledge, very much like a sage. His idea of being a man isn't like, get a job, get a woman—none of those cultural norms. He told me that to be a man is: control your anger, control your emotions, always be kind, never hit a woman, always treat women like they are gold. Always be who you are at every moment, or you're not being the man you are. He told me, never give up your morals, never give up your beliefs.

He was a very good dad. A strong-willed man, kind of like a monk. He never talked unless he needed to. People thought he was absent, but it was more like he only spoke when he saw that I needed to be spoken to.

My mom's idea about being a man is kind of similar to my dad's—you just have to make sure you're constantly doing what you need to do for yourself, and not let other people destroy what you believe in, not let other people put you down, not let other people stomp on your self-esteem. Basically, to be a man is just to be yourself.

Meanwhile, the culture around me was basically, to be a man you have to be physically strong. You have to be extremely reclusive and set back, like a brick wall. Don't exude your emotions all the time. Don't let anyone in. You have to do all the things a man does—love a woman, be into sports, be into baseball and basketball. You have to get a car to take out women. Have a job that pays really well, or you're not a man. All of those silly norms.

⁓

It was probably in 7th grade that it hit me I couldn't just be me. Gym class—if you're not aggressive in sports, the other boys think you're not manly enough. Many times I felt overpowered by the energy of other boys, really violent, rude, brash. I was a wallflower kind of guy. I liked observing. I can do sports like swimming, running and stuff, but when it gets to the point of competition, I quit. I hate competition. I don't like having to prove that my body can do things, because I know it can. I don't like having to prove my manhood, as opposed to just living it.

The other guys saw me as a girl because I didn't like these things. The girls loved me, because I was a completely open person, so tapped into my emotions, into being friendly. Guys saw that as being sissy. Probably they were threatened, because I was constantly around all the women the guys wanted. I was best friends with them, sleeping over with them, just chillin' with them, and guys saw that as very unfair I guess. Like, how come this guy gets it? He doesn't even play sports.

In those years, I survived by music—listening, and making it. I literally had headphones on five or six years of middle and high school. I was almost blind to the outside world. I completely overpowered myself with sound until I couldn't take any more emotion, and then I'd pass out, exhausted. When I'd wake up, the sadness I was feeling would be gone.

I started out with angry rock music, trying to exude resentment towards what was happening around me. I think I was also trying to prove to people I could be strong. They'd be, like, "Man, what are you listening to?" And I'd take off my headphones and show them, and they'd be like, "Whoa, dude, that's hardcore." I'm like, yeah, that's being a man, right there. That's manly. Then when I realized I was only doing it for the attention and acceptance of other men, I started morphing into more gentle music and ambient women vocalists.

I was about fifteen or sixteen when I finally started delving into that side of myself, listening to Enya, Imogen Heap, all these very nice, subtly beautiful women voices. At first it was very frightening, because people would be like, "What are you listening to?" It'd be Björk or something, and they'd be like, "That's really weird that you're listening to that, dude." I was sixteen years old and a guy. I wasn't supposed to listen to Björk.

So many rules. That's why I was constantly in my own space. Like, if you don't accept what my rules are for myself, I put on the headphones.

I was completely supported by the girls and by my family—my dad, my older brother—so I was free to be me with them. My brother did sometimes make me feel bad for not doing sports. As a kid, he would beat me up, chase me around the house and put me in headlocks because he knew I wouldn't fight back. When I was around sixteen or seventeen, he stopped because I started to fight back. At that point, my whole family accepted that I was who I was. I do what I want, and I'm not weak in doing it.

In 8th grade, I met my first best friend, Amy. She was the first kindred spirit I really had. She was a tomboy, not wanting to conform to the girly aspect of society. Didn't put on makeup or prissy herself up. She was just Amy. She would tell me, "Don't try and be like all these guys, you're perfect the way you are."

~

First grade. I knew I was gay, but I didn't know what it was. Because of something my brother did in school, we moved across the city to a new side of town with different looking people. The boys there were more attractive than the ones in my old neighborhood—basically, my personal preference of being attracted to Caucasians. I was like, "Wow, why do I feel this way about this boy that just came up to talk to me, so attracted?" I knew something was different, because I saw other guys looking at girls that same way. I'd be like, "Why am I looking at these guys like that?"

I didn't know what the word gay was. I didn't even know what the idea was. It was just a feeling. There was nobody at all to talk to about it.

In 6th grade, someone turned to me in recess and said, "Faggot." I went and asked someone else, "Why did he call me that?" It was just curiosity at that point. They said, "Oh, he probably thinks you're gay, dude." I said, "Yeah, I like guys, but why's he saying that?" And they're like, "That's like being gay. They call the gay guys that." "Wow, okay. I guess I understand what being gay is now: being wrong."

In 8th grade, I finally really came to terms with it—the feeling and the words and the identification. That's when I got my first crush, my first infatuation with a guy, a straight guy, and I had it for a whole year. I told my best friend Kim about it. I hadn't met Amy yet, so I told Kim, and she blurted it out to *the whole school*. She didn't say about the guy, but everyone knew, and I could see that *he* knew.

That boy started acting rude to me, telling all his friends I was weird—that I was the gay guy who was in love with him. His friends started bashing on me, constantly trying to start fights. This guy Victor literally rammed me in the hall, pushed me against a locker and called me faggot. I turned around and gave him a really hard shove. I don't think he expected me to be that strong, because I gave him whiplash. One of my girl friends came running up, cursing and yelling, and started pushing him. My girls all came in and just got on him, basically, and so for the rest of that year there was a battle between the people who hated me for being gay and all of my girls who were defending me. Every time there was a dance at school, it was like, boom! Battle time. I would be standing there going, "Man, I just wanted to love people." It was a silly, silly experience in middle school.

≈

My relationship with my mom changed for the better when I met my second boyfriend, Peter, who was one year older than me. She saw that I was able to have a stable relationship with another guy. I'd had one boyfriend before that, and all she saw in me at that time was the rebellion, such as skipping school for two days to be with him. She hated that dude. She thought he was ruining my life with his lifestyle. Then she saw the difference with Peter. He was smart and handsome and she saw him taking care of her son, so she let him live at our house for seven months.

Peter's family didn't accept him. His dad was abusive and crazy, and just made him live in a sort of Harry Potter closet, so I told him to come live with us. After a time, things fell apart, and my mom finally kicked him out. I was like, "If you kick him out, you're kicking me out." She was like, "Fine, you're kicked out, too. Leave!"

Peter was my first real adult relationship. It was dramatic, and also traumatizing. After we got kicked out, we were homeless together, living in his truck. Then we found an apartment together, and lived there for five, six months. It was bliss the first few months. Then, of course, the normal relationships problems came into play that I'd never dealt with before. I'd been repressing love for so long that I didn't know how to be with someone. All sorts of abuses happened during that relationship that tore us apart. Emotional abuse, mental abuse, all sorts of craziness. Neither of us loved ourselves. Especially him. As a gay man, he was more repressed than me. His family hated him, and I resented him for being so checked-out all the time. "Man," I thought, "is this how gay relationships are? Is this what gay people go through? Or is this what everyone goes through?"

No one had an answer for that. I was like, "Man, being gay sucks ass, man." Peter and I moved apart. We didn't talk for years.

When I was eighteen, I moved to Austin. That was when my sexuality really started expressing itself. I was finally able to be who I was, and had wonderful experiences. Eighteen was when I felt comfortable in my skin.

Finally I no longer felt terrified being out in the world. The only thing that terrified me were my mom's fears. She would constantly tell me horror stories. Even to this day, she'll still try to inject certain fears in me—not about being gay, but just in general, such as, "Be careful, the world's dangerous." I have to tell her, "Mom, stop. I don't live the fear life anymore."

The reason I love women so much is that women have been the catalyst to everything I am as a man. They're powerful beings, and they're going to teach men to come back into their own power. Not the kind of power over people we see in the world, but the power to express who they *really* are, being truthful and heartful with each other. Gays are a bridge between masculine and feminine. Straight men are obsessed with women, with how they are. Why? Because of their emotional body. How is she doing that? They want that. They don't know how. Men have that, too. They just *forgot* it.

I've had this instinctual knowing that the Earth created gay people for a reason. The Earth did it. Gay people didn't just pop up out of nowhere. I believe the Earth created gay people for two reasons: to fix the overpopulation problem, and to teach the world unconditional love. That's it.

≈

The real fear in my life has been of not being understood. I've been bombarded with so many judgments. "Oh, you're the gay guy." You're not the guitarist, you're not the writer, you're not any of these. You're gay. My struggle wasn't really to be accepted for being gay. I just wanted someone to look at me for being myself.

It's been very empowering to realize how much strength I actually have. Because of what I've lived through, I feel I'm ahead of the game. Now, I need to help people. We need to stop the bullshit right now, and start loving. What people think of as unconditional love is actually conditional love. They say they love someone for who they are, but really they love them for who they *think* they are. So that's all I'm here for, learning how to love authentically and showing people that.

I'm not here to judge myself anymore, or validate myself. I'm here to show everyone that we're all in it together. None of us are getting out of here alive. Even if nobody accepts me, I have to accept myself. It's like the lover you've been looking for is in the mirror. People get in these relationships that fall apart the way mine have because they're searching outside of themselves for someone to save them and validate them. Validation is fake. The answer is not there.

After dealing with so many different situations for so long, nothing hurts anymore. It's not a numb feeling. It's just. "Okay, I've dealt with that." Complete trust. In this world, we're all projecting our existences onto each other, so when someone does something hateful towards you, you have to understand it's because they're in pain. They're inflicting pain because they're in pain.

In my future, I see a lot of love. I see a lot of helping. I see myself pulling people out of their hells. That's what I'm here for.

I Feel Like I'm Faking It

"I don't want to be that guy. So I lie."

So many men were expressing the feeling of not being fully authentic that I finally added it to my list of questions: "Do you feel like you're a fraud or an imposter? Are you afraid of being found out, exposed?" I wanted to know how common this was. And the most common answer I got was, "Of course!" And even, "Yes. 100%!"

Occasionally, I heard something different from guys who "want people to pull the curtain on me and see who I am" and "have no fear of being found out. I've had my covers pulled. A lot."

A few artists, when they're doing their art, didn't feel fraudulent. And often, guys nearing seventy didn't either. These few exceptions aside, most of the men I listened to said they feel like frauds. "My worst fear was being exposed for not being as big as my 'man' hat, what I was pretending to be."

They were telling me that it's not even an intentional, "I'm putting this on" kind of thing, because there's a sense that the whole male role is a performance. Even though virtually everyone was feeling this way, few realized that everyone else felt like a fraud, too.

As a girl growing up, I started to notice that the boys who had been my playmates and friends were suddenly puffing themselves up. Exaggerating. A lot of the men I was listening to spoke of this as well. Pretty soon, they said, you've told so many lies about yourself you don't remember what the truth is. "It's hard to know what's true and tell it first of all to yourself," said a man in his 50s. "Please don't be angry with me when I tell the truth," a man I loved once asked of me. I looked into his face and saw the boy who had tried to tell the truth about something he'd done and been punished for it, and so began to hide and scatter.

When these men were feeling safe with me, I could see that there was an impulse to be honest, to tell the truth about themselves and be known. I had made a commitment to myself of "no blame, no judgment," no matter what they said. I wasn't raising my eyebrows or dropping my jaw. A number of men shared that they didn't want to tell the truth because they didn't want to be found out to be the person they deeply felt they really were. Where there are secrets there's shame. The recurring refrain I heard was—"I won't be liked." "I won't be loved." "I'll be abandoned."

This coping behavior that had been so frustrating and puzzling to me was now becoming a curiosity. So I asked, "Under what circumstances are you most likely to not tell the truth?"

≈

I'm not much of a liar, except when it comes to protecting my friends from getting in trouble. I've figured out a lot of ways to feel safe and get along. That's what you have to do.

(11 yr.)

Boys start putting on more of a cover so they look tough and more scary and then they think they'll be safe. That's kind of what it's like for boys growing up. I've noticed some kids tag along with bullies since they feel safer. What I do to stay safe is—everyone who gets really angry with me or wants to start a fight, I just really ignore them. Then I walk in the direction of a recess monitor. Basically, it's the survival of the fittest for them then.

Most of the people I've known who act all tough and stuff have been fairly abused by peers. When I see other kids acting all strong and mean, I think you aren't really a man. A man is what you are yourself. You have to act yourself to be a real man.

(11 yr.)

I kind of exaggerate to impress people. But then it's weird, because sometimes I won't be exaggerating and they won't believe me, and sometimes I will be exaggerating and they will believe me, which is annoying. You want to impress people because they might already be good at something or you want them to think highly of you. Then they might hang out with you more.

(14 yr.)

Omission and obfuscation's the same thing. I'll lie to keep my job.

Outcast [a rapper] says, "The whole world loves it when you're in the noose. The whole world loves it when you're looking down." So, I might lie about that. "You got paid today?" "Yeah, but you know, money's gone already." I mean, usually it is though.

(20s)

In my relationship with my partner, I have a weird tendency to beat around the bush when it comes to finances. I don't necessarily lie, but a little bit of smoke and mirrors. Absolutely. It all has to do with the insecurity of feeling that I don't always have enough money to get to the places I want to go or do the things I want to do. It's an emotional thing. The reason for fudging around definitely comes back to being accepted and loved. She might not want to be with me.

My partner definitely makes me honest because she's the opposite. She's very straightforward and blunt most of the time. And she calls me out on stuff like that. It's really good for me. Really good.

(20s)

Am I good enough? Am I good enough? Am I good enough? A lot of pretending, puffing up, posturing. Lack of self-worth. It's always there, but it's *not* talked about among guys.

(30s)

I think there's probably some insecurity in me that people at work will find out I'm an emotionally sensitive guy who's got liberal politics and who doesn't maybe have as much knowledge with certain tools or been in construction and things like that. But deep down inside I'm worried about not being adequate enough for the job. As a paramedic, I'm concerned about not being the smartest guy on the scene. It's a dog-eat-dog business I'm in, and there's always that fear. Maybe in other professions you're able to hide your intelligence weaknesses. With mine it's all out in the open. You've got to diagnose a problem, assess the situation, and do something right away. Either you're a good firefighter or a bad firefighter, a good paramedic or a bad one. Guys judge it more quickly.

(30s)

When I lie to myself and try to force the universe to my will, boy, things really don't work. I tried this with my first wife.

(30s)

I really, really don't like to lie at all. I almost get physical pain. It makes me so uncomfortable. If anything, I actually have a problem with divulging too much and instead of lying I'll just try and bowl somebody over with so much information that I distract them with truth.

(30s)

It's kind of liberating telling the truth. And even then I feel that knot in my throat because it's not easy to say the truth all the time. There's something wrong with that, you know? I must have learned that somewhere. When I feel like lying at first, I've been practicing catching myself and saying the truth. I can still feel the pain of it.

Sometimes I keep things ambiguous. Like, if you're in a relationship and you have another relationship, not physical, but you've allowed it to become too intimate. So you're not really being unfaithful, but I can talk myself out of the greater truth, which sucks. I should—I mean, I wish I could be more up front.

You can't control someone you're completely honest with. And, to be honest with you, that's scary. I compare myself to other people I care about and come up lacking. And when you don't want to be that person, you lie. You have secrets.

The fear behind that is wanting to keep my options open. And behind that — needing to be in control. Fear of being vulnerable, I guess. Afraid of being caught, afraid of being discovered for being an unrighteous person. And then I won't be loved and accepted.

(30s)

I can certainly be much more honest and let down my guard with my wife, for example, than I can with most of the people in my life. But even with her, there's a certain way in which I don't want to demonstrate too much doubt or insecurity. I want to keep up a strong sense for fear that she will be disappointed and no longer see me as a strong enough partner and leave and go find somebody else. So I do it to keep that connection, by being strong for her.

(40s)

It's hard to look closely at something you're getting a paycheck for being.

(40s)

Oh, boy. I lie when I've probably done something really stupid or inappropriate or when I don't feel good about myself. I'm protecting myself probably from being inauthentic. "Ugh, that's just not who I wanna be." So I'm gonna lie about it, you know?

(40s)

It's a game, and the stakes are high. You're doing your darnedest just to play the game right. You go and go, but there's this little niggling sense that this is not the right game. You put all this money and time into your education and you've got a job and you'd better know what you're doing. You're feeling, "Shit, but I don't know." You get scared to death. You've taken a wrong turn here, Dude. Do I do less or more? In this life, you cannot do less, so you do more. You think, "I'll bluff my way through." You puff up your chest and make like you know what you're doing. You're thinking, "Maybe nobody's going to guess that I'm really an asshole."

(50s)

We spend a lifetime creating this illusory self to hide that we're frauds, then the illusory selves are duking it out somewhere, and you go, "Oh, God." There's no place to get a break from it except sex. Therefore, we men are so dependent on sex, and therefore, dependent on women and, therefore, pissed off.

(50s)

If I feel like behind the curtain I'm a fraud, then I'm weak and I'm about to be discovered. It's not just a curtain anymore. Now, it's a wall of bricks and mortar and it's so deep inside this protective place where no one is going to realize I'm a fraud. There's no room for connection spiritually.

(50s)

What scares me away from telling the truth is judgment, and behind that judgment some kind of punishment. Where the quality of actually listening isn't pure. If I say green it will be heard as red or whatever. So, if by speaking the truth, it's heard as something different, then it's not really the truth, you know.

(50s)

The way guys get treated coming up—it explains a lot of male behavior. As they say in AA, "I don't drink to feel good, I drink to not feel." You start lying to yourself. To keep out the bigger reality. You lie to get ahead. For self-gain. It becomes a habit. You don't even know you're doing it. Don't Even Notice I Am Lying. D-E-N-I-A-L.

The guys I met in recovery, we had to tell the truth with each other. Very few famous people are good role because of what they had to do to get there.

(50s)

You're so busy pretending to be something that you're not, you forget that you're pretending . . . and boy, then you're really in trouble!

(60s)

As a man, there's something you're constantly proving. And you're always failing because who knows what that is even? It's an impossible job to live up to, right?

So there's a lot of shame about that and then you have to hide, you start telling lies because you don't want to be that person. You're trying to constantly prove to the world that you can be something that it is not possible to be.

(60s)

Women can fake orgasms. Men can fake entire relationships!

(60s)

I think virtually all men feel like frauds. It's a heavy, heavy burden, because it [the idea of "being a man"] is made up. That's why we need denial, a system that's extremely strong, but also as fragile as glass. Many people in denial feel, "Better get away from me with that shit! Get away from me with the truth, or I will beat you to a pulp. I got a system of denial here I'm going to protect. If I have to, I'll kill you to do it."

(60s)

Men puff themselves up, but other men know that the other guys are puffing themselves, too, and so—it's just a kind of play. Some information is being conveyed and the rapport is maintained, and that's why people do things like that. To stay connected.

(60s)

As a boy, I was always trying to impress everybody. Always wanting to be everything to everybody. Then I realized—just figure out who you are or wanna be, and be true to yourself. The way you manifest things is be yourself. And if your mom's an alcoholic and the only parent you've got, you find someone who isn't alcoholic to listen to.

(60s)

Learning how to use language is such a powerful tool, for good and evil, because when my neighbor asked me if I was mad at him, I thought, "Well, I just won't be mad at him right now." But a microsecond before and a microsecond later, I was. So I convinced myself that it's my truth. A lawyer's truth. You know what you're doing. And if you don't know what you're doing, then it's only a lie to him, not to yourself. What the hell, he doesn't count, he made me mad. See how that is—it's what we do to justify our human behaviors.

(60s)

If I don't tell the whole truth, if I'm vague and ambiguous, giving mixed messages, it helps me feel in control. It's an illusion, but sometimes it helps—for a while. It was a control I didn't even know I was needing until after I started to do recovery work.

(60s)

My first love ended terribly and painfully. I punished women for years after that—it was awful. I kept repeating it. I wasn't violent or anything, I just—I was very careless with their hearts. I remember one in particular who was divorced and had a boy named Mike. She was attractive and I just wanted to sleep with her, really. She fell in love with me—boy, which scared the shit out of me. And her little boy . . . I finally had to—I'll never forget saying, "We've got to talk." I remember sitting in a restaurant in Los Angeles telling her I just couldn't do it. I've never seen a woman become more emotional and sad, look so wrecked and destroyed. She had a bad first marriage. She thought I was going to be good. That stayed with me, and I really felt her pain, so I stopped. She was the last woman with whom I did that. I became more considerate and compassionate and honest with what my intentions were. So if I just wanted to bed somebody, I would say right up front, "This is sex only, right? No emotional stuff." The smart ones said, "No, thanks."

(60s)

My wife is Spanish-speaking. The first time we went to counseling, my Spanish wasn't very good. The counseling worked. Years later, I was more fluent so I could bullshit. It took longer.

(60s)

I don't lie, but I withhold. Don't say what I really feel. I didn't want to upset my mother or she would withhold her love. I'm the same way now with my partner.

(60s)

I lie when I have to protect somebody but, really, I know in the end I'm just protecting myself from having to go through it. Imagined protection, imagined safety. Genetically, women are more honest. They get to hang out with the kids, traditionally. Kids demand unflinching honesty. Their emotional radar is so accurate. Helps you open up. It's not like in the business world, where you have to shrink in.

(60s)

I was 38 years old when I first smoked marijuana. You can't smoke with someone and not be honest. It doesn't have to be marijuana, but whatever gets you to honest. How can you do business with someone who isn't honest? Honesty is just communicating.

We'd smoke and brainstorm about work — never at work, but afterwards — throw out ideas, no matter how stupid they were. Listening to guys from all levels of the company. That's when you hear what's really going on. We'd get so creative. Nothing was too stupid. That's when the company took off.

(60s)

I don't tell the truth fully about the pain and the financial stretch I'm in. It's not a good idea to take my wife over into that worry and pain. She can't go there with me. It doesn't help, either, because then I'd lose her love and affection, which is based on my strengths, and I would get this guilt pain, which is disempowering. I'd much rather be the "Big Guy" for her, even if Big Guy is stretched out of my mind at the moment, and get the love and acknowledgement for that.

(60s)

I was in a men's group for twenty-seven years. We acknowledged at the beginning that men are liars. We lie to each other, we lie to our wives, we lie to ourselves, we lie, right? We have problems with the truth. So we were going to form a club and try to get past all of that and stop lying to each other and to ourselves. And that took us twenty-seven years to get. I've done a lot of group stuff in my life and I think that men's group is probably, hour for hour, the most valuable time I've spent in a group.

(60s)

You start sort of weaving a web of enchantment. That's the art. Being somebody other than who you are. Or, being something that you are, but you make it look much bigger than what it really is. Falsifying the whole thing. So you get to be a little boastful, a little bit self-aggrandized because you have to be. You have to look a little bigger than the other guy.

Guys don't tell the truth because of the feeling of inadequacy. It's knowing underneath how small you really are, and what a klutz you really are, but you want to come off not being that. The whole thing isn't authentic.

(60s)

If "being a man" is being trained away from authenticity, it's no surprise women feel disappointed when they fall in love with someone who can't be who they really are. As long as he's being duplicitous with himself or avoiding himself, a man's not going to be authentic and connected with anyone else. If we're not telling the truth to ourselves, it bleeds into all other relating.

(70s)

All men feel like frauds. Leaders especially feel this. Being a man is synonymous with feelings of insecurity. The general theme of uncertainty, insecurity, and ambiguity is part of being a man. Period. It's one of the reasons men form alliances and relate to each other the way they do, which is to try to learn to trust each other and, the most important thing being—*Can* I trust you? Can I count on you to watch my back? Soldiers are the most extreme example of that. Policemen, firemen, mariners—but just *any* man.

(70s)

Zack (18 yrs.)

"How can you play the game
if you don't know the rules?"

I went to a prestigious, private, all-boys school called Colton, probably the WASP-iest school in the city. My dad, uncle and older brothers all went there. I loved my experience, but it is definitely not for everybody. Colton breeds competitiveness. It encouraged people who learned quickly. It encouraged athletes, and if I wasn't in love with sports from such a young age, it would have been a lot more difficult.

At age fourteen, going into high school, you're expected to be macho. You're expected to know how to ask a girl out on a date, be good at sex or making out. Sexuality is what we're constantly thinking about. If you're born a girl and don't like a feature about yourself, you're allowed to use makeup to change that, and it's a positive thing. It's like, "Oh, she looks very pretty today." There's no makeup for guys. It's that simple. You are what you are, which quickly gets internalized. So you check your reflection three hundred times a day. You're being judged completely on your outside things.

My background—all-boy schools and no sisters—gives me a unique perspective in being able to see exactly when these changes happen and why. For example, identifying why it can be so hard to flirt, as a guy. And all the other contradictions—how you are expected to be a leader in groups and in classwork. Then you see girls be labeled bitches if they step up as leaders. You don't have that in an all-boys education. In high school, you're mature enough to be like, "Oh, that wasn't bitchy. I wanted to say the same damn thing she did."

Being a guy is definitely not easy. I'm an entirely different person now than when I entered high school, and it's really all because of one class—Human Development (HumDev)—and one teacher. Karen Dennis is when it all changed. When I was a freshman, here's what she wrote about me. I still carry it around in my wallet:

> And then there is Zack . . . He watches carefully in class, listens with an open heart, but seems still to be deciding what he is going to do with what he hears. He is keenly aware of his surroundings. I feel that down the line, one of his challenges will be determining where the needs of others end and his own begin. He is kind, the real type of kind. The sort a young person can't bullshit . . . he is the kid that reminds you why you do what you do for that tiny paycheck.

Yeah, my mom cried when I read that to her. And what I can say is, at some point I decided this stuff mattered. My number one goal this year was, how do I continue Karen's legacy?

~

When I was a sophomore, my friend Marky and I got invited to a senior girls' party. We were super excited. We were going to hang out with seniors—we're cool. We'll have a bunch of fun.

Marky ended up not going, but I did. There was this senior girl I start talking with. At that time, I was exclusive with another girl in my same grade. Anyway, the night goes on, and I'm getting drunk, very drunk. I'm sitting on a couch with this girl, and she was being flirty with me. We were watching "American Pie" by ourselves, and she's nibbling on my neck or whatever. Eventually, we start hooking up, and it happens—me a sophomore, she a senior. I was definitely more drunk than she was. We had sex. I was a virgin.

After it happened, I told nobody except Marky. I told him everything, and it was fine.

Two years later, I was a teaching assistant in a group session that was led by Karen. The topic was consent. There was definitely a hunger for it. I was like, I don't have any experience with consent. And then this story came up. I was like, wait—was I raped? As a sophomore boy, I had never considered it. If I were a girl, would I have thought I was raped?

I'm still not sure whether I can call it rape, because I knew what I was doing when I said yes. But at the same time, I was so drunk that it was in that gray area. As a boy, I had never even thought to consider I could get raped by a girl. We're boys. We're supposed to want it. So I lost my virginity to a senior who I didn't really know, basically blacked-out drunk on a couch.

Afterwards, oh my god, so awkward. I would see the senior girl from time to time, and she would be like, "Don't tell anybody." I agreed.

The hard part was, I considered what I did to be cheating on the girl I was seeing at that time. What I told her was, I woke up next to this other girl with her shirt off. I lied. I still regret that, too. I eventually came clean, I think. Yeah, I did. Still, I felt so guilty for so long—like, how did I cheat on somebody? That's not who I am. What the fuck?

Even after I did, it was like, "No, I'm not—I don't—I'm not ready to call that rape." I told Karen, and she was like, "Think on it some more." I have best friends who don't know this story. I was like, "I fucked up." Now, I would never have pressed charges. But what I'm saying is—as a boy—I was brought up thinking *go for sex.* That's what you want. And then I was a victim of an abuse of power, an abuse of society. I wasn't taught to protect myself in that sense.

The whole experience gives me insight into women who get raped. I've been offered sex in the last month from a girl I thought was too drunk, and I said no. I'm very clear with that. Even last night it came up, and I was like, "Are you sure?"

～

Men are expected to have deep voices. Basically, what it'll come down to is you're supposed to be really everything—a long list of different contradictions. Whether that's being gentle but dominant; smart, but not overtly smart; confident, but not cocky—and you definitely can't be insecure. It even goes to your looks. It can get into everything. You're supposed to have the V—tall, broad, big, but not too ripped; you don't want to be intimidating. I mean, girls get the hard end of the stick there, too. That's just a double-edged sword. We're harsh on each other.

The sad thing with that—girls are harsher on girls, and guys are harsher on guys. It's like gender self-discipline. If a girl is dressing too sluttily, guys aren't going to say anything. Guys probably won't even think about it twice. It's the girls that will harass her, abuse her, put her in her place.

When you insult a woman, you don't generally insult her womanness. You don't insult her by taking away her gender. When you insult a man, you usually insult his identity in some way, taking away his gender or his masculinity. "You're a pussy." "You're a homo." "Be a man." "Man up."

I'm a skinny guy. Once when I was younger, I went to a party over Thanksgiving break at the home of one of my older brother's good friends — all older people. The girls are like, "Oh, you've grown so much. Nice to see you again." And the guys are like, "Wow, you need to gain some weight." Literally, verbatim, the quote was, "You could pull if you gained weight." Meaning, get with more girls. I'm like, "I haven't seen you in three years, and the first thing you think of saying is, you need to gain weight?"

~

My dad is a political consultant. Sure, I was brought up going to sports games with him because that was his interest, and that was my brothers' interests, so maybe that's why it became mine too. My room was blue. So we can contribute to some of those early stereotypes about guys. The only directive I was really ever given was, be kind and be honest.

My mom was less of a blank slate. She was the more around parent when we were young, because my dad works a lot. Oh, she definitely was feeling a little cooped up being the only female. Especially when we were teenagers. I think she got a little sick of it. She's been a trooper for sure.

When my mom would yell at me, that's when I would cry most often. I remember being downstairs, she was yelling, I started to tear up, and she told me, "You can't just cry whenever I yell at you." Eleven or twelve. Also, my parents never argue — at least not in front of me. My scariest memory of my entire life was my mom screaming at my oldest brother at the kitchen table. I still don't remember what. Blocked it out. I just got up from the table and went in my mom's closet, when I was like eight or nine years old. But these are like the extreme rarities—the times that stand out.

As the youngest in the family, I was very tuned in to my mom. That's always been who I am. I'm always watching people, and I'm good at reading how they're thinking, what they're feeling. My mom's very proud of everything I do relating to the HumDev work.

I'm really close to my dad, too. The men in my family are gentle. My mom does the handy work around the house. My dad knows how to change a lightbulb, and learned how to grill three years ago. We're not a stereotypical family in that sense. But being a man was providing for your family, I'll say that much. My dad was the breadwinner when we were younger. I was always told I was going to get a job. There was never like, "You're going to be a domestic dad."

There's always been a lot of academic pressure. My dad went to Princeton, my mom to Wellesley. B+ is not okay. I was never allowed to really slack off, because my parents would say, "I'm not spending this much money a year for you not to care. You're not allowed to not care about education, or not care about being smart." That was always the biggest motivator for me.

~

I'm one of the most competitive people I know. It was cultured into me—in my family, but especially at Colton. My earliest memories, I'd play games with my brothers and there was definitely winning and losing. I was always trying to keep up. Like we weren't singers or dancers or—things that don't have a score. I agree with Lance Armstrong one hundred percent—the joy of winning comes nowhere near the pain of losing. It infiltrates every part of my life, not just athletics. I'm competitive with myself.

With boys, there's always a score. This explains a lot of our sexual and domestic violence problems—consent problems, too. Have you heard of the pizza metaphor for sex? Oh, my god, it's this TED talk, and the guys is saying we need a new sexual analogy. The baseball diamond doesn't work. One, there's a winner and a loser, but in sexual activities that shouldn't be. Two, this whole thing of running the bases doesn't make sense. Do I have to hit a home run every time I want to have sexual activity? And three, everyone knows the rules already. On the other hand, when I order pizza, at the very least they're going to ask me if I want the regular, and I get to say yes or no. Or, you can do a half-and-half pizza. I want pepperoni, my friend wants sausage. There's room for variation and a discussion between you and your partner. It's not a race. There's no winner or loser eating pizza.

I think the whole game issue comes from the trust thing—can I trust you, or can't I trust you? I think men and women both want a simpler version of what it can really be. It's hard letting people be the way they want to be. It scares people.

～

The joy for me in being a boy—ah, it's got to be the friendships. What Colton does so well is teach the male friendships. Guy friendships are unbreakable. If you get in a fight, it's gone by the next day. That's just a gift that our society gave us. I don't think it's innately guy necessarily, or it's innately girl not to do that. It's just the norm. As far as fitting in goes, I've been more in than out. I've been lucky to have good, safe friends from early on. Losing my friends is my worst fear. I don't know how it could happen, but if I fuck up so bad that I lose these people that I love so much, I must have really, really fucked up.

As a gender, we're definitely worse at listening than women. Why? Well, as a boy, when you speak up you're almost always immediately validated, so we are taught that our opinions matter. Girls, on the other hand, when they speak up, even in our class, they almost always raise their hand first. Then when they're called on, it's, "Sorry, may I go to the bathroom?" Why are they saying "sorry"? Because they're taught to apologize when they speak. Boys aren't.

I don't know what it would require for me to listen better. Guys are so busy—"I have to be somebody. I've gotta get my game," whatever it is. Our biggest fear is being a nobody. It comes back to legacy. Was I a somebody? Was I making a difference? Did I waste my life? Everyone's judging. It's the people who live ten doors down. It's your best friends. And it's yourself.

We need more education about human development in schools. It's not group therapy, but it provides a space where you're learning how to be human. You're learning all the most important lessons that you don't learn anywhere else. When I wasn't doing it for six months, I noticed I was feeling less happy. There's got to be a greater desire for change among men. You have to tap into it early, before someone tells you it's stupid. I was taught in time, saved in time.

Oh, my god, Karen tells this story about being at the grocery store with her young children, and there's this jerk in line behind her. She's taking a while, clearly a mom with two kids trying to get the job done. The guy behind her tells her to hurry up. Her little son turns around and tells the man, "You probably have sadness inside."

~

I don't believe I've ever actually expressly told anyone this, but every night what I say is, "Thank you, God, for another day." And then, "Thank you for continued protection," because I don't want to fuck up and have my parents kill me if I mess up the University Merit Scholarship I just got. I say a prayer for the next day—a wish, basically. And then just say thank you.

I've only believed in God for about a year and a half now, two years, probably. Don't really know what inspired it. I just kind of just started to pray. It might have been when I was feeling guilty about breaking up with my ex-girlfriend when she was in the hospital. Maybe that prayer was my valve, releasing that pressure.

Fundamentally, I definitely was a trusting person, and I'm working my way back. I guess I went from trusting everyone, to trusting me more.

I have trouble being alone. Not many people know that. When I'm alone, I'm almost always listening to music. Silence is a little bit trippy for me. I just got approved to go on a Vision Quest next month at my high school. I'm scared. I want to do this because I think this will be the most challenging thing I've ever done—to be alone for three days and no technology. I'm a city kid is what it comes down to. Never really related to camping. Bugs, snakes, raccoons—not a big fan. But I'm really happy that I get to go. I'm hoping it solves this hole that I find in being alone, without noise. We'll see how the Vision Quest goes. If I see a scorpion — I'm gonna flip.

~

In my sophomore year, I cheated once more on the same girl (not the older girl I lost my virginity to). In group sessions with Karen, we wrote letters to ourselves. Then, at the start of the next year, we opened and read them. Mine referred to what I call "the sophomore slip-ups." I wrote to myself, "What the fuck is going on with you? Why are you doing this?" I felt so bad for so long about the cheating that I decided to tell her. Was that just of me? Would it cause her pain she didn't need? We had already broken up. Finally, I told her. She was very upset for a while. Then, when I had worked out the whole rape thing, I told her about that, too. She said, "I never knew that those were the circumstances. I'm sorry I was so harsh on you."

I don't often lie, but I don't always tell the truth, either. I'm pretty good about saying, "I don't want to tell you," and if they're my friends they understand they're not getting it out of me. Part of HumDev is teaching ourselves to avoid regret or shame. It might sound selfish, but I didn't want to hurt them because *I* would regret it and *I'd* feel shameful about it, more than because I was scared of how *they* would feel. Maybe that regret about it comes from knowing their pain. So I'm protecting them, and myself, from feeling it. I think it's kind of a human nature to not want to feel certain things. It goes back to the Karen letter again about "where his needs begin and others end." That kind of sadness I've bottled up for a long time. I was totally a rescuer. Having to break up with my girlfriend when she was in the hospital was probably the most painful thing I've ever experienced. I equate pain with sadness, to be honest.

Before I'm going to date somebody, I've got to be damn sure it could be serious or good because . . . I don't know, just . . . I don't want to get hurt. When my ex-girlfriend and I started dating, I had a very different feeling about who she was than she turned out to be. So I need to really, really know the girl if I'm going to put myself in a place where I can hurt her or be hurt, because how can you play the game if you don't know the rules?

If Men Are Going to Change,
Women Have to Allow It

"It's a real challenge for women to get clear what it is they really want [in a man]."

When my son was about to go to kindergarten, we were encouraged to bring along a pillow for naptime. I decided to make one. I invited him to come with me to the fabric store so he could choose any fabric he liked. He made a beeline for a bolt of bright, gold fake fur. What led me then to steer him away from his first choice? And then again, from his second choice, the gold lame? He did wind up getting a very soft, slinky fabric that felt good, but it wasn't furry and it didn't sparkle and it wasn't gold. What was I afraid of?

I was beginning to recognize all the ways we women—as girlfriends, wives, colleagues, mothers, sisters, daughters—are complicit in perpetuating limited notions of male identity. By what we value, by what we *expect,* even *need* boys and men to know and to be. "The way men are required or conditioned to behave with each other is profoundly influenced by the presence of women," a man in his 60s told me. Listening to these guys, I was reflecting on my own assumptions about men, and the ways in which I'd been unaware of how boys are treated in this culture. It's painful and sad to see how I've been part of creating this.

As mothers we have an immense power, whether we recognize and acknowledge it or not. To love or withhold love. Or, to just not know how.

Relating with men, I often feel the presence of their mother or primary female caregiver, and sense whatever degree of peace has, or has not, been made with her. Boys' earliest years are usually spent with women, who may not quite appreciate who a boy is. We may *assume* we know, and not listen. Who is *this* human being right here, right now, in front of me? A man in his 40s told me, "Half of our male role belief system comes from our mom. She is the forgotten contributor." I began to wonder if maybe "womanizers" are men who, missing that early attunement with a woman and longing for it, keep searching for it in one woman after another.

Are we, as mothers, handing our sons over to the prevailing culture for fear that they won't "be a man"? Are we giving up our say in what "being a man" is?

I noticed as my son grew older that sometimes I second-guessed my own guidance, feeling hesitant about the male world he was entering and, at the same time not wanting to handicap him. What was that about?

When I shared my feeling with a 64-year-old his face got soft with knowing. "You're sending him off to battle." And a woman friend said, "It's hard preparing your son for a party you know you're never going to be invited to." Though it was becoming clear to me that "party" is not really the word for it.

So I asked, "How do women participate in your idea of "being a man"?

≈

I grew up in a house full of women, and from overhearing their conversations and understanding them so well, I quickly learned that the guy who's beating down their door and sending them flowers and ponies and cherries and shit, they don't give a fuck about him. But the guy that won't call them back is the one that they're in love with.

(20s)

I think women participate in the idea of being a man by desiring me. A lot of who I try to be is somebody desirable. My notion of what is desirable to women is power. So as long as women go for power, it reinforces that. That's why these gross old-looking guys get these young babes — because they can provide. You would never see that work in reverse, or very seldom.

I like to get attention. I'm used to behaving seductively. It's power. I'm beginning to see that seduction is really about control and that what I'm really wanting is connection. Intimacy.

(30s)

I don't know any woman who can handle that life itself doesn't make sense. Like at some basic level none of it makes sense. But, I think that what it comes down to is, if you're in a relationship, if you want to tell the truth to the woman—"The truth is, I don't know what the fuck is going on"—then all of a sudden it's threatening. She feels, "If he can't go from A to B, he won't be able to provide this or that." She's not comfortable with not knowing. It's all defined through somebody else—the man who's supposed to know things. That's why men don't talk as much. Sometimes I'd rather just stay quiet because they can figure out whatever the hell they want me to be. When women are on men wanting them to express themselves, it's felt as one more pressure. One more thing I'm *supposed to be*.

So that's what I think of as the mantle of manhood, or the mask—and people are tired of it. They want to put it down. The reality is that means accepting complete responsibility for your life. Very few people are willing to do that.

(30s)

I feel like I've been lucky. I had a very educated, aware, feminist mom who provided a space for me to be more expressive and in touch with my emotions. She made it okay to talk about those things; while at the same time, through other things, like sports, I was able to "play the game". So I don't have to worry too much about performing masculinity in other ways. I could do the things that were expected of guys. And frankly, if my wife and I have a little boy, I'll try to make some concessions to the rest of the culture's expectations, like okay, we'll be athletes and you can be masculine in that way.

I hear about men in progressive circles complaining that they're in some sense of crisis because they have been told that women wanted men who are more sensitive and then they became sensitive and found that women felt that they were not strong enough. Even from more progressive women in my life, there are still those same traditional expectations. It's so deep. Frankly, I have never really noticed women actually wanting men to be more sensitive. It's always been, in my observation and experience, the more traditional conceptions of masculinity. Men who exhibit those characteristics have been perceived as the leaders, the charismatic ones, the ones who got the girl.

My partner and I talked about it. She says one of the things she likes about me is that I'm not a SNAG — a Sensitive New Age Guy. She and her friends see such guys as silly wimps, irresponsible navel-gazers. There is something so profound and forceful in our culture that the image of a man who's strong and tough and exciting, someone who people want to be around, is what women are attracted to.

(40s)

Compassion, empathy, kindness, listening — those aren't feminine, those are *human* qualities. "To be a man" is to be trained out of those. You know, tough it up, shrug it off, whatever. That's not kind. If you don't use a muscle, it doesn't develop. Women in this culture expect the man to always be "on." Where can I *let down?*

(40s)

Something's broken, you fix it. There's a question, you answer it. A place to go, you go. Men do all this to be more attractive to women, and I think that's where women will collude the most, choosing fairly consistently those men who are the action ones, the quarterback, the smartest guy in the class, the whatever. They're not choosing the sensitive, shy kid who decides to paint instead of sports.

(50s)

What women really want in a man is very confusing to men. Mixed messages. I think women are confused, too. They want intimacy and love and connection and nurturance, but they also want to be taken and commanded and even dominated sometimes. It was very confusing for me as a young man to see women go for the bad boys. The hyper-masculine jerks.

It was hard to believe when my girlfriend told me that the more vulnerable I was with her, the more of a turn-on it was. That gave me permission to be more of myself.

(50s)

With my last partner, I took care of her. She would call me a saint. I loved taking care of her. But there was always this hope that then she would feel safe and see that I'm not like other men, blah, blah blah, and then she could open up and we can have this wonderful intimate relationship. But she can't have that wonderful relation that I hoped for because she can't. She can *receive* caretaking. She can be held, helped to talk and open up, but she doesn't have the wherewithal to come after me, to ask me questions, to understand me.

There's a way, as the caretaker, that I feel in charge. But, as that caretaker, I feel dreadfully alone and missed and dropped and hurt, so I don't feel powerful. I feel like my needs aren't being met. So it kinda runs both edges of that sword.

(50s)

We're taught to be frauds at an early age. My mother wanted me to be more than what I was. She had greater ambitions than I was capable of, that I could not live up to. But to get her off my back I had to say I was doing it. If I had been the perfect son I would've been married, had a job in some respectable institution or business. And I didn't do either those. She wanted me to be what she felt my father wasn't.

I can trace all of my relationships back to my mother and my attitude toward her. My mother got very seriously ill when I was 14 and she never really recovered. She got increasingly angry about her life and how it didn't work out. I had to be more her vision of what life should be. She projected her unrealized things on me and didn't realize perhaps I was in fact doing just that, but in my own way.

(60s)

I would say that there's still a huge expectation on our culture, with rare but increasingly larger exceptions, that the guy who wants to be married to a really amazing, loving, together woman has got to have his money-making, professional skills together. And if he doesn't have it together, and I'm talking late 20s, early 30s, he's not really in a position to choose to commit. Because he doesn't know who he is becoming really yet.

Everybody seems to be a little confused. Nobody is expected to compromise. The woman is not expected to compromise anymore. The man can't compromise because if he compromises too much, he has no balls. Combine that with easy sex and it doesn't mean anything . . . There's a sadness in the air.

(60s)

A lot of women talk behind guys' backs about how big they are, how well they perform, how long they last. There's a really mixed message coming from a lot of women. On the one hand, they like their guys to be soft and emotionally in touch and ecologically aware and spend time with them. And on the other hand, they want them to be out there making the really big bucks. But in most of those jobs, you have to sublimate your feelings and rape the environment and screw over your fellow man. I think it's a real challenge for women to get clear on what it is they really want to nurture, and what the costs and benefits are.

(60s)

Pete (30s)

"If I could change one thing . . .
I'd make it bigger."

Men are supposed to be strong and tall. You don't want to be wimpy. I remember having competitions as young as probably third or fourth grade about height, before any of us had even come close to establishing where we were going to end up. Back to back, with the tape measure, you know, bragging about, I'm taller than you. One friend I grew up with—we were always very competitive with each other—ended up becoming 6 foot 4, so he beat me. He still likes to bring it up when I see him, which isn't very often.

It's that silly, and that's where a lot of automatic manliness comes, from your size. If a guy is big, it's just an automatic for him. He's got that taken care of. He doesn't need to prove himself. And we've all heard about the Napoleon complex, the aggressive, quick to anger little guys because that's how they need to prove themselves in the world because they're automatically a step down. I'm 6 foot 1 so I don't think about my height as an issue, but I've heard a lot of shorter men talk about how they're not taken seriously, women don't find them attractive. They live in this shorter man's world that is really humiliating, and nobody really talks about it. I'd have to think for a lot of people their lack of self-worth starts 'cause they feel, I'm already wrong from the get-go just by my physical being. I feel like there's a few different ideas of an attractive man; one is that you want to have the underwear model's body where you're slender but very muscular and fit. The other is you want to be really big, so that you know you're alpha, and a lot of women are attracted to that. Maybe because they feel protected? You know, we are still animals at the end of the day, and in many mammal species the biggest male gets every female in the herd. I think there's still a bit of that in us.

I remember being as young as fourth or fifth grade and having slumber parties with a bunch of boys. We'd all give ourselves erections and compare our penises and make fun of each other for it. I don't know if I've ever told anyone that, and the odd thing now is being grown up and seeing these same guys and never, ever once have any of us ever brought it up that we used to do that.

It was just totally part of being a boy, pre-testosterone. Everybody likes to get in on it, even if it's a friend, you still love to be in cahoots with others and take somebody down. Maybe that's just being kids, but it's happened to me where I was the one who was made the fool of and I was the party to it many times too. It's just something that we all did. It feels so good when you're not the one it's happening to that you're more than happy to do it to somebody else. At that age it made me more eager and at this age it would make me less eager. As a kid, you're just looking out for yourself to a certain extent 'cause it's a little rough out there.

When I really think about it they were just a bunch of little kids' wieners, they didn't look that different from each other. Luckily probably because if somebody had had one that was way bigger, I'm sure they would have gladly lorded it over the rest of us. I remember in high school people very openly making fun of the idea of an uncircumcised penis, which I have, and girls and boys together like sitting around talking about how weird that is. And then what I realized was that most of the kids from town had circumcised penises, mostly kids from the Lake didn't, and so I started to feel a little bit of pride about it.

It's ruthless. For something that really we have zero control over, the penis thing is—I mean, people are obsessed with penis size in this culture, just totally obsessed. I hear about it almost every day in the media, in conversation, I hear it, I hear it, I hear it. Both men and women. I think it's a way for women, whether it's subconscious or not, to maybe feel a little bit of power in having a preference or in taking guys down. And then guys who want to feel good about themselves, if they do have an above average penis, they'll want you to know about it.

As a young man, you're thinking—am I the right size, am I a man, is this the right thing to have or do or be or whatever? As young men, the only penises most of us are ever going to see are going to be in pornography, which of course they're picking good-looking penises. You're like, hey, mine doesn't look quite like that, is something wrong with it?

Thank god there's that unwritten rule in urinals that you do not look sideways. But I've had people look. You get a look, and you're like, hey! And you'll see little signs in public bathrooms, funny little signs like, "We're trying to keep this place clean, step a little closer, it's not as big as you think." Little funny things like that, or different foot marks on the ground that say: small, average, extra-large—further and further away from the urinal, that you have to then go step on. It's not like every bathroom has that, but you do see things like that. It's a deep shame that a lot of people feel. I mean, I have an average-sized penis, but I would never want anyone to know that because nobody wants to talk about their average penis. I wish it were bigger. If I had a magic wand and I could change one thing on my body, I'd probably make it bigger, because it's such an obsession. You've got to wonder, when you're with a woman, well, does this just not feel good because they've been with someone so much bigger? It's totally cruel. I can only imagine what I would feel like if it were smaller than average, and a lot of people are, of course. Millions. And they're not going to be able to perform and feel good about themselves during sex if they *already* feel inadequate before they even start.

I've heard groups of girls discuss very intimately their partners in front of me. I can only imagine what they say when it's just girls. I've slept with someone in the friend group and then known that, well, she's probably told everyone all about me, so I hope I did okay.

It's the same thing with guys. We say things that we would never say in front of a woman. I notice how my whole vocabulary changes when it's just me and my close guy friends. I just start talking differently because it's a different kind of atmosphere that we're creating amongst ourselves. Certain things feel more comfortable. A lot of the rules fall away, but the new rules crop up. You don't tell how sensitive you feel unless you really want to talk about it. It's almost an unwritten rule. You keep it more surface, kind of raunchy—sports, sex, hot girls, bullshit—and you make each other laugh. Women are apt to be discussing real things more often than guys are. But it depends on the guys. I have some guy friends that I can almost talk to the way that I imagine girls talk, but I think that's fairly unique.

~

There is so much pressure around sex for men. First you have to be a certain size, then you have to be able to get hard, then you have to be able to last just the right amount of time, not too short, not too long. A lot of the time you end up forgetting that it's supposed to be enjoyable.

The pressure's always there. Even with me and my partner, she's like, "I don't need to have an orgasm every time." I'm like, "Oh yes, you do." It's this strong sense of we haven't accomplished anything yet. It's a terrible feeling, and she's right, of course. There's no destination, it's just enjoying being in the moment, but it's totally ingrained in guys to feel that the job isn't done until the woman has climaxed. I purposely will do things during sex to make sure it's not feeling too good for me because I don't want to have an orgasm before she does. Which is fine, 'cause it's nice to make it last, but it's also like you're really in your head instead of just being in your body, which is what it's all meant for, you know?

With newer partners, there's more and more of that. I really feel like I have a lot to prove and want to make sure it's perfect, and I'm not thinking about my own pleasure at all. Which I think is what women sort of want, because when a guy's only thinking about his own pleasure, it lasts about ten seconds and then he rolls off of her. You don't want to be that kind of lover, but you also want to find a balance because there's a lot of pressure on the man. I mean, you can't really do the act without the man being up and at 'em.

I want to preface this by saying that I do think it's worse for women in general in our culture when it comes to body issues. Women get more exploited by men, but there's a public conversation about it. Our culture has a disease in regards to women's bodies. Perhaps because of that, even the women in my life who I think of as very sensitive, with a feminist ethic and all of that, will more likely say disparaging things about men's bodies than I think they would ever tolerate for a guy in their company to say about women's bodies. Maybe as a reaction to the patriarchy—like we put up with this shit so much, why should I be sensitive? They can be really insensitive and it hurts for the guy to hear certain things. I think penis size is the one that'll get the deepest into your head, as far as just really messing with your mind.

I think power probably has a lot to do with it. And a lot of it's probably subconscious—they're not even thinking about it as something that might be hurtful.

You know that quote "Men are afraid women will laugh at them. Women are afraid men will kill them." (Margaret Atwood)? It's like that.

～

I wouldn't be surprised if a lot of white racism towards blacks doesn't stem from the fact that black men are generally so physically superior to white men. That is oversimplifying, of course, but that may be part of the underlying psychology. You are bigger and stronger than me, so I better control you and make you feel less-than before you realize you are the dominant one. And your penises are bigger and we don't want you getting near our wives. You know—once you go black, you never go back—that whole thing. Most white men are super-threatened by black men. It's just a big body issue. And what's behind all this behavior? Fear. The deep fear of not being okay. So we do all this compensatory stuff to try to make ourselves feel better, bigger, stronger, more dominant.

It's insecurity. I need to know who I am before I really have room to be able to listen to somebody else. A lot of it has to do with what models you see around you. I think it comes more naturally to some people and probably more naturally to women in general than men, but it's totally within all of us to be just that much more considerate of each other and realize that we're different and that's fine. Things like listening and empathy can be can be taught earlier, encouraged as a value in school, you know?

Even if you have this little sheltered home and your immediate extended family, you're bombarded by the media and you really need somebody to help you translate what it does to boys, and girls. The mastery of the advertising is that you don't even know you're thinking it. You don't even know they got into your head. Just part of your thoughts forever, and you don't even know where it came from.

PETE

II

Violence

"Violence is a failure of the imagination."

— ADRIENNE RICH

"Because it is learned, it can be unlearned."

Any woman who has given birth to or nursed a boy, or anyone who even just looked, *really* looked, into the eyes of a newborn knows—there is no violence there.

So much of "being a man" sounded like a violence to the spirits of these young boys. Emotional as well as physical. The so-called "ordinary violence"—the daily violations that interfere with their being who they truly are. When I shared some of what I had been hearing with another friend in his 60s, he listened quietly, nodding in recognition. Then he leaned closer and spoke softly: "Yeah. And then, you have to *be a man*."

I am well aware of the fear and violence that many women live with, but I hadn't really let in how it is for men. The stories I heard when I asked the question— What was your first experience of violence?—changed that.

So many of these boys were beaten, yelled at, tickled to the point of tears, teased, mocked, put down, humiliated, hazed, called names. They suffered from absent, neglectful or abandoning caregivers, insensitive schoolyard bullies, mean big brothers, abusive coaches, unaware fathers and mothers passing on what had been passed on to them. In many instances, the brutality of their welcome to the world. A man in his early 60s told me, "I was found unacceptable. It's hard to find your way back from that." If your caregiver is a source of terror and pain, where is safety? An 11-year-old said it simply: "I've noticed that if parents are mean to their kids, their kids are mean to other kids."

Moment to moment we are impacting these boys by who we are and how we are. What do they see when they look in the mirror of our face?

I heard the bestselling horror writer Stephen King's name mentioned several times in connection with childhoods. One man had even thanked him personally for making a film (*The Shining*) that he felt must have been about his own childhood!

From another man I learned about something called the ACE study (Adverse Childhood Experience) done by Kaiser Permanente in San Diego. By their count, *half* of the people just coming in for a bad cold or a hangnail or whatever had significant adverse childhood experiences. Things like physical, emotional or sexual abuse or growing up in an alcoholic home.

I was trying to understand what it might be like to always be on guard, afraid that something violent is going to happen. What does that do to a boy's natural curiosity and creativity? How can you feel free to play and discover? It's heartbreaking what men have to go through to "be a man"—the uncomfortableness of it. I'm amazed at how much more limited the range of expression is for the men and boys I know than it is for women and girls. How easy it would be to pass on that uncomfortable feeling, without knowing why. Not out of malice, but because it doesn't feel good, and maybe nobody showed you another way of dealing with discomfort.

If you could have the imagination and a way to express whatever you need to express—would you need to be violent?

My Dad Used a Belt

"Kids pick it up"

My younger brother was picking on me. He's four years younger. My instinct was to fight back. That's what brothers do, they fight. I guess you could say I won. But I didn't hurt him. I could have, but I didn't. You need someone to wrestle with to satisfy whatever you're feeling. Like if it's anger or happiness. If it's happiness, it settles you down and makes you happy that you have somebody to play with, that you get to be a boy with.

He wants me to get in trouble. That's why he does it. He wants me to snap. But I usually beat him mentally. Having a brother to fight with, you get practice for how life is and what the consequences are.

(11 yr.)

I was in the car in New Mexico and my grandpa wasn't feeling good and my little sister was constantly annoying him, so my grandpa just got out his belt and hit my sister, just once — but I felt so bad I started crying even though it wasn't me. I could just feel the pain on my leg when she got hit. She was like four and I was about nine.

My dad when he gets angry — he'll get his belt out, but he wouldn't hit me, he'd hit the stuff around. My mom was right there. She didn't say anything. If I had kids, I wouldn't hit them. I will talk with them and then I would do consequences.

(12 yr.)

Watching my parents scream at each other almost every weekend, I was keenly aware of emotional violence long before physical violence. I had these really, really insane temper tantrums when I was a very small child. I think part of it was because I got almost no attention at home. I felt like my mother was incapable of hearing me or listening to me or really fundamentally caring about me.

I was put into group therapy at the County Mental Hospital with a couple of other kindergarteners who were behavioral risks. Once a month I went with two other five-year-olds, and we just talked about how it sucked that everybody made fun of us all the time. When I got to a place where people did that — school — it just, everything erupted out of me. And, of course, I'm five years old; I have no understanding of being able to control it.

I know, it's a little weird, maybe it's a little different for a guy to say, because I feel like everybody I know at one point in time had physical violence. I never really did. I can't think of a single occasion where I've actually been in a fistfight. But the emotional violence is absolutely every bit as destructive. It's absolutely amazing what kids survive. What a "normal" weekend was for me.

(30s)

My dad drank a lot my whole life, until very recently. For my entire growing up, he was extremely reactionary, really volatile. He never hit me. Yeah, there were a couple of token smackings for foul mouth, but he was never actually violent toward me physically. Verbally sometimes, but not physically. He would smash things in the house, that kind of thing. He didn't know how to get it out. All that pain. It was scary to see my dad be violent. I'd usually just be silent. I'd totally shut down.

(30s)

My first experience of violence was fighting in elementary school — because it was expected, and also because I was hit by my older brothers when I was a kid. I didn't have my dad around. My oldest brother especially would take it out on me. Or, if I did something wrong, I'd get the belt. So I think that I got in fights because I was already violent.

(30s)

My father had a barber strap, one of those thick straps, and they believed in hitting so, I surely remember that. Only in the later years was it restricted to the buttocks. Before that it was . . . well, never around the head.

(50s)

My first experience of violence was getting beaten on the legs hard with a fly-swatter by my mother when I was probably four years old. Who knows for what reason?

(50s)

My mom had no tolerance for our suffering. If she was pissed off at us and we were whining or something, she'd say, "I'll give you something to cry about." She'd been hardened somehow. She ridiculed our "blubbering" when we cried or when she'd slap us. It was like—just suck it up. Unfortunately, I internalized that behavior. When my kids would get hurt when they were little, I'd say, "You're okay. Get up. You're alright." My wife would look at me like, "No, no. They're not okay."

(50s)

It was a threat, "Wait till your father gets home." I was maybe five, playing with matches. I got spanked. It was always intimidation. My brother was always intimidating me too, threatening to beat the crap out of me. We've been estranged for the last 28 years.

The only physical abuse I ever suffered was a couple of strikes from my father and the spanking. I'd say in my life, probably less than twenty spankings, but I don't remember that that much. He was a man of not many words.

(50s)

My first experience of violence? Oh my god, it's so early. What was scary to me as a boy was—my dad, my older brother, werewolves, Frankenstein, Dracula. Losing a fight was scary. If I'm not strong, I'm vulnerable, people see that I'm weak. I used to win my fights 'cause I would go berserk, Tasmanian Devil-like when I felt vulnerable. I used to love that feeling of invulnerability. And it didn't matter how many times I got hit, I just wouldn't stop. So I won.

I don't know if I would have done that if my brother hadn't beaten me up.

There were two fights I lost. In one of them, bigger, older guys beat me up and then laid on me. I bit them both in the belly, broke the skin. I walked home crying that they had beaten me up, and feeling so ashamed, so humiliated. Like I was nothing. I felt castrated. I was not a man anymore. Whatever that thing was that I long to be so I feel safe, it was taken from me.

(50s)

My eighteen-months-older brother and his friend beat me up daily and got a big kick out of that. Violence was never my way. It becomes clear at a certain point. I assume it's like a rape victim. After a while, you just lay there until it's over. They get tired of beating on you, because you're not reacting and you're not scared anymore. You're just laying there. The thrill is gone for them.

(50s)

My father would hit my mother or my sister and me. One time we were driving on some kind of family trip. Sandy and I were in the back seat playing one of the billion games we made up 'cause we spent so much time in the car. They must have said something about how we should be quiet. All I remember is my father flailing and whacking both of us back with his arm. It was mayhem. I didn't know what it was coming from, I didn't know what I had done. I'm sure it was a little bit physically painful, but it was the random violence of it more than the actual physical pain. I was around six or seven. Sandy must've been three. My mom didn't protest at all. Utter silence. Because if *she* protested, she'd get hit.

In fourth grade I had rheumatic fever. I was supposed to call out if I needed anything. I'd call out in the night, gripping my hands like this, thinking, "Oh god, I hope it's my mom and not my dad that comes," you know what I mean? Sometimes it would be him, but when it was her, I would just sigh. At least I had her.

Basically, fear ruled, and that definitely shaped me. As impulsive and spontaneous as I was, I learned that by managing my behavior around him I could avoid calamity. I could bring something up, and I might hear back how wonderful I was, or I might get, "You stupid fucking idiot. You don't know?"

It was liberating to go away to school. And when I started playing sports, I got strong and could take him on. I would come home and I'd stand up to him, and most of the time he would just go into his study and slam the door.

He died at 60 of a massive heart attack . . . just bam!

The thing about him was he could be utterly charming — that was his public persona. So it was a true cathartic moment in my life when, after his funeral, I went to hang out with the other professors in his department. They started talking about him the way I would have talked about him and about how impossible he was and what a bastard he was, and how he made all these rules that he didn't have to follow but everyone else did and what a tyrant he was. I always thought that only happened at home. I thought that he ran this perfect life — outside.

I just hugged these guys. It was really amazing.

(60s)

I lived with my aunt and uncle who didn't want me. Every day I lived with the fear of being thrown out. I became extremely hypersensitive to faces and sounds because my uncle would go from being lovely and caring to being this schizophrenic crazy man. He'd take this table in front of us and throw it into the wall. So, I am very alert to people's body positions, facial expressions, tone of voice. I also gave myself away a lot just to be at peace, sold out some of my own wishes or thoughts so I didn't create controversy. I mean, the acting out I've seen in other kids, you can only do that when you have loving parents. I never had the freedom to be a bad boy. It's a privilege.

(70s)

I always had my share of fights. I don't know why. Just pissed off at something, I guess. We used to have BB gun fights. I got a BB right above the eye, so that was the end of that. It was wartime then. It was what was around. Kids pick it up.

(70s)

They had this long clothing brush and it was actually brown, but they called it the black brush. So they would just say, hmm, do you want the black brush? Was it effective? Not with me. Incidentally, I never, ever touched my children. It didn't work with me, why would it work with them. Right?

(70s)

My dad used to have a punching bag on the bottom of the deck, under the house. He punched it so hard the whole house shook. He never broke out and yelled at us, but that feeling of rage in him, about to break, was terrifying. It never broke so, in a way, it became more and more terrifying throughout my childhood. What is this thing he's constantly struggling with? It's right there, you can feel it, but it's never allowed to get out. Incredibly intimidating. Even just a look.

(70s)

My mom slapped me. I was about three or four maybe. I was totally shocked. My mother told me many years later that I was so shocked, that she never did that again. She was astonished that she had done that. She's a very smart woman.

(80s)

There was no violence in my life. The good thing is—this is my computer up here [points to head], this is my mouse [finger] and I could go like this [puts finger to his temple] and I can relive anything I want. But I crossed out all the bad things, only kept the good things!

My dad used a belt, but that was what everybody did and you didn't feel it hurt you, so it didn't feel like violence.

(90s)

Thomas (40s)

*"We don't collude on violence,
we collaborate on peace."*

I grew up in a dysfunctional household. Violence, alcoholism, inappropriate behavior—it was all mixed together. I was already like, "What can I trust? Can I trust myself? How do I even know what's normal for me?" I had to find out the hard way, by doing it wrong and suffering the consequences.

When I was growing up, I lived primarily with my mother and a series of fairly violent and abusive men. I didn't actually see my mom get struck by anybody, but I heard her screaming and crying. Most of the behavior that was modeled for me was from my stepfathers, or relationships my mother had. My birth father—he's from the Middle East—provided sort of a backdrop in my life, an attitude. There is definitely the patriarch there, where dad's in charge and he runs the household.

In 2005, I was arrested, charged and convicted for domestic violence. That brought to my attention a life-long pattern of behavior, and a connection between me and my father and the other men in my life growing up. I was taught to control and dominate my partners. It always came down to me calling the shots, me being in charge. My definition of violence changed from that point forward. My idea of a violent man was someone who fought with other men all the time, and was physically abusive to women. I wasn't those things, but I was using different types of coercion in my relationships that I wasn't aware of. After what I witnessed from my stepfather and the other violent men in my mother's relationships, I vowed to never hit a woman. I have kept that vow, but I wasn't aware of all of the other kinds of violence that I had been doing.

My life came to a screeching halt. I was engaged in a heated argument with

145

my partner at the time. I was drunk, and we were fighting. She pushed my buttons, and I pushed her against the wall and threatened her life.

I was forty-three years old—in jail with four felony charges. All the trappings of a successful life had fallen away as a result of my alcoholism and my addictions I found myself embraced in this very violent, tumultuous relationship with a young lady. Looking back, she was an amazing woman. She had started graduate school. Successfully employed, smart, funny, attractive. I didn't appreciate any of those things at the time.

We were trapped in a cycle of violence that was very dangerous. There wasn't any hands-on, but there were a lot of threats, and a lot of physical violence around her, breaking things, throwing things, screaming and yelling. That's the behavior that was modeled to me, and I never really questioned there was anything wrong with it. I thought I was justified. There'd been a couple police contacts but no arrests made, and I didn't even think anything of that.

The night that I laid hands on her, I realize now that what she was doing was setting limits with me, boundaries with me in saying, "You can't come here like this. You can't talk to me this way. You need to leave." For a lot of men, when our authority is challenged, that's when we tend to be the most violent. That's part of the male role belief system. We're trained that being a man is being in control and dominant.

This time, I went to jail for six months. It was a time for me to really, really reflect on my life. I ran groups in there. Then a court-ordered program to help men stop violence came in, and that's where it changed. When I left jail I was able to get in with a group of guys and get sober and nail it down.

I thought I knew what it meant to be a man. There are certain things that seem to be hard-wired and genetically part of being a boy or a man. We have the ability and the upper body strength to control and dominate. We think we're the big shots, that we're in charge, *because we can be*. If it's a Nerf gun or a pink bicycle with training wheels and tassels, you know, my son goes for the gun. The way I treat his mother is the biggest factor in how he learns to be a man. It was for me, looking back. If I treat her with respect, if I value what she has to say, if I listen to her and invite her into discussion and into decision-making, that's what he's going to notice.

It's really the rules of engagement, how you treat people. Now I say, "Equal is equal is equal." And that's something that takes a long time to soak in, because I always reserve the right to, if all else fails—I'm going to put my foot down here. Because somewhere in the back of my mind is the idea that I'm the boss and this is the way it's going to be. Looking back, I see that forcing things to happen and forcing others to do my bidding left me an unhappy, broken man with unfulfilling relationships, disappointment, regret.

~

A lot of guys, when we're first getting help, we try to minimize or deny responsibility for our violence. Blaming, really. It's culturally acceptable. "She freezes me out. She gives me the silent treatment. She isn't affectionate to me." There are a lot of kinds of violence—physical, verbal, emotional, economical, sexual, spiritual. Statistically, women are the guilty party 48 percent of the time. This is a real statistic. Men, 52 percent. A 50/50 split. Of course you're going to recognize that in your partner before you see it in yourself

I got good at being passive-aggressive. I was losing control of this person. When we up the ante, when we're challenged and our emotional or verbal or economic authority doesn't work any more, as happened in my case, I finally crossed the line. I shoved her against the wall, and I threatened her.

She didn't call the police immediately. She waited, and gave me a chance to explain myself. I remember the look on her face. She shook her head and said, "No, you're not going to do this to me." There was a quiet understanding between us at that moment—a pivotal, life-changing event. That look on her face, in her eyes.

Over the last few years, I've seen that look many times. I've seen it in my own mom's eyes when I raise my voice to her. It's a look of being hurt so deeply, and frightened. Fear of my rage. In my mother's frightened eyes, I saw myself as a terrified young boy. I felt ashamed, a very uncomfortable feeling, which was quickly followed by anger to justify myself. Men, we do that. It's a habit. Emotional violence—what it does is spiritual violence. It leaves a person worn down and off-balance.

The most difficult thing to deal with is when I feel justified. It stems way back. Growing up in a turbulent and unpredictable alcoholic household was emotional violence. I remember as a boy when I had suffered humiliation and violence, I said, "This is not going to fucking happen to me anymore." This emotional bomb shelter where you go into, it's a protective mode. Years and years of, "You're not gonna fuck with me. I will not let anybody control and dominate me or challenge me ever again." I carried that attitude all the way up to domestic violence.

That little boy is still there, and he's still afraid and he still doesn't want to be hurt again and he still doesn't completely trust people. I have to keep reminding myself, "You can trust her. She loves you." My default position is not to trust, not move towards intimacy, not be vulnerable. I have to make a concerted effort to overcome that automatic response.

⁓

My mom grew up on the East Coast—very strict Victorian Protestant parents—and she eloped with my father, who was a non-English-speaking, handsome young dishwasher. They met in Washington DC, in the early '60s, and she fell in love with him, or the idea of him. She didn't even know him. My mom told me that she was brought up to believe that women are supposed to be barefoot, pregnant, and in the kitchen. Children are to be seen and not heard. Being with this kind of mysterious Mediterranean guy was exciting for her. Unfortunately, he learned to speak English, and she got to know him and realized what he was all about.

My father is a micromanaging, controlling dictator, and he can be very cutting in an emotional way. He's a retired doctor now. Very smart, lonely and isolated. It's kind of a sad story. His father passed away when he was really young, and he had to go to work. When he was sixteen he moved to Paris, and was conscripted into the French army and served in Algeria.

We tried to camp once and it was a disaster. My father would say stuff to me like,

"You take up space. You use up air." Once, though, he really stopped and listened to me. That was when I quoted John Lennon to him: "Life is what happens when you're busy making other plans." It really gave him pause, because he's always been making other plans and not living. He had no model of how to be with me. I'm going to break the cycle. I hope my son is going to have a different notion.

～

When my stepdad was violent to my mom, I felt defenseless and angry, like, "I'm going to get this guy." One time, I actually did. I attacked him.

I was thirteen, something like that. My stepfather had been molesting my sister for three or four years. When I found out, I unleashed on him with all the anger that I had toward a lot of men. I remember chasing him out of the house and throwing stuff at him, including a bottle. Over the years, I made threats to this guy, and he basically laughed at me. Like, "Come on, you're no good. You're like your mom." He eventually left. No charges were filed, and he went on to abuse another child. I carried a lot of guilt and shame for the longest time. Thank God that in recovery I was able to do an inventory and deal with it—more than anything, the guilt I felt for not being able to protect my sister. I had a sneaking suspicion that my mom must have known about it, so I carried a lot of resentment against her, too.

It wasn't my responsibility. I understand that now. I didn't have the guidance I needed during that period of time. I needed the framework of the twelve steps to finally let go of all that responsibility.

Alcohol saved my life two times, one was when I was about that age and I would have killed myself if I didn't have that relief, that ease and comfort I got from a drink. And, surprisingly enough, the second time was when I was clean and sober, but I didn't have a program in recovery.

～

The recidivism rate for violent men is high. Once you become aware of your behavior, that's just the beginning of a long process of changing it. I've only been physically violent to a woman one time. After that disclosure event, I got involved in working with other men, and I've had to say, "I'm sorry" to my partner and my son for being verbally and emotionally abusive.

When men get together, it's a Super Bowl party. You wouldn't believe what they talk about in the firehouse. The first time I went fishing with some guys that I really liked, it was just a matter of time before the racist or sexist joke or the off-color remark would come up. We would all collude. For the first time in my life, I said, "I'm not really comfortable with that." It was something sexist or racist. The response I got was a sense of relief from the other men. They said, "You know what? I don't like that either." Even the person who made the remark regretted it. For a man to be able to be able to admit when he's wrong—that is huge.

We get a lot of mixed messages. I think we're kind of confused, men in general. We need to take a class on how to listen. We're trained that being a man is about not paying attention to your feelings, not listening to yourself. If you don't listen to yourself and don't have empathy for yourself, how can you do that for anybody else? I was a controlling, violent man *by habit*. We have a lot of work to do as men.

You know what we're telling our boys? "Man up." Those are the words used. "You can do better; this isn't good enough. You can work harder. Don't cry, you can take it, be strong, shrug it off." And what we're telling the girls is, "You're all right just the way you are." Or, "Don't worry, it's okay." Or, "You're so pretty." We've set the bar way down here for them. We even get down on their level and tell them that. Meanwhile, the big guy looking down at the little guy who's hurt is saying, "Don't feel empathy for yourself. Don't trust yourself. Don't complain. Be a man." That's the message we're giving.

When my nine-year-old son gets a scratch, he takes care of it. He doesn't like pain, and he avoids getting hurt. I'm afraid that he's not going to be prepared for when he gets tackled or some bully comes after him. I tell him there are always alternatives to violence, and that the peaceful way to resolve a problem is always the best way. He prefers hanging out with girls. I don't know exactly what that means. He's handsome and he's charismatic. I guess there isn't the same pressure to be a guy. He's seeing that it's okay to enjoy things like cooking and things that traditionally are female gender roles. Those lines are blurred now.

My son brings out the childish in me. We laugh a lot and have fun together. We play. He's amazing. I asked him if he thinks girls are better at certain things than guys. His answers were startling. "We're both the same." Or, "Girls are even smarter at mathematics than men. Girls can run faster than boys." I think the change is coming from the bottom up, where it should—from the little people.

~

I'm a certified substance abuse counselor now, and a batterer's intervention facilitator, so I get to meet and help guys in both areas. The crossover effect is really good. We have the opportunity to have a safe place, confidential place, where we can finally let our guard down and actually relate. What I've learned is that all people deserve to be treated with a fundamental, basic sense of dignity and respect, and that I don't need to check their motives. I don't even know if they want recovery or not. I just know if a guy's hurt, he needs help. If he's hungry, he needs food. I have people who have killed their wives—manslaughter and so on. I'm trying to help men go from not killing to the point where they can listen to somebody. We don't collude on violence, we collaborate on peace. That's what we do. That's exciting to me. Peace is a moment-to-moment decision.

When guys first come into the recovery program here, they name their "hit man," which is a learned behavior, and they name their "authentic self." They find out they don't have to live in the belief system they've been taught. We so elegantly and easily can describe the way we vision ourselves. The way we like the world to see us is what we want to see in our partners. And it's polar opposite from what our hit man is and what we've been *trained to be*. The only guy I can't help is one whose authentic self and hit man have the same name. I don't think that's ever going to happen. Even the most hardened people have both sides to them. There's that innocent open boy, very alive and wanting to be, in everybody.

As a young boy, I remember that I always felt bad for somebody who wasn't treated fairly. I felt empathy for people, and also disappointment if I would go to his aid and he'd turn on me. I didn't know how to be patient, and see that this guy is being inappropriate because someone has picked on him. "It's because they've been hurt before, son." I wish I'd had someone to tell me that. No one ever did.

I had that empathy as a kid. I think we all do. I just didn't know how to put it into practice until I'd suffered through a lot of stuff myself. Real suffering is when you've got nobody who's willing, or able, to tell you what's true. I think a lot of men who go for worldly power suffer from this. Oftentimes, the more "successful" they are, the deeper the denial and isolation.

~

My partner Gina and I met when we were in court-ordered detox. We were both addicts, emotional infants. She's witnessed my behavior first-hand. I decided to stay a facilitator when my fifty-two weeks were up, thinking, "Wow, I need to *pay attention.*"

I'm living amends — I'm trying. I wish I knew what I was doing more often. Especially with my son. I'm gonna break the cycle of violence. When he gets angry, my instinct is to match it. I wish I could provide him with a more conventional sense of security, and I'm working on that. Gina and I we're not married. I've never been married. It's hard for me to trust. That's a part of my wall, probably. I watched my mom get married and divorced four times. I've watched everybody I know get divorced. I don't have a whole lot of respect for the institution of marriage, but I do respect the commitment that I'll make to a person. On some level, I feel we're already married. For the first time in my life, I really feel safe with her.

I'm working with her on listening. I'll go, "Honey, is there anything you need from the store?" And she'll go, "This, that and the other thing." A few words into it, and I'm already distracted by another thought. And then, invariably, I call her from the store, and say, "Honey, I forgot what you told me to get." She says, "You didn't forget. You weren't listening." The more I listen to her, and listen with my heart, I'm starting to discover what a wonderful person she is, how smart she is, how creative, how interesting. Men, we tend to go "Okay, all right and the point is?" We need to have the answers—we need to know, be in charge and in control.

I go to a lot of stag meetings and functions that are just men. We get that safe ability to bond and express our feelings. AA is an amazing movement when it comes to bringing men closer together. In the men's groups we don't talk about our women, and we don't objectify. We talk about spiritual principles, feelings, step work. It's amazing.

With the circle of friends that I have in my recovery fellowship and my family, I feel that I don't have to be the strong pillar of emotional stability. Under the old rules, everything was pressure, trying to live up to what I felt society's image of a man was or what an image of a man was supposed to be—tough and strong, and be able to handle situations, not be afraid.

Now I don't have those struggles. I can be vulnerable and ask for help, and it's a relief—a big relief to not always have to run around like I know everything. Not run people's lives, and be in control of everything—the center of the universe. It's like, welcome to being a human being again—just another human being, another well-intentioned person trying to do the next right thing.

"Boys Will Be Boys"?

"I have people to talk to.
That's why I'm not a bully."

I kept hearing about a profound violence being done to a boy's basic nature. A man in his 60s summed it up for me: "Violence is normalized. 'Boys will be boys,' meaning—boys will be violent. And if you're a little boy, you just have to learn to take it and fight back. Cowboy up. At great personal cost and at great cost to the human race."

It was becoming clear to me that, even if these boys managed to avoid violence at home, when they stepped outside they were going to meet a bullying world. It was just expected, *it was going to happen*. So they had to figure out a way of dealing with it. What would it be like to have physical violence an expected part of daily life—simply because you're a boy?

For many of the guys, athletics were spoken of in a fond way as a polishing and a chance to bond. But as I listened, I began to also see how, in many situations, violence was being inflicted on the guys who participated. Controlled violence, maybe, but violence. A 62-year-old said, "I used to dread recess. I'd go outside and here goes kickball or dodge ball. There's a lot of hidden violence in those sports games."

I wonder if men who have experienced violence are more apt to be drawn to watching violent sports, and experience some kind of temporary relief from watching it? Especially when they identify with the winners.

One of my favorite things as a young girl was running—it just made me happy because I liked to go fast. We lived in what had been a cow field so there was plenty of space. I'd take off out the front door, screen banging behind me, and run full out as hard as I could until I collapsed from exhaustion and delight or reached the end of the field. I know these guys are drawn to the same sense of aliveness—the pure joy of being in our bodies. But then there's competition, proving oneself a man, being tough, not feeling vulnerable or needing help even if you get hurt. The training tends to bleed into daily life and pretty soon everything can become a competition until, as one man said, "Winning is everything."

Something is getting lost and something *else* is getting passed on.

∾

At the beginning, they hurt you and do stuff to you and then, how they stay a bully or how they actually be a bully is, they do it once, nobody tells them to stop. And then they're like, okay, what if I do it again? They do it the first time to protect themselves 'cause they're afraid they're gonna get hurt.

(9 yr.)

There's one guy who kind of always has to be on top and goes around and bugs people. But he only does that to, like, first-graders. I don't hang out with him. He's mean. He doesn't pick on me, or any of the fourth-graders. I don't really know why he does it. Maybe he doesn't have a good life at home so he takes it out on other people. I think it's just to act cool in front of his friends. There's a lot of kids at my school who like to act cool, because they don't want to be like left out, you know?

(10 yr.)

The bully is scared and that's why he picks on people. He hasn't really had much practice of violence with his brother or he might not have anybody to talk to or he just doesn't feel welcomed. I have people to talk to. That's why I'm not a bully.

(11 yr.)

When I was in pre-K, there was a kid who was obviously supposed to be in first grade but he was still in pre-K. He was much taller than all of us. I tried to stand up to him so my friends wouldn't get hurt. Finally, one morning he threw a punch, I threw a punch back, then he threw me right into a little playhouse and that was the last of him, thank God. He did it because someone didn't do what he wanted them to.

It's better when you learn how to avoid fights like that. Sometimes someone tries to start a fight with you so that you get in trouble and not them. They say you're a moron and then they keep insulting you and insulting you. Finally they say, "You want to start a fight?" And what you have to do is just say, "No, I'm good" or "I'll pass." That really throws them back.

(11 yr.)

My first experience of violence was when I was in fourth grade, so maybe nine, ten? I was walking home from the bus stop with my gingerbread house and this kid, who was bigger than I was, in a different class, says, "Hey, give me a piece of your gingerbread house." I said no. And he says, "You better do what I say, because I know karate." He busts out this little stance and shows me a couple kicks and punches. I'm like, oh yeah? Well, so do I! I did my fake little roundhouse kick and all this stuff. And he just, bam, chopped me in the back, punched me in the stomach, and pretty much beat me up. His dad came over, and yelled, "What the hell are you doing?" Grabbed him by the neck, and smacked him around a little bit. I was like, whoa. I can't believe this kid just did this. Luckily, I had my brother hold the gingerbread house while we were fighting. So I got to eat it.

(20s)

School was survival of the fittest for sure. The boys were always competing. The most insecure boys were always the toughest, biggest bullies, the meanest guys. In the gym class locker room there was lots of name calling and teasing and hazing going on. They didn't mess with me too much 'cause I was their same size. There were a couple of the biggest, baddest bullies that I didn't really know, but they were always pushing people around, especially if you were an outsider. There was this one kid who totally came from a different place, and he was a little bit smaller. They really laid into him much harder. One day, in the locker room, one of the big, tough bully guys just got this guy and threw him up against the locker and scared the daylights out of him. He didn't know what hit him. He just looked at him with a white face. His expression said it all. He said, "Why did you do that? That hurt. Don't do that." You know? And the bully guy, if I could draw cartoon bubbles of what he and his buddy were really probably thinking in their minds—you know, I don't think it's what either of them wanted to do. They didn't get the training wheels they needed when it came to emotional growth.

(20s)

When I was a little fella, I had this incredible sense of innocence and freeness in the woods. Then that feeling started to get smaller . . . I had a cousin—two years older—who was also very big very early and very tough and very rough. I knew that there were just things you had to watch out for before I ever really had memories, because he was probably the most consistent bully in my young life. I was really a good wrestler in high school. And I remember the first time I pinned him. Oh, God, that was satisfying! Oh, it was huge. Probably one of the biggest moments of my adolescent life was that accomplishment. 'Cause he was such an albatross growin' up. Violence with hillbilly kids is kind of—it's not questioned. It just kind of is.

(30s)

Really early in grade school I did some terrible things to a kid in my class. What the hell is his name? He called me up years later, I think it was at the behest of a therapist or something, as part of a counseling program he was in at college. He called Serena who was my accomplice, too. We both had really awkward conversations with him.

I never beat him up or anything, but I remember I wrote nasty letters about him once and put them around the school, and then his parents came. It's just horrible. And they found them. It was a terrible thing to do. Terrible, terrible, a little cruel thing. So that's certainly very violent.

I think when you're young there's curiosity and power and you don't know what it's gonna do. I think there's a kind of cruelness in humans and I don't know how to deal with that. I don't know how to speak to that at all.

(30s)

One of the worst things is to be chicken. I wish I had wanted to fight. It would have been better. I felt like I had to live with being a chicken. In junior high there were some situations where you obviously weren't gonna fight the kids with the knives and the chains. You didn't wanna tell anybody, so you just modified your daily schedule and went and hung out in Ms. Grabowsky's English class or went to study in the library. It is sort of shameful. I wish I'd had the strength to do it differently, or even to confront them, let them kick my ass or whatever. But I just didn't know what to do.

(40s)

In third grade, in the arts and crafts segment of our school, I started to make an emergency bag like one the firefighters' I'd seen on TV. There was an episode where a guy repelled down a ravine to get somebody who had crashed their car and pull them back up. He had this big satchel with a bunch of emergency equipment in it. That was really cool. I wanted to have an emergency satchel like that.

So I started to make it — just sort of a bag with a strap over it — and this other boy started teasing me saying it was a purse. "Simon's got a purse. How's your purse, Simon?" It's so classic. Of course, I insisted, "No, it's like a firefighter's bag," but — whatever. It didn't matter. That had a big imprint.

(40s)

Low-level violence is part of the enculturation process. It's a big factor when you play sports. From a young age, there's an expectation that you're going to get hit, and you're going to deal with the pain. There's a whole language around it. Suck it up. Shrug it off. Walk it off. You want to intimidate your opponent into thinking they didn't hurt you. They gave you their best shot, and you just rubbed it off.

The first time I played with a hardball — you know, baseball was just terrifying. There are some cases of kids who died by getting hit in the head. But they teach you to put your body *in front of* the ball, *even though it's a goddamn rock and it hurts.* Some guys maybe leave and don't play sports anymore. Others just steel themselves and shut down emotionally.

In football practice, we had this exercise called "bull in the ring." It was about direct collision, somebody running full speed into someone else. What I most remember is the shock. When you get hit that hard, you go kind of numb for a second. It's almost like a smell. Later, I hurt like hell, but it was kind of a badge of honor. My mom would've been ecstatic if I'd said, "I'm scared. I don't want to do this." She would've said, "Okay, you don't have to do it."

I was standing on the sideline. My coach came up to me out of the blue and shook my hand. "You took a lot of hits today. I'm proud of you." and walked off. This guy was an asshole, a total maniac. Yet I remember it today, over twenty years ago. I liked the positive reinforcement, but it was always very mixed with this sense of fear and anxiety about imminent pain.

(40s)

No, you didn't cry. I think sports does that a lot. Excuse me, that ball is going 100 miles an hour and you want me to stop it? Or, football—I'm holding the ball and that's why everybody wants to kill me? Who came up with this idea?

(50s)

I used to play soccer a lot. I love playing soccer with these guys. The competition—you know, that's the level of taking the towel off. I'm going to go full tilt against you and you're going to go full tilt against me, and let's see what happens. There's really something about meeting a man like that.

(50s)

I read somewhere men interrupt 90% of the time, women 10%, just to keep a place. It's always who's on top. Violence is a means by which to feel like I have a place that you're not going to take away.

(50s)

There was a kid who would bully me. He was in a grade above me, and we used to wait for the bus together. He was always hitting me and shoving me and stuff like that. One day, we got into this fight and I managed to get him—I was a wrestler at the time—in this hold. I got dominance of him, pushed his face into the dirt, and then all his friends made fun of him. I remember feeling terrible about that, because—I mean, I was defending myself for sure. Me and my friends had been at his mercy for a long time. But afterward, I just felt terrible. And I went to a Quaker school, so there was not a lot of that going on. Going to Quaker schools all my life was actually in some ways a disadvantage, because when I left them—I was amazed at the aggressiveness of the other men in my life. Actually, men, and women as well. You realize that a lot of times nothing is done. Men do not see a society that feels there's anything wrong with it at all.

(50s)

I wasn't good at competition. I was afraid of baseball. I took a line drive foul in the belly and was hit on the head with a bat. And when I was playing basketball I ran down the court and executed a brilliant lay-up—for the wrong team! Everyone laughed. I was a very sensitive kid. It was humiliating. I was always the last kid to get picked. I was pencil thin and called "sissy." I went away—mentally, physically, psychically. I took my books and sketchbooks and just left. When I was nineteen I had a loaded gun held to my head for an hour. It diminishes all fears in comparison. I became an artist.

(50s)

The worst place in the world is the locker room. There's this energy. I still hate to be around men who talk about beer and pussy. Drives me nuts. In order to increase intimacy, you dis somebody else. But he not only disses me, he disses himself.

(50s)

In sports, like in the military, you don't ask questions. Total submission to the coach. Winning is everything. Hurting the other team is of *no* consequence. No room for feeling. In training, the coaches would say, "We got to break you down before we build you up." Don't let the other guy know how much he hurt you. Don't show your weakness. They *taught* that. It was training for socioeconomic behavior. That's what the country needed after WW II. I've had seven surgeries on my knee. Would I do it all again? You bet! Playing in front of forty thousand people was the most exciting thing I ever did.

(50s)

When I was a little league coach there were a lot of single moms who didn't have a man in their life so they were bringing their boys to baseball practice to get some "man" training. You know what we did with those boys? To play baseball they needed to wear a cup over their privates. The moms always bought them too big 'cause they were so worried about offending their son's "manhood." I mean, these boys were maybe six years old! We'd tell them to stand up next to the wall. Then we'd walk down the row with a baseball bat and hit them lightly where their cup oughta be, so they better be wearing it. That was "man training." With these little six- or seven-year-olds!

And we'd tell them — when you're out on the field you have to *pay attention*. You can't be looking at clouds or looking around at all because the ball might smack you in the face. We'd tell little 7-year-olds this!!

(50s)

I went up to a drinking fountain in elementary school and, as I was drinking a big kid came up behind me and smashed my head down and it chipped my tooth — and then you're afraid the rest of the duration.

(60s)

There was a kid down the street who was a bully. He got mad at a friend of mine and sent me up to the house to ask if this little boy could come out and play, so he could hit him. I did that, but I didn't know what was gonna happen. That was my first experience.

One day the same kid chased me home. I was sitting on the front porch and he threw rocks at the house. We had a trellis with vines on it. The rocks were coming through the vines and one hit me in the head. That's my first *personal* experience. I was probably five or so.

(60s)

I was a jock. I really loved athletics. But I didn't get along that well with the other athletes. They appreciated my speed and skill, but they didn't really like me very much. One night, when I had kind of longish hair, this football team pinned me down and cut my hair off and yelled really ugly things at me. It was real violence.

I think they meant it in good fun, like they were bringing me into their tribe. But there was something a little off about it too 'cause when the quarterback walked in he was appalled. He screamed at them and came over and apologized to me. I always figured that's what women must feel a little bit. There's something kind of scary about male culture.

(60s)

The culture of athletics tells you anything you can get away with in the service of winning is okay. In water polo, 70% of the game goes on under water. The referee can't see, so you do illegal stuff. If you get caught, you throw your hands up and take the penalty. Then, when you go back to play, you get away with whatever you can again. Winning is everything, and it's okay to cheat. That's the training. In later life, it caught up with me.

(60s)

Sports encourage competition. Good coaches try to channel competition into a positive force. You get to be competitive *and* have teamwork at the same time, working side by side with your comrades and combating something else. I had one coach I hated and I knew it right away. I quit football because of him. Became a lacrosse player. In practice, when you were working out and hitting the sled, he would literally say, "Kill! Kill! Kill!"

(60s)

I don't know what the real root is of that greed and that total disregard for the rest of humanity that's causing us to destroy the planet, but I would not be surprised to find that it was some sort of significant childhood abuse of the people who are in power, who would have some effect, and who are predominantly males.

(60s)

One of the first experiences of violence I remember is some older girls who force-fed me garbage. It was terrible. Awful. I have no idea why. Two held me down, and the third one pushed it in my mouth. They were like six years older than me. I was maybe seven, maybe eight. I felt like I wasn't able to breathe.

(70s)

There's a dominant repetitive dream now. All the sex dreams are gone and my libido has disappeared, at least in my subconscious, but I have bully dreams.

I'm not a little boy in them. I'm my age right now. People are trapping me, threatening me. They're bullies — always men, of course. Not on a playground or at school. No, the guys are in suits. They're going to beat me up.

(70s)

When I was seven, four guys who were bigger and older caught me in a vacant lot and threatened to beat me up. I had an uncle who was a professional boxer, and he had taught me a few moves, so I stood up to those guys. I said, "Okay, I'll take you on, one at a time." They chickened out. That incident — facing up to those bullies — was when I felt I became a man. I never got beat up in my life.

(80s)

Arnie (40s)

I did bad things. From the age of seventeen, I was a racist skinhead, a white supremacist. I don't believe anyone has an excuse to be violent, but I had absolutely no excuse. I came from a privileged background in the Midwest, born into the middle class. I had everything going for me, although I grew up in an alcoholic household where emotional violence was the norm.

My parents were pretty miserable, and that made me want to distance myself from them. It also got me lashing out. I was a bully on the school bus as early as kindergarten. In elementary school, I started getting into fights in the schoolyard, and by the time I was in middle school, I was committing serious acts of vandalism. As a teenager, I started drinking. I got into punk rock music, which I still love. I appreciate the D.I.Y. attitude and "question authority" aspect of punk, but back then it was just about smashing things and hurting people and lashing out. I was lead singer in a white power band, putting out violent, hate-filled music.

From my earliest memories, I was obsessed with being a warrior. I learned to read early, and read stories about King Arthur, the Greek myths and Norse myths, all these heroes. Being a lethal holy warrior was incredibly appealing to me. My thrill-seeking needed constant cranking up, so when I encountered racist skinheads, I knew I'd found something far more effective than punk rock. I joined up for the kicks, and to make people angry. Here at last was my chance to be a warrior for a magnificent cause—to save the white race! I truly believed white people were under threat of genocide at the hands of some shadowy Jewish conspiracy. It fell right into the torchlight ceremony that Hitler used. It made total sense to me, probably because nothing else in my world was making sense. I assumed an identity where all that mattered was the color of my skin.

I remember one Thanksgiving dinner when I was vehemently and drunkenly spouting my views. My mother said, "Well, Mr. Nazi, did you know that you're one-sixteenth Indian?" That completely shut me up. Later that night, I went back to my own house, and drank beer out of glass bottles until I broke one and slit my wrist with it. That's how convinced I was that my racial identity was all I had.

I wanted to make the world hurt like I hurt. Initially, I donned a swastika for shock value, because it was the most effective way to piss people off. I wasn't a racist looking for other racists. I was just a bored, angry kid looking for something to make me feel worthwhile—a cause to join up with. I found very quickly that once I started radiating hate and violence, the world reflected it back. This, of course, further validated my paranoia and conspiracy theories. I wallowed in violence as a means of self-destruction and stimulation.

I became very proficient in aggression. With my bare hands, I beat other human beings to the point of hospitalization, simply because of the color of their skin, their sexuality, or for the adrenaline rush. I broke a gay man's face with my elbow, then spat on him as he lay in a crumpled heap in the corner, laughing about it with my buddies all night and for many nights thereafter. I practiced violence until it seemed natural. Kids who tried to emulate me did much worse. I was living in a reality of terror I'd created myself.

≈

There were two milestone events in my leaving the movement. One was becoming a single parent. The second was, a couple months after that, a friend of mine was murdered in a street fight. By that time, I had lost count of how many friends had been incarcerated, so it struck me that if I didn't change my ways, death or prison would very likely take me from my daughter. I was twenty-one years old when my daughter was born. They put her in a little hamburger warmer thingy, and the first time she opened her eyes in her life, they met mine. That exchange was a huge moment in my life that I'll never forget. A week later, after coming home drunk and covered with somebody else's blood, I got in an argument with her mom. I didn't have any response other than trying to cut my left hand off with a dagger. I almost died. Still, single fatherhood is what really started to change me, taking me away from the movement. Of all the awful physical violence I did, the worst thing was being drunk or hung-over during the bulk of my daughter's first eleven years. That's my biggest regret, something I still struggle with every day.

I was twenty-three when I reached a point where, like, "I'm done with this. I'm not a racist anymore." The more I opened myself up, the happier I was. I went from being a White Power skinhead to being a raver—an absolute one-eighty. While there was still a lot of drug use and irresponsible behavior, there was also a lot of forgiveness. Going to rave parties helped me to relax. You love everybody. My daughter turned me on to Buddhism. When she was having emotional problems in middle school, she learned to meditate, and started going to retreats and asking me to buy her Dalai Lama books and stuff. Later, that inspired me to learn to meditate, too. I was carrying a huge, heavy grudge against myself.

The realization hit me: self-forgiveness could be possible. Through meditation and studying the Dharma, I began to go from just trying to survive my past, to healing from it and actually helping other people. I was thirty-eight.

The music of a Brazilian female singer was a refuge for me. It helped me get out of the depression. For so many years, the music I've been used to is filled with aggressions—powerful enough to drive people to kill each other, to hurt themselves. But this woman's music is even more powerful—delicate and gossamer, at times, but also powerful enough to move mountains and the gravest of souls, all without the slightest hint of aggression. Gentle power. To me, the embodiment of everything that's beautiful about being a human being. It was symbolic of finding the gift in the wound. It touched some deeper part of me and helped me, as I was writing about my past, be strong enough to relive what I needed to relive.

≈

I come from a culture of thousands of years of war. That's what's shaped me as a man. It defines who I should be culturally, and what it means to be a man. And it all has to do with war. My dad has the same fascination. When I was a little kid, he would watch a TV series called "World at War"—World War II battle reels—though he never served. I'd watch with him. He was in the NRA, and I was raised around guns. It seems I could shoot a gun as soon as I could hold it. We used to have a pistol range in our basement, and a gunroom full of guns and swords and knives. I was fascinated with that stuff from day one.

My mom loved me a little more than life itself. To this day, I like the smell of Noxzema because when she tucked me in at night, it was just after she had washed her face. My mom's message of who I was supposed to be was less about manhood, more about being a human being. She is an absolutely amazing artist, and I drew a ton as a kid. I'd draw war scenes, and spaceships blowing each other up—gory stuff. My art was kind of where my mom and dad met in me, applying my artistic talents to portray the warrior I wanted to be.

As a little kid, I was constantly told how smart I was, how gifted I was, how I could do anything I wanted to do in life—that I was the best kid on the face of the earth, so amazing, so wonderful. You start to think of yourself as above and beyond everybody else. That's lonely and isolating. It's pressure, and you can't live up to it. The young Arnie was bristling underneath, saying, "No, that's not who I am. I'm not wonderful. I'm horrible. If you don't believe me, watch this." By horrible, I didn't mean weak or small. I meant horrible like Attila the Hun, like the Third Reich and every war wound into one.

I was bored in school. Just too much bullshit. Now that I work in education, I see things like Montessori and project-based learning, and I truly believe that had I been exposed to that growing up, it could have completely changed the course of my life. I loved martial arts. I was super good at it. But I didn't continue because my parents couldn't afford it. Man, if somebody would have come to us kids when we were fifteen and said, "Hey, do you want a free membership at our MMA gym," and really gave our aggression and testosterone a healthy, somewhat agreed upon outlet. . . .

I was presented with healthy challenge after healthy challenge, but I kept rejecting them. "I don't want all your attention. Go to hell, and leave me alone."

My running away began as soon as I could run, and culminated the year before I became a skinhead.

I had a lot of anger I didn't know what to do with. I was running away from parents' mundane suburban existence, and from my pain. Trying to get away from the person I thought I was supposed to be. I wanted to be in the city, where things were grittier and realer.

By our neighborhood's standards, we were poor. By world standards, I now know there are literally billions of children who would have happily traded childhoods with me. I wasn't aware how privileged I was.

I work with a Latino man, Mexican and Mescalero Apache, who was born into extreme poverty and addiction. He went through the most horrific sexual, emotional, physical abuse that you could possibly envision. Since he was let out of prison, he has become an amazing source for good in the world. When I sat down to talk to Lenny, the first thing I said was, "Well, I feel like a real asshole complaining about my childhood after hearing about yours." He looked me right in the eye, and said, "Suffering is suffering. There's no hierarchy."

The first time I remember fear was getting woke up by my mom screaming at my dad at three in the morning. I was five or six. That scared me. My mom was working two jobs and taking care of this hellion kid, and she didn't want to deal with her drunken husband. My mom was always literally at the end of her rope, but as a guy I couldn't let people know I was scared or hurt.

When I was much older and had been dumped by my girlfriend, I told my mom I wanted to kill myself but couldn't because of my daughter. I was expecting her to say, "Oh my God. Oh, my boy." Instead, she said, "I know how it is. During your whole childhood it was like that. The only reason I'm still here is because of you and your younger brother. Otherwise, I would've killed myself." I took on her pain. Her pain and my pain were all mixed together.

≈

People ask me what turned me around. There's no real simple answer. Exhaustion? It was really exhausting to have to keep suppressing this inner knowledge that what I was doing was wrong. This was complicated when people I was try-ing to hate would treat me with kindness. There were times when black people, Jewish people, gay and lesbian people treated me as a human being, even though I refused to acknowledge their humanity. I didn't change on the spot, but those acts of kindness did plant seeds that stuck with me, and built on a growing sense that what I was doing was wrong.

I remember a kindly African-American woman at McDonald's who greeted me warmly as she took my order. The next time I came in, I had gotten a swas-tika tattooed on my finger. I tried to hide it from her. She looked me right in the eye, a look of sadness and genuine concern, and said, "I know you're better than that. That's not who you are." I got my food, went and ate it, and never went back to that McDonald's. I never saw her again. Twenty years later, I haven't forgotten that moment.

Once, a kid who looked up to me came bragging about how he just punted a little ten year-old Latino boy in the stomach. He was telling me this like a kid would tell his dad he got straight As on his report card. My first thought was like, "That's fucked-up." But I didn't have the courage to say that. It would have destroyed every-thing I'd been preaching, this whole identity I concocted. So I had to say, "Well, you know, uh, little ones grow up to be big ones."

I started drinking more, cranking up the heavy metal music. I couldn't put out of my mind the people I'd beaten up so bad that only their parents could rec-ognize them. And I couldn't put those acts of kindness out of mind. It just kept building up and building up, until I couldn't suppress it. I don't think that courage is the right word. Looking back, it was just about better self-preservation. "You're on fire. You'd better jump in the lake."

I started realizing how enslaved I was to the ideology.

~

I had effectively been on a ten-year bender. Once I quit drinking, nine years ago, I had so much guilt and remorse for the harm I'd caused. I felt the need to really make a positive impact and speak out publicly against racism and hatred. And we need more women in charge, more consideration of women. I'm very much a feminist. But at the same time, pretending testosterone doesn't exist is not going to accomplish anything. We need to acknowledge it, find healthy ways to deal with it. I would like young boys to know that having your life revolve around sex will absolutely make you miserable. When I was a skinhead, I was lucky if I was able to get an erection, because I was so drunk all the time. And when I did, it was just like, bam and done. Bottom line: sex is not the most important thing on earth. If it's part of a genuine relationship with someone, it can be amazing. If you don't have that context, to be really blunt, you might as well just jack off.

I don't really ever feel unsafe—physically. The biggest challenge for me is emotional safety. When I hear people say they don't think I'm genuine, that hurts. Ninety-nine people are telling me it's time to forgive myself and be gentle with myself. But then one person tells me I'm full of shit and still a racist and not sorry enough. I'm like, "Okay, maybe I should go back to beating myself up."

I need to learn how to be more gentle, more mindful of what it feels like to be on the receiving end of rough language. When I say, "Fuck you. Fuck this," apparently it scares the shit out of some people. Because I'm not threatened when people talk to me that way, it doesn't occur to me how it might affect others. It's cool to get glimpses of what it's like to not be you.

My daughter is my greatest mentor. While she was growing up, we lived with my mom. My daughter wants to be free of me now. My friends Lenny and Bikram have been big mentors, too.

Bikram is probably the most important man in my life right now. I talk to him every day. We say, "I love you," to each other. His relationship with his dad was very much like mine with my dad—not very close. When I hang up on my dad, the first thing I think about is Bikram and his dad, who was murdered by a white supremacist. I'm 100% on the same page with Bikram on everything, including the call for gun responsibility.

I feel like I should say my dad is the most important man in my life. I have all his issues, and all his gifts. I owe everything I am to my dad. At the same time, the last time I talked to my dad, I hung up on him after an hour long screaming match about guns. It drives a very personal stake through my heart that my dad is expressing the same fear and paranoia that I did back in the movement.

~

I've come to realize that responding to aggression with compassion is much, much more difficult than responding with anger and violence. It takes much more strength to say "I don't know," to approach something without judgment. When I was younger I created my challenge by declaring war on the world. If I could speak to four-year-old Arnie, I'd like to tell him to challenge himself to really consider what bravery is all about.

I can talk the talk a lot better than walking it. It helps to have a meditation practice now, and to understand impermanence and interdependence. My daughter introduced me to that. The more I practice kindness, the better I get at offering it to people who least deserve it, like I was. I was given unconditional forgiveness by people who I once claimed to hate. They demonstrated for me the way from there to here.

Innately, I am a warrior. I believe I can live up to that title now, for the first time in my life. We're trying to break the cycle of violence and get kids to understand that their decisions and actions have consequences. Get them as excited about being peacemakers as they would be about being an athlete. We still get afraid, yes, but we find the wisdom in that fear, and inspire other people to move past it and be fearless also. To me, that is being a warrior.

The Hidden Epidemic

"To be accepted for your most vulnerable thing . . .
it's priceless, priceless, priceless."

I was astounded and heartbroken hearing the amount of violence these boys are experiencing growing up. I kept listening and, as my openness to hearing them widened, so did the kinds of stories I began to hear.

One in six. By the time boys are sixteen, as I learned reading an article by psychologist, David Lisak, one in six have been sexually abused. That means, in America, nearly 20 million adult males over eighteen have suffered unwanted or abusive sexual experiences. And that's just the reported instances. I'd been aware for quite a while that the numbers in girls were even higher (one in three or four), but until the scandal in the Catholic Church broke, I hadn't thought much about what boys' experience might be.

I was learning—staying up late into the night, reading online and weeping. One in six seems to be relatively true worldwide. There are so many men growing up with abuse or affected by someone who has been abused and hasn't addressed it. More than one-third of those abused never disclose the abuse to *anyone.* Yet children and families are immediately affected by it, often throughout their entire lives.

One man said that in the projects where he grew up, probably 90% of the guys he knew were sexually abused. It was just expected. You knew it was going to happen to you. Another man I interviewed, a forensic psychologist, said that *all* the death row inmates he's worked with had been sexually abused; some were in prison for killing their abusers. More often than not, the offender is a trusted, known person. Only 10% of the abusers are strangers. There are no toll-free numbers, no abuse hotlines for men. Can you think of any publicized cases of male rape? So where to go for help? A man in his 30s told me, "As horrific as it is for the victim, it's almost more horrific that it's so hard for people to find support in their communities."

The behaviors that our culture assumes are simply normal and appropriately masculine are the same as those that an abused child feels he must have to survive: don't acknowledge your pain, don't express it, don't talk about it with anyone else, don't show feelings of vulnerability or helplessness. Boys and men are warned away from the very things they would need to begin their own healing. The training begins early and runs deep, which leaves a whole lot of boys and men living in shame and secrecy and silence. Suffering *on top of* the suffering.

So many "incidental" stories: The family's handy man who invites a six-year-old to help with some construction work and instead drives him to a remote field, parks, pulls down their pants and jerks himself off, gives the boy a silver dollar that fills his whole hand and tells him not to tell. The friendly ferris wheel operator who climbs into the bucket seat with a ten-year-old, covers the boy's eyes with his hand and has him hold onto his exposed penis while the wheel goes up and around and around. The welcoming neighbor who offers a place to hang out after school and carefully grooms an eight-year-old for his own needs. The admired camp counselor who generously offers the comfort of sharing his bed with a homesick ten-year-old. The beautiful, needy aunt with a prurient interest in her young nephew's private parts. The school counselor who listens to a third grader's words, but not his heart and takes advantage of his vulnerability.

Loss of innocence. Fear. Confusion. Even if, in some instances, the encounter is "pleasurable." And, most of all, the misuse of power and profound betrayal of trust.

"And the hardest part for me, was having to . . . pretend nothing happened. I was way too scared to say anything," a man in his 50s told me. Because their experience is often less heard, several of the men felt an urgency for it to be told, so I've included longer excerpts of some of their stories. A couple of male readers of an early manuscript draft didn't want one of the stories to be included because they found it too disturbing. I know the feeling of wanting to turn away. But, as a man in his 50s said, "We may not want to look at it, but it's the reality of *many* boys." Another man, after reading the same story, looked up from the manuscript and said, "Is that all?" Sexual abuse is far more common than most of us would like to believe. Survivors of abuse often become obsessed with proving their masculinity, when what they need instead is care. A safe place to heal and get support.

I was inspired by those who are willing to come out of denial, reclaim their lives and, by naming the violence, stop passing on the pain. Although the suffering of these survivors is often more apparent and intense than for other men, it speaks to the violence and trauma—*of all kinds*—that so many have had to endure. A wide range on a continuum. Again I was hearing, "There is no hierarchy of abuse."

To me, these men who are doing the work of revealing and healing are pioneers.

Most of the men I spoke with spontaneously offered to show me a photograph of themselves taken before they were abused. One said, "This is who I was supposed to be."

John (70s)

"I felt safe. She understood what I'd been through."

The sexual abuse occurred when I was sixteen. My father would come into my bedroom in the morning. I'd lie there in terror, thinking, "Where the hell's my mother?" This happened four or five times, until finally I put an end to it. One morning he came in and started making his advances, and I just picked him up and sat him down over in the corner of the room and went back to bed. That was the end of it.

During that period, he sent me to spend the weekend with one of his friends, and he's telling me how much I'd enjoy it. Well, obviously he was sending me to have a sexual encounter with this man. After the first night, I left and came home. I expected my father to be very angry with me. Never said a word. I didn't realize at the time that my father was bi-sexual. He was off having homosexual affairs in Milwaukee, Madison, Chicago.

My mother, because of my father's position in our small community, he was a Protestant minister, thought our family was special, a step above the others. Meanwhile, all these awful dynamics were going on. My mom was no more available emotionally than my dad. I had the feeling she was worried about my welfare, but it came through as agonizing, not as nurturing me and taking care of me. My mother used me for emotional support—surrogate incest, emotional incest. The whole thing was a big emotional mess.

Where was my mother when the abuse was going on? That's what I kept asking myself. Sometimes the mothers were the perpetrators, but that's a fairly small percentage of the cases. It's so confusing and heavy duty. She's supposed to be your primary source of care and trust so it has devastating consequences.

There were no boundaries in the family, so I did not know how to be assertive or ask for what I wanted. I didn't know how to say no, either. The only way I knew how to deal with situations was to be passive-aggressive, and I was very good at it for a lot of years.

An example: I went to college on a football scholarship, and I was in pre-med, as my father wanted me to be, although I wasn't very interested in it. I started drinking, picked up with a girlfriend and became sexually active. The drinking and sex sort of took over, and I wound up flunking out. I think that was my way of saying, "I'm not going to do what you want me to." Claiming my own integrity.

I wound up enlisting in the Army. This was during the Korean War. Three years in the service as an enlisted man on a heavy artillery gun crew. I was stationed in Germany for a while, and still drinking a lot. If I went more than two nights without getting drunk, people wondered if I was sick, or what was the matter with me. A lot of anger. Inappropriate anger that I didn't know where it was coming from. People used to describe me as being stoic, which is a euphemism for being emotionally shut down. I just walled myself off from the rest of world, and lived in isolation. I didn't have any friends. The hallmark of my childhood was loneliness. I never had friends my whole life.

The Army was a real wake-up call for me. I realized I needed to get back to school, so when I got out of the Army, I did. I didn't get grades good enough for medical school, but I got turned on to physiology and went to graduate school in that, finally getting a Ph.D. During those years, I was a weekend drunk.

I got married, and my first wife was the daughter of two alcoholics. I found myself taking care of her and making things all right, which was my role in the family with my mother. Of course, that didn't work. We had two children, and the best thing I can say about my parenting is that I didn't abuse them sexually or physically. But emotionally? I was certainly not available to them, and very authoritarian. Speaking of which, because of my father's anger and his authority over the years, his control over me, I was always intimidated by authority figures. If I saw a police car two blocks away, I'd break into a sweat—"What have I done wrong now?" Any kind of confrontation was always a hostile confrontation.

I embarked on an extramarital affair that went on for maybe five years, with all the lying and sneaking around. You know, an extramarital affair is primarily a sexual affair, not real intimacy. There's a confusion between sex and love. I wound up getting a divorce, then remarrying. Ever since my parents left me alone in the hospital when I was five years old, I've felt like an orphan, emotionally. I was always looking for the home I never had. The first marriage didn't satisfy that, so maybe this new one would. She had five kids, and again I was going to take care of her and help her with the kids. Don Quixote tilting at windmills. A real rescuer.

My second wife's youngest son became a drug addict, and I was having real trouble coping with it. I thought she was enabling. Whether what I thought she should have done was right or not, I don't know, but it was certainly a source of conflict. I began to go to Al-Anon, and began to see behaviors in myself that I didn't care for—inappropriate anger, passive-aggressiveness, hostility, lack of boundaries.

I decided to do some family-of-origin work, and went to a therapist. We were going through all the family dynamics, and one day he said to me, absolutely out of the blue, "Were you ever sexually abused by your father?" I was about sixty years old, and up to that point it had been completely suppressed. In all those years, nothing had triggered it. Apparently, that's not uncommon.

When he said that to me, I had an instant flashback—my bedroom, what happened there, the panic, where's my mother, all this sort of thing. I was stunned flat, yet I was still unemotional about the whole thing. About that time, my mother died. I thought, "Well there goes my last chance to ever have a home." My father had died a year or so earlier.

I began looking for resources, and found the AMAC group—Adults Molested As Children. I attended on a weekly basis for about two years, and things began to improve some. I stopped thinking about suicide and picking out a place to drive the car off the road. I'd had recurrent nightmares for years since I was a child, and those finally disappeared. I thought I was doing fairly well at getting some things worked out.

That was when I met Marilyn, a former Miss America and a survivor activist who speaks out about her own sexual abuse. My wife, who worked at the same university where I worked, went to hear Marilyn. My lab was just across the street, and my wife called me and said, "You have to come and meet this woman." Television people were waiting to interview Marilyn. We walked up to her, and my wife simply said, "My husband needs to talk to you." Marilyn put her arm around my shoulders, and we walked away. I felt safe. She understood what I'd been through. Finally, some recognition. I still get very emotional just talking about it.

Marilyn's understanding and acceptance just completely broke me down. It was the wake-up call that finally opened the emotional box for me. Initially, I had a lot of anger more than anything else, but it was anger directed primarily at my parents for having had to carry their emotional baggage for them.

I still have a lot of sadness for what I lost. For sixty-five years, there was no place for this in my life. Now that there is, maybe I have trouble acknowledging that this is just the way things are. As close as I can come to that is loss of self, of being denied the chance to be myself, from the time I was a child. When I feel sadness now, I don't try and drown it out. I just experience it. When I go to lunch with this survivor friend of mine, or go to meetings, we talk about anything. We can cry together. I come back from those meetings feeling so energized, so good. Just pure kindness, you know?

≈

Why do you think I lived behind those stone walls all these years? Didn't trust anybody. If somebody was nice to you, you wondered what they wanted from you. In isolation, nobody can get to you. That's one of the common threads that I hear from male survivors. Also, the more "successful" men are, the more isolated they get. Who do you trust? There is a sense that the universe is not a friendly place, nobody's there to support you and care for you, so you've got to just buck up. And, for me, it goes back to boundaries. As a child, not knowing about boundaries, you have no choice but to go into seclusion because that way nobody can get to you. If you have healthy boundaries, then trust is not a problem because you can take care of yourself.

After I recovered the abuse memory, I went into what I call a mourning period where I just sat and sat in the dark. Essentially, I cried for two years. I was just so overwhelmed. My career was winding down, and I didn't have to relate to people a whole lot. It's scary. You wonder, "Is this bottomless? I haven't cried in sixty or sixty-five years. Is it all going to fall apart? If that happens, can I get it back together again?"

Many men, we feel we can't really tell the truth. That's because we're basically creating this persona all the time. When it starts to come out about the world leaders who have been in positions of power and you realize what their history is, what they went through, there may begin to be more compassion for the silent suffering. Otherwise why would they go for such power? It doesn't excuse the behavior. It just gives it a broader human context. If those stories would start to be told, not with condemnation, but with more honesty and empathy, we might start to see a change in behavior.

≈

I asked my therapist about doing some volunteer work. He said, "You like to cook, you felt homeless, go cook for the homeless." So for about three years, I went a couple of mornings a week to St. Vincent DePaul. They were doing lunches for homeless people, feeding two hundred a day. A group of us men came at 6:30 a.m. and did all the cooking and kitchen work.

What I learned from that was revealing. I saw how short on empathy I was, always pointing my finger at other people. Always somebody else's fault. Cooking for the homeless, I finally realized that everybody has a story. It doesn't matter who they are, they all have a story and it deserves to be told and heard and listened to.

The other thing I did was, I started volunteering for hospice. Again, it's the homeless connection. People should not die homeless or in isolation. They should die at home with friends and family and in comfort, if that's what they choose to do.

I sit with the terminally ill person while the caregiver gets out for a couple of hours. It's amazing the connections you can make with people, and how appreciative they are that somebody will just come and sit. You don't pry into their lives, but they open up. Being there is a mutual gift. I remember a hospice chaplain saying that you don't have to do anything or say anything. He called it "the ministry of presence," which I think is a wonderful phrase.

≈

In his book *Not Trauma Alone*, Steven Gold says that the worst, most heartbreaking stories he hears are about abused children who have never walked in the front door and had a parent hug them and say, "I love you, I'm so happy to see you." I never had that in my life—encouragement to just be who I am. I would have loved to have loving, nurturing parents, and to have grown up with boundaries, people skills, empathy, honesty. My parents didn't have a clue.

I would love to tell boys that feelings are all right. Feelings are feelings, that's all they are. Nobody has the right to tell you that you're not feeling what you're feeling. "Oh, you can't be feeling that way. You shouldn't feel that way." Pardon the vernacular, but that's called a mind-fuck, and people do it all the time.

What boys need is somebody that they can talk to in confidence, someone who will be non-judgmental and who will encourage them and maybe get them to start some kind of recovery or some way out of the situation. I honestly don't see any way until kids get in trouble from acting out.

≈

When I was in the middle of my struggles, I did some volunteering at the rape recovery centers. The coordinator there mentioned to me there was an organization called Male Survivor, and that they were having a retreat. That was when my recovery began to accelerate. Up to that time, I thought of myself not as a loner but a solitude person. Well, I got that straightened out. I really was a loner.

After that first weekend with Male Survivor, I did something momentous. My Ph.D. diploma had been sitting in an envelope for forty years. I never had any pride in it. I was still judging it, feeling it was second best because I was supposed to be a doctor, which was what my father had planned for me. Well, after that weekend, I finally got it out and framed it and put it up on the wall.

About that time, I had my second encounter with Marilyn. There were over a hundred women at the club where she was speaking, all of them sitting there drinking their white wine. I was the only man there except for members of the board of the sponsoring organization. At the end of her talk — she's always very careful how she does this — she asked if there were any survivors of sexual abuse in the audience, and would they be comfortable standing up. Well I wasn't very comfortable, but I did it. Later on, I realized what that did for me. It gave me a chance to take off the cloak of shame and put it where it belonged, on the perpetrator, my father. That was a huge step for me. I continued going to the weekends of recovery, and things just kept getting better. The world opened up.

I have a sense of color and movement and joy and sorrow now that are so different from anything I ever experienced before. The sky is bluer, the grass greener, and sounds are better. You get rid of all this other shit, and it gives you the space to enjoy where you are, what you're doing.

I gave a talk to a Rotary Club breakfast group recently. I told them, "You see before you a man who can laugh and cry and love." It's been a lot of work. A long journey. I have no confidentiality issues. What I care about is just getting the message out. What would I tell others? That the sooner you can share what you've been through and start on the recovery trip, the sooner you will get your aliveness back! You got a lot of years ahead of you. Don't waste them.

Where Did That Boy Go?

"I left myself."

Like most of us, probably, I've experienced the effect of the unexamined trauma many men suffer from. Because I was hearing so much about violence I became intensely curious; I listened more closely and began to learn more about trauma itself.

You get hit, you get yelled at, you get ignored—the body registers pain and starts to contract, sometimes leaving scars too deep to easily access. "It just gets stored in the body," a man in his 20s told me. And our bodies are always talking. Trauma fragments the brain and body. The nerves wire differently. Especially if the trauma happened when the brain was still developing. Finding a way to make friends with the overwhelming body sensations left by trauma, abuse and neglect requires kindness to oneself. Smells, sounds, memories—many things can trigger a flight, fight or freeze response, taking up the parts of the brain necessary for empathy and attunement. A traumatic memory isn't a story, it's a reliving. Facts don't matter. I was learning how, when trauma has not been addressed, it makes it hard to listen and feel at ease in the world. As a vet told me, "PTSD is a normal reaction to an abnormal situation."

How natural, when trust has been bruised, to weave a cocoon of self-protection around oneself and begin to see the world as threatening. But that cocoon can become an armoring, a habit of defenses, guarding a sense of unworthiness, inadequacy and shame—words I heard so often.

I have new respect for the attention and effort it takes to fully reintegrate in a way that can let the light shine through again. And for how painful and challenging it can be, and how necessary, to keep coming back to the body as it's recovering its natural ease and wisdom. "I was scared away from myself as a young boy. We're trained for efficiency, not authenticity," said a man in his 60s. Not easy to hold onto that boy in the daily wilderness of life and a world that is always telling them to be something other than who they are. Rare and wonderful when that quality of innocence, openness and aliveness survives the brutality of "manhood".

How do any of us bear unbearable feelings?

One of the readers of an early draft of *BOY* gave it back with very thoughtful and helpful feedback. One comment was about: "your all too obvious agenda, to do a book about fucked up men." When I responded, "I don't recall interviewing *any* fucked up men or boys." He continued, "Really? I guess we differ on what is meant by 'fucked up' because I know of one man you interviewed who is thoroughly fucked up. Perhaps you didn't ask the right questions." I searched my heart and mind for who that might be. He e-mailed back, "I'm the thoroughly fucked up one. Of course, we didn't talk about that part of my being or my history." We got together and continued the conversation.

Sooner or later, we all experience some kind of trauma in life. We fall apart . . . and in comes the rest of the world.

These men were helping me to listen more deeply. A man in his 60s said, "We live in a culture dominated by traumatized men, who are frightened and don't have any idea what to do about it." Hurting behavior comes from people who are hurting.

The training that goes into making a boy a "suitable candidate for the male world" seems to require him to deny pain and suspend his trust in life. "You're supposed to be a man—so you separate," a man in his 50s said. And if you can't feel what you feel, how can you heal?

A lot of the behaviors I'd experienced with men were beginning to make more sense.

～

When I was a really little kid I used to daydream about being able to change bodies with somebody else just so I could see what I looked like to the outside world. Sometimes I think — how can you love me the way you love me when I see so many bad things in me?

(30s)

I wish somebody had told me I wasn't alone.

(30s)

I have this vivid memory from when I was in my late teens or early 20s. I went to a baseball game with a bunch of my guy friends. We were sitting in the bleacher seats, the cheap seats — you know, the kind that sort of fold up. Maybe two rows in front of us there was a group of older men, and one of them had his little son, must have been around five years old, with him. The boy was playing on the seat. He stepped back too far and the weight shifted, so it folded up and he fell off. You saw him have that classic moment of hitting the ground, realizing it was all right and then pausing. The shock wears off and he starts to cry, right? The father looked down at him, picked him up and quickly saw that he was not injured. He was fine. But then immediately he said, "Don't cry. You can't cry."

There was nothing remarkable about the interaction but I remember having this very memorable insight that this is very common. On one level, the father's disciplining his son away from a certain kind of ability to express weakness and pain. Just think of all the negative consequences that that boy will have by not being able to acknowledge pain and be honest with himself about it. But, at the same time, even if you understand the negative consequences of that, I think we have to be honest and acknowledge that the father may actually be making it significantly easier for his son in other ways, given the reality of our society and that if a father doesn't do that, that's going to give a lot of other pain.

(40s)

Mr. Rogers liked us "just the way we are." But Mr. Rogers is no guy's guy.

(40s)

The part of my mind that thinks, strategizes, gets anxious — is programmed by the culture. The training started so early I didn't even recognize it. I believed that's who I was. The busy mind we *think* we are and are trained to be, locked out from our more human qualities.

Very little training in actually being *present* with whatever arises.

(50s)

When those first tender, vulnerable feelings come up, for sure there isn't usually a lot of help available for boys about what to do with it. Other than stuff it or turn it to anger. Because our fathers didn't know how to deal with it.

Like my dad got pummeled when he was seven years old the first day he was at his new British boarding school. He got accosted by a bunch of boys, young hoodlums who decided to rank him, you know? They bloodied him up and left him in the ditch. It was the first time he had been away from home. He was all by himself.

That was his indoctrination into manhood and it made him a very insecure guy. He spent his adult life trying to deal with that. Not just that single event, but that was big. There might be some unusual characters that grow up without that violence stuff, but most kids, most young men, got in a situation where they were going to have their noses flattened by somebody else. And they had to get out of it somehow. Some guys ran, some guys talk real fast, and some guys punch back. An awful lot of boys grow up with a feeling of fearfulness and develop all these compensatory behaviors. Guys have a hard time talking about it amongst themselves.

(50s)

I'm five years old. I feel it in my body, I can feel his hand on the back of my head and I can feel myself gasping for air because his penis is in my mouth and I think I'm going to die because I can't breathe and he's saying shhh, Sammy, shhh, Sammy, shhh, Sammy, shhh. And I'm just wanting to please him, not knowing what's going on, freaked out, thinking I'm going to die and here's this man, my grandfather, who I trust and who's wanting me to be quiet when I think I'm dying.

There are two tornadoes inside, spinning in opposite directions. One positive spiral pulling me into this warmth and safety, where I can relax and trust, be spontaneous and joyful and play. But then the other spiral spinning me outward in a frenzy of anxiety and fear. It's a pattern of push-pull around intimacy that drives the women in my life absolutely batty.

For a five-year-old brain to deal with that kind of complexity and those kinds of conflicting emotions and energies — love and trust and innocence combined with betrayal and fear and terror for one's life, combined with secrecy — it created a kind of meltdown in me. I think that was what the ADD was about. I became painfully introverted and shy. I didn't know where to go, so I went away.

A lot of people will say, "Well, so you were abused when you were five. Okay. When are you going to get over it?" I think it sets up some basic wiring in the brain. The least thing can trigger me into my animal brain. In extreme examples, it can create schizophrenia or double personalities. When I get triggered, it's not *like* I'm five years old. I *am* five years old.

Here's this image of a boy nursing, and he's so wide-open and so vulnerable and so trusting, right? How does a boy go from there to the other image — which is a fortress. What I learned with bullies in the playground was, "I've got to be vigilant. I've got to protect myself. I'm going to build a wall against the bully."

Then I have this abuse experience where, all of a sudden, I can't trust the people in my own home, right? I have the outer wall against the outside world; but then all of a sudden, I withdraw into the inner bastion. I fortify myself in there, away from even my family. I can't trust my mother and father to take care of me, I certainly can't trust my grandfather.

What I learned, in my abusive situation and what you learn as a man is, you're not supposed to feel all these emotions. You're supposed to be a man — so you separate. You can't trust yourself; you can't trust your feelings. Here you are, the king in the castle, separated not just from the outside world, but also from your family and from yourself, from your inner world. You're somehow going to have to be this invincible king, who is going to take care of everybody — take care of the women and the children, and the little ground there.

You start to tell lies. And once you start telling the lies, then it's hard to get out of those. How do you keep the boy alive?

A guy like Desmond Tutu or the Dalai Lama — they've been through so much, but they're still able to laugh and joke around and have this incredibly boyish sense about them. It's a real triumph to remain that open.

(50s)

The trust issue is always gonna come up. It's really about trusting me. Which is scary. I'm used to running. Away from what's happening. That's peace for me. I dissociate. "Oh, meet us down at the Chinese place for a beer. We're all gonna be there." Well, I'll text 'em back and say I'm late at work. So it's hard to make plans. That's another reason I don't get into relationships. Putting myself into a position of possibly having to tell what happened to me, and having that person say, "Holy shit, I'm getting out of here." It's fear of rejection, absolutely.

(50s)

We're not who we are because we think the world needs us to be something else. Men aren't meant to dwell on the pain, we can't feel the hurt, and if you can't feel the hurt then it becomes anger and often violence — to oneself or others.

(50s)

From everything I've read and heard from other survivors, the effects of the abuse are almost universal: lack of boundaries, inappropriate anger, isolation and intro-version, inability to advocate for your own needs, loneliness and being cut off from the world, being really emotionally shut down, a lot of substance abuse, sex-ual acting out, passive aggressive behavior and blaming, extremes sense of inad-equacy, body dissociation. Pretty much the traditional characteristics of being a "successful" man. A lot of guys turn their feeling of inadequacy into hypermas-culinity by becoming very successful, macho, or joining the military. Imagine the number of young men who have already been abused (and therefore suffer from PTSD), entering the military and being given loaded guns, trained to kill, and then returning home with further PTSD.

(50s)

More and more men need to make the personal decision to be open about their experiences. Talk to one other man who's been abused. Start there. Same thing as women have done. And then pretty soon young men who have been abused or who are being abused will see that this isn't something necessarily that has to be hidden, that it is so shameful that it can't be shared and talked about. It needn't remain a secret. You know, we have all these boys we know are being abused and they see no way out. Every single one of them thinks they're the only one. Every single one. This organization, Male Survivor, does these weekends of recovery where they bring 40 to 50 men together. And the most overwhelming moment is when at five o'clock on Friday the men congregate. You watch as they walk in and start looking around and realizing that there are all these men and they've all been abused. There are men who just walked in the room, looked around, and started weeping. Because there is no public presence for this. Knowing that there were all these men who had been abused was so freeing.

There are far more men who were abused who are very successful, so there's a tendency to think — Well, geez, they're fine. You know, it's not true and it doesn't capture it.

(50s)

I remember the time my dad spanked me. He asked me if I brushed my teeth and I hadn't, but I didn't want him to get mad at me or not like me, so I told him I had. He went to check my toothbrush and it was dry. I was busted. The look on his face was like a monster. I'd lied to him and he had to teach me about integrity, and the way you teach somebody to do the right thing is by scaring them into the right behavior. He came and grabbed me, put me over his knee and began to hit me. In that moment, there was very little distinction for me between, "Oh, this might hurt a little bit," versus, "This guy could kill me. I don't know how far this is gonna go."

You clam up. You divide the world subconsciously into two factions: the people who are being controlled and threatened, and those who are doing the controlling and threatening. You want to make sure and get on the side of the controllers. When my dad was spanking me, I was powerless. And in grade school, I became the toughest kid in my class.

This is the exact dynamic that people who are acting out on the entire world got traumatized into in childhood by male figures in their lives. And, to a large degree, by women because women want a strong-seeming man.

(60s)

Men are angry because—they don't know why. They're angry because their lives are taken away from them when they're children and they don't even know it, and there's nothing they can do about it. But they—they know. We know. We look around and look at our lives and we know this isn't what we want, but we don't know what we want. We just know we don't have it. We don't know how to go about getting it because we don't know what it is that's missing, and we know that, Goddamn it, somebody is to blame for this. And who is to blame? Somebody's gonna pay for the fact that I'm about to die and I never got to live. And when we're in the middle of our life we're thinking why am I doing this? What am I doing? We think we lost our life. It was taken from us, and that's why there are so many angry men.

(60s)

The boys I knew in grade school, most of them had tender hearts, right? After awhile, I began to wonder, what became of their tender hearts? Then I asked myself, "What became of *your* tender heart?"

This world is loaded with men who are in the closet. We're all going around afraid of men coming after us. We're afraid to stand up as full human beings in the presence of other men.

(60s)

It's really hard for men to name or describe what's the highest purpose of their life. Because they confuse that with the tasks of what they imagine the life of a good man to be about. The belief is that I have to provide for, I have to X, Y or Z for my wife, for my kids and then I . . . That's where the tragedy is. And there's almost no permission to step outside of this belief system.

Last May I took a month, first time in my life, I went off by myself. And I came back, transformed in my own eyes because I did something I wanted to do. For me, by myself. I stepped out of the boxes of all the scheduling stuff. And all I did was get up every morning and walk in a moving community, the Camino de Santiago in Northern Spain, a 500 mile ancient pilgrimage route. While the landscape changed, almost moment-to-moment, I lived in a whole different experience of the world. I had never felt permission to be, to do what moved me. This was a huge breakout for me.

I'm doing it again next year because I want to walk it slower. Not like I usually do my life — here's the goal, got to be there, got to be here, on this date. I want to just enjoy the moment.

For most men, being in the moment makes them extraordinarily anxious because they lose their frame of reference for being who they're supposed to be in the future and for who they think they are in their past lived life. To be clear, being in the present, being in the moment is very, very hard for me. Very hard. Because of all the expectations, assumptions, everything I'm supposed to do. It's not easy for guys to relax and enjoy their lives.

I have hope for men when I see their tears.

(60s)

Jimmy (50s)

"Telling people helped."

My mom would say, "You used to be such a happy boy." I look at a picture of me when I was twelve, and it's unbelievable. I remember walking out my back door. My brothers were playing basketball in the backyard, and I was feeling life is great. I'm a good person, and I got a great family. I got these really cool friends, and I'm going to go to heaven one day. Life is great.

It didn't quite pan out the way I expected.

I was in the FBI for twenty-two years. Retired last year. Before that, I was a prosecutor in New York City. I worked on the Child Sex Crimes Prosecution team in the Bronx for the New York City Law Department, and then I became an FBI agent and profiler, specializing in child sexual victimization and child abductions.

When I was a prosecutor, my brother called me up one day and said I should do something about the director at the camp when we were kids. I said, "What do you mean?" He said, "Well, one day I snuck in his office, and I found pictures of him molesting boys." And I said, "I thought I was the only one."

The next day, I went to the FBI/NYPD Sexual Exploitation of Children Task Force. I told them what happened. As I told the story, I started shaking. They started an investigation, tracked the guy down to thirteen different Catholic schools over the course of twenty-six years. Every time there was an allegation against him, he just resigned and walked a few blocks to the next school and kept on doing it. Nothing was ever said, ever done. This guy directed camps and, handed out towels in kid's locker rooms. He did everything he could to get access to kids. Taught and coached—everything.

So they did this investigation, and they were having trouble finding somebody within the statute of limitations who would talk. They interviewed all these kids, and nobody said anything. Then they asked me. They wanted me to go undercover, wear a wire and talk to him. I flat-out refused. There's no way I'm sitting down to talk to this guy, you know? They said all right, but as the months went on, the investigation stagnated.

Meanwhile, I went on with my life as a prosecutor. My boss walked into my office one day and said I was behind on filing my paperwork to be admitted to the Bar. I hadn't done it because you have to list every place you ever lived, and I would have to list the camp and I didn't want the perpetrator to know where I was. I thought they would do a background investigation, and talk to him. Even though I was now twenty-five years old and the molestation happened ten years prior, I was still afraid of him and of my secret.

My boss was pretty pissed. She said, "If you don't get your paperwork in by the end of the month, you don't have a job." I agonized over it all night, and called in sick the next day. I used the time to fill out my application—twenty-five pages long—then went to my law school to have them attach my transcripts so it could all be sent in to the Bar. When I walked into the registrar's office to have them process my application, sitting behind the desk is the guy who molested me, working as a night clerk. I didn't know it at the time, but he'd just been fired as an eighth grade teacher two weeks before.

I had just convinced myself my fears about this guy were ridiculous and I was being an idiot, a child. And there he was. I thought I'd walked into the Twilight Zone. I mean, my jaw hit the floor. I was frozen in place. I didn't know what the hell to do. Fortunately, the Dean walks in, and I used my upset to say, "Look I'm going to get fired if we can't get this application in right away. Can you personally handle it?" At that point, I didn't want to hand him the history of my life.

When I came back out, the guy who molested me said, "Oh yeah I noticed you graduated from here a couple years ago." He's sitting right next to the alumni file. "Oh, and by the way, I'm sorry about your mother's death." That really got me. He had ruined my relationship with my mother. She had known something was wrong, and kept saying, "You used to be such a happy kid. What's wrong?" I would push her away. Then she died of cancer, and I never told her what it was.

For me, that did it with this guy, because now I was pissed-off. I walked outside, called up the FBI, and said. "Look, I know where he is right now. Come and wire me up." They did, and I went back in, arranged a meeting, then met with him on six different occasions, and ultimately helped get him locked up.

～

When you are a teenager, your parents are so un-cool. So you just look to other adults who you believe are cooler and more hip than your parents. My father was very quiet. He's a lawyer. Does all sorts of speaking, but at home, totally quiet. I learned more about him from the stories he told friends of mine or relatives, than from what he told me. I don't know what it was, but he just didn't feel comfortable talking to us. Anyway, the guy who molested me was very demonstrative, very in your face, a tough-love kind of guy. Everybody liked to play basketball, and he was the coach. He played as well, and he was the ref. If you did anything, bumped into him or whatever, he'd call a foul. But then he'd punch you in the stomach, and just walk away like nothing happened.

One time, while we were playing ball, a truck got stuck in mud. We all went outside in the heavy rain, and were putting rocks under the tires. You know, passing them from one to the next, and I dropped one. It splashed up mud on him, and he just punched me in the solar plexus. I went down in the mud. He just got in the truck and left me there covered in mud, gasping for breath. That's the kind of guy he was.

Other times, he treated me nice, with respect. He told me, "You're the hardest worker in the camp, the guy I can rely on. I want you stay on and help me close up camp." I thought I was special, you know? I thought all my hard work had paid off. Wow, little did I know that wasn't his plan.

When I got home, I wanted to tell my father what had happened so he'd beat the guy up with a baseball bat, yet knowing I'd get in trouble just for saying the words. We didn't talk about sex in my house. So I went into the shower on the first floor, and turned off all the lights. There were no windows in the room. I just huddled in a corner, turned on the water and cried my eyes out.

When I got back to school, I told the priest about it, and he told me, "I absolve you of your sins. Don't ever tell anybody else." He told me to say ten "Our Fathers" and ten "Hail Marys." Fifteen year later, I helped conduct the investigation that got this priest locked up. He was molesting other kids in my class. By the way, he was the one who had sent me to that camp in the first place. I had gone to him to tell him, "You can't send anyone else there. You've got to warn these kids."

~

When I met him that first night, I was wearing a wire. They had prepped me. I didn't think it would work, but they knew. They said, "Just tell him that you have something to talk to him about. That he's the only one in the world that you can trust with this information."

We went to a bar, and we're sitting in the back booth. We order beer, and he says, "So tell me, what is it? What's up?" I say, "Come on, you know. I've never talked to anybody about this." He says, "You always were a wimp. You never could stand on your own two feet." He immediately tried to upset the power balance again.

I understood what was going on now, so I played with it, and it was very effective. I sat with him two hours and forty-five minutes that time. He bragged to me about when he first started molesting kids. It was when he was nineteen, he was a volunteer at a children's shelter—the night shift because nobody else was around. He could do whatever he wanted with the kids. "Those kids were begging for it," he said.

One of the ways to get these guys to talk is to show empathy for them, to understand. He was looking for somebody to talk to about this. I was told to just say I was confused back then, I was sorry for my reaction in the past and yada yada. He told me, "You know, what's interesting is that of all my boys, you were the last one that I thought would come back to me." I said, "Why?" He said, "Because I hit you hard, and I hit you again and again. I was probably too rough on you." He wasn't talking about hitting. That was a metaphor.

"This has to do with sex, right? And kids?" I just let my jaw drop and looked at him. That was all it took. They told me to play as if I were into the same thing, like I was interested in it but I hadn't done anything—basically that I wanted him to teach me. It was disgusting. Two hours and forty-five minutes, I sat there with him. When I left, I walked back to my apartment. The agents met me, and took off the wire, and I immediately ran into the bathroom and puked my guts up.

Finally, after meeting him six times, I got enough information about a kid on a particular team that was within the statute of limitations, so an agent went out and interviewed all the kids on that team. Nobody disclosed. The agent went back to the school, and asked if there was anybody who got kicked off the team, anybody who didn't make it. They told him, yes, there was this guy who was the scorekeeper for a while. The agent interviewed him, and the kid disclosed and told him about another kid. The agent interviewed that one, and then we put them in front of a grand jury, after which they went back and arrested the perpetrator and locked him up.

He ended up pleading guilty. At the sentencing, I came out of the judge's chambers with the judge and walked up to him. He was like, "Man, you didn't have to do this. I was going to quit teaching." I glared at him, "You don't get it. This was a slap on your wrist. I'm going to be watching you the rest of your miserable life."

It was a total turning point, because now I could see him as a pathetic bastard instead of being afraid of him. That was great. After everything was concluded in the court, the agent and I went out to lunch. While we were sitting there, he hands me an application to the FBI. I said to him—this was very revealing—I said to him, "They would take me even though I was a victim?" I just couldn't believe that. "Of course," said the agent. "You did a great job. We need people like you." That's how I became an FBI agent.

When we were making the arrest, I sat my family down and told them, and told my father. He's always been supportive, but he's just quiet. One of the fears that a lot of boys have in telling their parents is that the parent might go kill the person. And that's exactly what my father said: "It's probably a good thing I didn't know, because I would have killed him."

Another thing that prevents boys from disclosing is the stigma of potentially being an offender, like because we were victimized we're going to grow up to become offenders. The Vampire myth. They don't want people to look at them that way. On top of that, the stigma of homosexuality, and the completely emasculating feeling that I wasn't a man in this situation. So many men live with that forever, because nobody talks about it.

While I was in the FBI Academy, the agent got transferred to his office of preference back home in Boston, so they put me in his spot on the squad that had just finished investigating my case. Full circle, basically.

It was good to be able to help kids who had been victimized, but also very difficult because I was constantly having to be enmeshed in it. But I had a degree of empathy for the kids that nobody else had, and also an insight into what they were going through. Knowing what they were all about, I got really good at interviewing them, getting them to disclose. I became a national and international expert in the area. That's all good, but you know, I didn't want it to define my life and it had become that, professionally.

~

I had a massive heart attack a few months ago. Almost didn't make it to age fifty-one. I made it through, but it's a stressful situation. I find that speaking out at survivor conferences was incredibly good. At first, the FBI didn't even want me to talk about it. Some agents said it would embarrass the Bureau.

I hate the Church for what they did, not just to me, but to tens of thousands, if not hundreds of thousands of kids. It's unbelievable. They've documented like 11,000 pedophile priests and 30,000 victims or something ridiculous like that. The average time spent from victimization to disclosure is more than twenty years according to the study they did at John Jay about the Catholic Church. So we're going to hear about it a lot more.

The perpetrator was like. "I'm a real man, and I'm going to teach you how to be a man." He was scary, but because of that I respected him and looked up to him. I thought he was a man's man—meaning strong, able to take it, able to meet any challenges head-on. So I listened to him. But what I lost was my teen-age years. What he did was completely undermine my trust—I felt like damaged goods, unworthy, like there must be something wrong with me or otherwise why would he be doing this to me? Even though I did a lot of fun stuff at camp, too, I buried it all. I didn't want to think about it.

It's very difficult for victims to separate out the good from the bad. You don't want to remember anything, so little things that would normally be wonderful are triggers to remember all the bad stuff. So you just close your mind off to it. What you're doing is basically hurting yourself.

A few years ago, at one of the Male Survivor conferences, I went back and reclaimed my youth. My young self deserved to have that guy as my mentor, not have him molest me. If he hadn't done that back then, I would have been a very different person.

I pictured what should have been. In my mind, I played it out as if that's what happened, and just sort of took it back. Amazing. As I went through it, I started, for the first time, remembering the names of the guys I hung out with there and the camping, the swimming, the fishing, the hiking, the campfires and all the cool stuff we did. I reclaimed all that, and smiled for the first time about it. A watershed moment for me. I finally could smile about my childhood. It took away a bunch of the pain of going back there, and the weakness and the vulnerability of being a victim.

One of the other things that really helped was writing it down. As difficult as that was, for whatever reason, having to actually physically write it takes it from the emotional side of your brain to the physical, practical side. No matter how big and bad and horrible it was, now it's finite, contained in this stack of papers. That made it somehow more manageable.

Once I did that, I said, "I'm not going to let it eat at me anymore. I'm not going to ever be quiet about it again. I'm just going to realize that I was a victim of a crime like millions and millions of other people, and I won't carry the shame any more." That's when I decided I was going to speak publicly. Over the last fifteen years, I've spoken many times at the Male Survivor conferences. Each time, more and more and more guys—people from around the world—come up and thank me.

You know how you say survivors are like pioneers? I think it forces us into a position like that. You're supposed to just deal with whatever comes at you and that's it, *because you're a man*. But that's not always the right thing to do. There's no format for that without some sort of trauma, you know what I'm saying?

One of the things that I find has been most destructive is that the whole experience left me with this need to protect myself from being taken advantage of again. You get hyper-vigilant. The people you love, they may do something that you perceive as disrespectful, and you immediately put up this wall and get protective. Intensity comes out in me and it works against the people that are closest to me, the ones I'm most vulnerable to. I hate that it happens, but I feel like I have to protect myself.

≈

I was on the Oprah show featuring 200 male survivors. When those twins were showing us their videos and talking about the priest who abused them, I was in the audience losing it. I mean, I am just bawling. I couldn't believe it. I felt so bad for them and it also brought up my whole thing again. I was shaking. I was shivering. That's what happened to me when I was being molested, and also when I told the cops about it ten years later. I have investigated thousands of child sex crimes over the last twenty-five years. I've seen it all, but never in a setting where I was allowed to be human about it. I couldn't believe that here I was physically shaking and sobbing. The man next to me said, "Do you need a hug?" I thought I had dealt with this all. I felt so much empathy for those two guys. I wanted to hug them, and I felt so much anger at priests and the church.

The Catholic Church is such a pariah because it is the only church organized in this way—a centralized controlling government, its own country, with diplomatic immunity. They can avoid subpoenas and search warrants. Outrageous. It's basically institutionalized child abuse.

The vast majority of those who are victimized grow up to abhor violence and sexual victimization. Even so, there were some who were already predisposed to being an offender, and do go on to victimize.

I don't know why people say that one-in-four females, and one-in-six males are victims. The most prolific offenders, by far, are adult males who offend against adolescent males. Those guys can go on to have hundreds of victims, whereas, there are very few rapists of females in the history of man that have reached even a hundred victims. Male victims are much less likely to report abuse. Too many stigmas, too much shame. These reported numbers are just scratching the surface.

You have to do recovery in your own time. But if you wait for your own time, you're probably never going to do it. It's just too easy to be crushed by the shame and keep the secret. But once you stand up and tell the world . . . It's like you're finally free to live again.

Boys Don't Cry

"I train myself to not feel it."

The word "safety" was coming up a lot in the conversations—a wish for a safe place to let down and be themselves, be seen and accepted and loved *as they are*. "I grew up believing that asking for help is not to be a man," a man in his 40s told me. You get punished by parents, peers, and others for experiencing your own vulnerability. If you're trained away from, even *shamed,* for tender, painful feelings—what happens to these feelings?

We live in a culture that traditionally allows men to not listen or be responsible for the effects of their actions, yet also tells them to be something other than who they are. Entitled and deprived at the same time! No wonder they often speak of feeling confused and angry. More often than not, no one showed them how to welcome those uncomfortable feelings, feel what they're feeling, and let it move through. And if we don't face our fears and pain they become violence—to ourselves or to others.

If you're scared away from tenderness toward yourself when you're a boy, cut off from empathy for yourself, it is difficult to feel and express it for others. And sometimes, they told me, they don't know how to find their way back to the openness of that boy. How can you cut off one feeling and not have it affect all the others?

I was curious about this, so I asked, "What makes you feel vulnerable?"

The younger boys wondered what the word meant.

≈

I grew up in a big family. I identified with my brothers and my father because it seemed like males had more access to a wider life than my mother and sisters and I. You got to go out in the world and *do* stuff. I also noticed that they didn't cry. So I decided I wasn't going to either.

I distinctly remember the moment, sitting at the dining room table, when a feeling came up and I held it back. This was pre-puberty. I actually suppressed tears. I was training myself. So I know a little of how it feels. As one guy in his 30s said, "It's got to be bad for your body. No wonder so many men have prostate problems. That's got to have something to do with blocked energy."

I was saved from a tearless life by the arrival of my menstrual cycle. I couldn't go through pregnancy and childbirth and being around the honesty of children—and still not cry. That was in my biology. It was a refuge. A gift. The ability to cry easily is a freedom most women have. Most guys don't.

What is it like when half of the human race isn't allowed to cry? And thinks that tears are a sign of weakness?

I didn't ask a specific question about crying but hearing so many stories of violence I wanted to include these voices too. Not being allowed the release of crying—for all the emotions under the tears—seems to me to be one of the most violent of the violences done to men.

~

If someone's parents died or something, they wouldn't make fun of someone who cried. I've seen my mom cry a lot. Not so much my dad. Maybe when you grow up you can deal with things without crying. Crying sounds like the ultimate solution, like, somehow it helps. I don't know why. It's just weird. I don't know why people don't do it then.

(10 yr.)

When I was nine, I remember getting a can lid cut. I just wouldn't stop wailing, even though my mom kept trying to comfort me. And then when I turned ten, it was totally different. I got a little splinter of pencil lead in my finger and I just kept going ow, ow, ow. When I went home and had to pull the last tip out, I felt I was a little bit more grown up—different as in the ways of what pain is like. I can handle pain better and not make a lot of noise. I actually found a way that helps me have almost nothing really hurt mentally, too. I do it naturally now. Whenever something's painful, I just instantly think—it doesn't hurt, it's not going to be bad. I train myself to not feel it. And now I just do it instantly. I don't do the same thing when I feel sad. I just cry.

(11 yr.)

I know a lot of people who cry and it's not okay. Like this one kid, he's considered sort of sissy, and then nobody wants to be his friend 'cause that's a girlie thing to do. And when he does cry, it just puts it over the top. You're supposed to be stronger and not show it.

(13 yr.)

Early on, anywhere from when I was five to eight, I remember talking on the play-ground—bragging about who hadn't cried for the longest time. "I haven't cried in a year." "What? I never cry."

(20s)

Crying on the playground was the most humiliating thing that you could do. You would just try to hide it at all costs. You do not cry. And if you can't cry, think what that does to your body. No wonder we clank around in all this armor! It's like an exoskeleton that should have been shed already.

(20s)

When I was in junior high school—13, 14?—there was a boy in my class who cried a couple of times. I remember witnessing him crying, and I actually admired that. Although I'm very susceptible to emotion, I don't cry easily. I guess lately that's changed a bit. It's interesting that inversion happened at that time, why I thought that was admirable. I remember harboring this desire, wishing I could cry more because I felt like that would be evidence for a richer response to life.

But things changed. I used to carry around the idea that somehow I had drier, less active tear ducts or something. I felt the welling up of emotion that would be sufficient to cry, but not actually crying.

My dad is stoic, so he never shows any emotion, but my mom is a real emotional whirlwind. My dad cried when he told me they were getting divorced. I was embarrassed by him.

(30s)

I got made fun of a lot. Called "crybaby." But I kept my ability to cry!

(30s)

What makes me feel vulnerable—really, truly vulnerable, not like "I don't have the right shoes on" vulnerable—is this feeling of, what if I let this person really know me, like *really*, all the insecurities, all these other parts of myself. Be real—and they don't want to be with me, they don't want anything to do with me? I think that's the true vulnerability. And what a heartbreak, because if we're all feeling that way, then—how come we can't pair off a little easier?

I feel like I've been doing it for years—getting that naked. I think I really try to get that naked and I wonder—Have I really gotten that naked?

It's scary. I mean, you get splashed. Because someone is going to leave you. The amazing thing is, is after having that kind of pain, that we keep coming back for more, isn't it? It's stunning.

(30s)

I had a lot of rage from my childhood. I've been working with it a lot. In my thirties, I trained to be a nurse. When I graduated, I was asked to give the address and I teared up. The response was women loved me for it. And the guys—some were okay, but some were like—our women like you, but . . .

It's a minefield. It's very tricky. There's an invisible line. If you go over it too much, you're out.

(30s)

I never learned to hold back tears. No, I'm a terrible weeper. I do remember holding back tears as a young child because it was easy to cry and I was aware that not everyone was sort of okay with that. It was kinda looked at funny. In my adult life, I've definitely held back tears because I didn't want to be a weeper in front of women, because then the power thing shifts. Yeah, better stop 'cause it's stupid. You don't wanna be pitied. You wanna be complimented for being delicate. At the same time you really wanna bring the thunder, you know. It's just really a mess. It's just—forget it. It's impossible. It's so funny, I quit.

My father never cried in front of us, well—one time, and he barely shed a tear. I'm not even sure he was really crying when his mother died. He went off and did that totally on his own.

I have this really vivid memory of my grandmother's funeral. She was cremated and a small plaque placed next to her husband's grave, my father's stepfather. My cousin was wailing, my aunt was wailing, even my uncle was crying. My dad, he took out a pocket knife and dug a small hole above his stepfather's grave to put some of his mother's ashes into, and all he said—with the whole family watching—was, "Here she is, you son of a bitch." I understood then what kind of father he had had.

My father has nightmares every night, and I think it's because he holds all that shit in. Every night he's plagued by nightmares. And I suffer nightmares when I'm stressed out. I don't know. I'm a weeper. I think that's probably how I let it out. And I drink too much.

(30s)

I'm probably a pretty typical, not very in touch with my emotions kind of guy, but—oh—put me in front of a movie or TV show about fathers and sons and I'm a basket case. I think a lot of guys feel this way.

(40s)

I wonder if I'm worried about being too vulnerable or letting people see me cry. And sometimes I'm worried that if I cry in front of someone, they're going to try to fix it, you know. Well, what's the point then? It takes me out of it. I would like to meet up with someone and have him say, "You cry all you want."

I just want him to listen and empathize. He is probably feeling like he doesn't want to go where my pain is because he might have to feel something.

(40s)

For men to get out of the "man box," we have to reverse an entire lifetime of training. It's much harder than for women. It's daunting, immense. You don't know where you're gonna end up. That's why more men don't take it on. You've got to have time and support. You've got to have that safe place, and some motivation. It's not like there's a tried and true — oh, come over here, the grass is lovely. It takes enormous courage. Most men don't want to be that vulnerable.

(40s)

A very close friend of the family, sort of like my grandmother, died. She was in her 70s and we decided to have a remembrance for her at our house. We all went around the room and shared a story. I got choked up and people jumped in to kind of stop it, like it would be uncomfortable if I cried. I was probably 19 or 20, and I do remember thinking, "God, if I can't cry now, when can I cry?"

I don't know why we do this to each other. What's the matter with crying? My grandfather, who was a major general, was at that wake, and I feel maybe his presence had something to do with it. He was one of the first to say something — I don't know what he said, but I felt squelched in that moment.

Something acting school taught me was that anger is a secondary emotion and there's always something behind it like fear or sadness. When you get mad at that person in the street or in the other car, you're basically saying, "You scared the hell out of me. You almost killed me." It's primal. There's a basic feeling in the body and then the story happens. And it goes to blame, judgment — all of those secondary things.

I think if every time I got angry I could decide, "Okay, what was that really about? What really is happening for me?" it would help.

(40s)

Health makes me feel most vulnerable. Once your health goes, that's pretty much it. I guess I feel vulnerable all the time. And I feel comfortable with that. All this is so fragile, so I've got to live this moment now. I mean, I don't sit around shaking either. This Is It. This is life. Vulnerable.

(40s)

Four years ago my marriage was destroyed in one sentence—by my wife. "You're just a nerd with a small dick." That was really the first time in my life I ever turned to friends and said, "*I need help.* My life is falling apart. I don't know what I'm doing. Nothing makes sense. I can't—I can't do it."

The culture has created us and then we re-create the culture, perpetuating this macho thing where we're all behind our own forts, just yelling and shooting at each other and not feeling safe.

And yet the only way out of that, I think, is to open ourselves in certain situations. In my men's group, we've been able to create a culture where we can open up to each other. But it's very fragile. It could be broken at any point by just a stray comment or a joke, or one of us making fun of each other or a competition. We just wouldn't do that in that group.

(50s)

There's an incredible tenderness and vulnerability that's on the other side of the pressure to be a man. I hide that vulnerable part to get on with life. One reason why women identify more with gay men is because they both know the fear, a certain kind of vulnerability. Women don't have to hide the vulnerability part to get on with life.

(50s)

I wish I'd had another guy to talk to. It was a relief, all these years later, to hear that it's not uncommon that the first time you're with a woman you've really, really wanted to be with—and maybe feel is "out of my league"—often you can't get an erection.

(50s)

I feel very foolishly young. To the degree to which I can embrace vulnerability as a source of strength then I think maybe there's something in that about being a man. But I don't think of myself as a man in terms of having reached some point of command of my world, not being scared.

(50s)

The key is asking. Asking is a very gentle and vulnerable place, like, "Honey, can, could we tonight? Or tomorrow? In the morning?" You know, there's an intimacy.

(50s)

There's real tenderness in talking about these belief systems around "being a man" and how hard it is for men to deal with them and figure it out. If you begin to dismantle them, and you don't really have anything else to rely on, there's extreme vulnerability. And then if someone comes in with this kind of new age language, "Oh, we're all one anyway, of course you'll survive," it's like, "You're not the one whose belief system is being dismantled here. This really sucks, and it's hard."

(50s)

When I was about twelve, I decided I wasn't going to cry anymore because I thought crying was for babies, and I had felt like I was a crybaby. Probably, I had been told that. So I shut down. I didn't cry until I was twenty-one, when my father died. I mean, I can almost count on one hand, unfortunately, the number of really powerful times that I have been able to tap into some deep sobs. And I'm not talking about leaking. I mean, like really, really good profound deep, orgasmic sobs. It is something I'm sorely missing. I've tried to figure out ways to tap into that. None of them have worked.

(50s)

I came out west when I was 24 in the '70s and I participated in high confrontation encounter groups. There would be people getting broken down. These men would be crying and I'd be thinking, "What pussies." 'Cause back in New Jersey, we got chewed up and spit out. Then, I started to realize, "Oh, wait a minute. I'm the one lost." I don't cry ever. I was with my wife watching a movie — *The Black Stallion*. There was an emotional scene and tears started to come out of my body. It was overwhelming to feel, "Oh, my god, it's gonna come." They came this high [points to eye rims]. Whatever channel had been shut, opened. I started to cry. Now I cry easily. There was something about the groups . . . and making it okay and now I can actually sob. Oh, my God. My whole body—I think it's healthy.

If that doesn't move through you — well, maybe that's why there's such a ferocity about the push for sex, because it is the only place of release.

My last partner could cry easily but it was this quiet cry, and she got head-aches. It was never fun for her to cry. When I would cry, it would be five minutes of intensity and then I would feel good. One day she said, "I wish I could cry like you." I thought, "How many men hear that comment?"

When I hurt myself, it doesn't hit me to cry. But with emotional pain, I will cry.

You know, they did research on tears, and the tears that came out from onions were essentially saline solution, but the tears that came out from emotional hurt was toxic material. So the body was actually excreting bad things.

(50s)

One of the things that happens with these workshops these guys go to, they cry and they're held by other men. It's a revelation, you know? It's just kindness. I had never had that experience in my life. He just kept holding me and saying "Hey, I'm here."

Someone actually held me and I sobbed for an hour and a half.

If you have to have it all together all the time, *literally*, it's this hardness. It feels like a misunderstanding of maleness that's gotten so rigid that it can't flow with what's happening. It's so old, like this big suit of armor clanking around.

(50s)

You're not allowed to weep as a man. You can't weep. Not even with your mom. It's rough on the body. Sure, as a little boy I could. But as soon as it gets into that junior high school space . . .

I got made fun of. I was a sissy. I mean, I was physically inept. I'm lucky to be alive. I had the experience of standing around when they're choosing teams. You know, it's one of the most humiliating experiences there is — you're on the play-ground and they're picking teams for baseball, football, or whatever. I'm there until the very last three or four kids are chosen. Maybe one of them is wearing a brace and then the other one is really fat, and I'm chosen just before those kids. And you really get it. I think about fourth grade, I would say, is when I got it.

I got that old lesson that they stop bullying you the more you stand up, and you can't weep. I embraced the space that tears up and I just didn't give a shit, but break down and cry? Now that is a fuck up. You lose your status incredibly as a boy, as a young man. You can't break down and cry.

My wife's dad, Jimmy, came to our wedding. He was a gambler, a pit boss at a casino in New Jersey, a handsome tough guy who got along with everybody, even the Mafia guys who came in. So she was afraid he wouldn't like me. "The Hammer" they called him. So Jimmy "The Hammer" comes to the wedding and meets my friends. He saw some of them tear up. He turns to his daughter and says, "Look, this is who I always wanted to be. No wonder you've fallen in love with this guy. I just didn't know how to let it out. These are successful men who know how to express their feelings."

My wife always said, "You know, my dad was a history buff and read a book just about every night. He was an artist and a painter. He was all these things and he was also 'Jimmy the Hammer.' She was afraid that, watching these men tear up at our wedding, he'd be freaked out. But no, he starts tearing up.

(60s)

I didn't hold back tears that much. Although every time I cry, I feel like I'm holding back from really shaking. I mean, you always feel like, as you're crying, can I cry more than this?

Humanity makes me cry. What touches me most is, in its simplest form, is a parade. "Oh, my god! This is all coming together." Something about the noble human effort — to put on a costume and walk down the street and belt out your song everywhere. And kid's performances — I just go weak. Oh, god! Every time.

(60s)

I don't think I was really in touch with my own vulnerability until the death of my dog. I let myself care more about that dog than anything. I didn't guard my heart whatsoever. If I could have, I would have stepped in front of the truck that killed her. I would have given up my life for her. I didn't ever feel safe enough with a woman to do that, because to be that vulnerable is terrifying. Well, there were times when I did. And then, I got the jugular cut. And I didn't have any tools at the time to know how to repair.

(60s)

Because of my size, the depth of my voice and the way I carry myself, which is often a little bit faked, I feel pretty safe in the world. But the important safety for me is not physical safety, it's emotional safety. That's around people I trust and love and know they love me, just as I am. I guess when I feel most vulnerable is when I realize I have to be dishonest about my real feelings. And when I'm not really true to who I am, or who I want to be. One, I don't want to hurt someone's feelings. Or, I don't want to admit that my baby gut has been offended or hurt. When I back away from something, I realize I'm being an emotional coward. Because I know I'm gonna be ashamed of myself for doing it. The vulnerability comes from facing myself and facing the reality that I'm not facing.

(60s)

There's no opportunity for men to fall apart. We just don't feel we can. I think every man falls apart. That's when a lot of men run off with young girls trying to hide from what's really going on. What a stupid thing. I did that.

I am so sympathetic to the power we have to delude ourselves — create a storyline. And believe it. I've been very far from reality most of my life.

(60s)

At my high school reunion, some of the most worldly, successful ones were some of the ones that were the most calcified. I guess because they have the most to lose. They just can't afford to have it fall apart because they believe that's who they are.

(60s)

You know, we don't feel our bonds. This is an interesting thing. We don't feel that we're stuck. We don't feel that there's more. We live being bound and gagged. We don't know that there's something on the other side. And this is the shame of it.

What seems to get us out of stupors is a good crisis. Maybe a little car crash, or a fire. Certainly, a death here or there or a pet dying, or something that's important going wrong. Not getting the job you want. You may soon have a flash of insight. Or being insulted just at the right moment, your psyche may open up.

(60s)

In our situation it was often about Molly's fears of living in such a wild place, so far from other people, the very circumstances that were fearful for her were the things that made it safer for me. It was what I felt I was lovingly providing. So I couldn't listen with an open heart because I took it as an accusation of not providing. Then she felt I was insensitive to her needs and full of myself. She'd get more and more irritated and pissed and not say anything but shut down to me emotionally. And then I would shut down even more to her by being even more full of myself (her words) — the vicious cycle. Almost always, it was about not feeling appreciated in one form or other.

I think it is hard for all of us to be vulnerable and probably harder for men than women in our culture. Although Molly made it clear that what she most liked about me was my soft side not my macho male side, it was often hard for me to fully accept that and to override my deep cultural male habituations. I didn't have the trust in the vulnerability. It's sad reading her journals after she died to realize she wanted something more from me and I didn't know how to give it.

(70s)

What makes me feel most vulnerable is the truth. Either from me or from the other person. I avoid feeling vulnerable. I don't want to be vulnerable. Next question.

(70s)

You can't be in this life without having a whole lot of pain. I love it when I cry.

(70s)

I remember my father telling me about he and my mother were divorcing and my mother was, in fact, in Reno getting a divorce. I was stunned. I didn't see this coming at all. I suppose I looked shocked and he said to me, "Don't you want to cry?" I felt insulted by this, actually. I didn't like being told I could cry. No, you're telling me you guys are divorcing and now you're going to tell me how I should feel about it? I really wanted my mother to be there.

And then he went back to his dinner party guests.

(80s)

David (30s)

"The survival systems that kept you alive will kill you now.
Everything you're right about, you're 100% wrong about."

When I was born, my dad didn't believe I was his, even though it was clear I was. He divorced and left my mother when I was one. Crawled into a bottle and never came back. I never knew him. My mom had such a sense of betrayal that the word "dad" was never even mentioned, and we never asked. She was sixteen when she got married and had my brother, twenty when she had me. She didn't want my dad back. That was the whole thing—"You're my sons, *my* children." It was like a lover kind of thing.

My grandfather was around, but he was kind of a ghost figure. I found out later he was an alcoholic. So there was no real super-strong role model. Now I can see clearly men who have strong male models and men who don't—a difference between night and day. My brother was god. I loved him. We were never allowed to go outside, so he was my *only* friend until I was nine or so. He was literally everything to me. That we don't have any contact now is still a source of grief, but the only way I know to honor him is to keep going forward.

My first memories of abuse start when I was about five. Every night, my mother would come home from work. It didn't matter if she had had a good day or a bad day, she'd always find some reason to make us go down and spank us. She'd make us hold onto the bookshelf. We're naked, and she's always giving me licks, generally twenty-five, and double up with my older brother, Jim. The rule was, if either of us did something wrong, we both got spanked. We got beaten every day because of something about me. She said it was always my fault, never his. Jim would scream, and if you screamed you got double licks. I never screamed. So she'd start over on him until she got tired and she couldn't swing anymore. When her arm would start to hurt she'd send Jim upstairs.

After the release of violence, she'd feel better, so then she would want to cuddle. Jim would be upstairs crying and moaning, hoping she would go check on him. She would want to tickle and play. At some point during this, she would hit me as hard as she could. She'll have her knees on my shoulders and keep slapping me as hard as she can as she tells me I'm the reason we're poor and dad left and she gave up on her dreams. I'm the most selfish person she ever met. I'm a man, and all men are worthless, lying shits who don't deserve to live. She was going to beat the worthlessness out of me. She never did anything to deserve a son like me.

Then, after she got all that out, the connection of the violence would make her want to make out. I remember sitting on the couch with an erection and my brother upstairs crying, knowing what was next. Her saying it was all my fault.

We'd go through this every single night. The same pattern. Then we'd have dinner, we'd watch TV, we'd go to bed, and then she'd hit her lows and start crying: "No one loves me, ah, ah, ah. No one loves me, ah, ah, ah." We'd get afraid she'd come in our room and get us. My brother would push me in there, and she'd be like, "You don't love me," and I'm like, "No, I do." It's really hard when you're five, and your mother's telling you that you don't love her. I know I did love her, but I tried to love her as little as possible. She would say if I loved her I would hold her. Squeeze her tight, butterfly kisses, real kisses, oral and then sex. Eventually my brother would get in bed, and I'd play dead and inch off the bed, hoping they wouldn't notice.

I know the textures of my mother's sexual organs. I know what my mother tastes like. When it was over, I would feel so lonely and ugly and dumb. Back in my bed, I would put the pillow in my mouth and scream. Scream as loud as I could. Cry and cry, praying every day to God to kill me. When I stopped praying, I gave up on God. You keep coming to in these blackouts. Your brain doesn't hold the whole picture. No one ever put me to bed or read me a good night story.

I'm never going to get to the bottom of that. I'm never going to get to the bottom of the things that my brother did, either. There's no like, "Oh, well, thank you, I graduated." I would love to graduate. I've spent my whole life wanting to graduate.

Jim was always so mad at me. He would put things inside of me, do everything he could to me. He loved hurting me. That was his goal, trying to get me to scream, but I never would. Then at the end of our time each day he would hold me underwater. I tried to escape, you know what I mean? But the thing I usually ended up with was just apathy, because if I fought the two of them, I would become them. I tried to give them nothing, ever.

I came home from school one day, and Jim started doing his thing. Then, for some reason, Mom just came home early from work that day, which never happened. She beat us like she'd always do. Then the next week, she started dating. She put all that stuff that she would do to us—she put it into that. I was eight-and-a-half when her abuse stopped. Five months later, she met her second husband, and he moved in before you know it.

He was a guy so he'd slap us around, but nothing compared to the stuff from my mom. It was a vacation, as far as I was concerned. He was never scary. My mom, when she got scared she got mean, and she would beat you with everything in her being. I remember being a kid, and I would disassociate, and all of a sudden I see my body flying in the air. I'm seeing the ceiling, and smashing into the wall. This guy—his being there kept her from beating us like that anymore. She tried once, but she didn't get in one lick. The guy was like, "Fuck that. Get your ass upstairs." So that was the end of the daily physical stuff. Thank God for that guy. He was around for nine years.

≈

One thing I'm proud of is how I confronted my family. I was nineteen and had been working on myself for six months. I started getting memories of the abuse. I got a counselor, and my mom and my brother finally agreed to sit down and let me say what I was going to say. I looked at them, and I just opened my mouth and said everything I needed to say. There was no sense of I'm going to get mine, or I'm going to punish you. I wanted it to be like a hand of love, a hand of forgiveness. I spoke clearly. I told the truth. A lot of the survivors I know want to get their child-hood back forever. They want to do things that will make the person pay. I don't see how you can get anything back. I never thought that way. The only way I can be free is to forgive.

I told them I'd pay for half of the counseling, or all of it. We can work on this, I said. We'll meet every other week. They wrote me a twenty-eight-page typed letter, my mom, her third husband and my brother. They disowned me, said the abuse never happened and moved away to another city.

When I was five and six, I would travel to now. I could see my life, and I could feel what love was like. I could feel the idea of the kind of dad I wanted to be, and the kind of relationship I wanted to have. I couldn't see it visually, but I could feel it. Love's like this, my wife's like this, my daughter's like this, life is like this. I held onto that and believed in that—for no reason, and not on a lot of evidence. Every day my mom would say, "No one will ever love you like me. I love you more than you will ever imagine." Inside I would say, "No—love is not this."

You carry the memories of the abuse around always. You just don't know what's going on. For example, I was getting into these screaming arguments with my first girlfriend, and she'd be so hurt, and I couldn't stop myself. I know I'm 100% right, and yet I'm 100% wrong. I was destroying the greatest thing that ever happened to me. She was sort of like my childhood. But I had to end it, because I can't keep this darkness from coming on. You have no idea where it's coming from. Next thing you know, you're saying things that you can't take back.

The people in your life, whatever your triggers are, because they love you, they're going to stand on those triggers. Now at the moment, it seems like they're trying to kick your last nerve in. At the time, you think they're out to hurt you or whatever, but it's the conflict that gives you a place to stand, and heal bit by bit.

Was my relationship affected by the abuse? Absolutely. Was I aware of it? Absolutely not. But I knew something was tragically flawed. Whether you have memories or you don't have memories, it doesn't change. You are still living completely out of the effects of the abuse, even if you try to repress it, you're always living out of it. You just don't know it. So it's just no wonder we live in the world we do.

I attempted suicide. I've made unbelievable mistakes.

The problem with most survivors is, we feel we're shit. Why am I speaking in the third person? I said, "most survivors." Own it. I always saw myself as the lowest of the low. The shame and the sense of less-than are so profound. You fear that if everyone really knew you, knew the secret . . . And the reality is none of that.

My grandmother lived near us. She was God, safety, sanity. She was the stake that I held onto instead of falling off the cliff. When she died, I could not get it that she was gone. We were so connected. I could smell her. Everywhere. I was nineteen. I quit college, moved out of my mom's house. I didn't know it, but somehow I thought if I moved out and dealt with my shit I would lose my grandmother. You know, if you break the covenant—don't talk, don't trust, don't feel—you're out of the family. So after she died, it's like I started my life the way that I always wanted it to be.

One day, I was at a restaurant, and this person said, "I'm taking an acting class." Boom, I was into that. Living on my own. New job. A person in that acting class was like, "Wow, I'm going to this adult support group. Would you come with me, because I'm nervous?" I went. She never went back. I never stopped going.

The adult child group was created by a church. It was a Jesus-based, 12-steps thing about adult child issues. From that group, I went to incest groups and all the other types. I am always amazed at how strong women generally are and how they engage and dive into the traumatic events in their lives. The guys in the groups, nowhere close. Most of the guys don't have as many skills, and usually no support group. Many years later, I started a support group. I mean, I annoyed five to come hang out with me. A little over two years ago. Now, if I have this going on, I can talk to Will. If I have that, I can talk to Pete or Todd or Ramon. It all helps—groups, therapies, workshops, acting.

Women don't see that the idea of intimacy for me is—like you want me to be naked and walk down this alley and all these people that could, you know, violate me? Like what? That's what you want me to do? Why would I want to do that? It's the most vulnerable place. For most men, violation is the loss of all things they hold sacred—safety, all that stuff. But you try and try 'cause that's where the freedom is.

DAVID

~

To me, the most abjectly violating thing is neglect. Parents so busy with their own lives, their kids are just some kind of augmentation. Like someone who never told you they love you. They never held you. I can't think of a more cruel thing.

I'm just really grateful that I get a chance to be a parent—to be the parent I know my dad wanted to be, my mom wanted to be. I'm going to make mistakes and all that kind of stuff, but I hinge my entire future on this one little thing that I hold onto—an act of faith like when I was a kid, I guess. I'm going to give my child issues—like any parent. It's a given. But I'm not going to give her trauma.

My wife Gabriella has access to every part of me. My daughter Mercedes, too. It's like stuff is getting burned off and it's cool, but it's definitely work. Certain things kept me alive, but now they're killing me. They're not going to work anymore. And they're not good for Gabriella, either, so I've got to let them go. The two of them have gotten so underneath everything I ever held onto for protection. We've been together sixteen years now. Gabriella is so gifted. Takes your breath away. She's perfect in so many ways, it's just astounding. I know I am a gift in her life, but the fact that she has had to put up with my shit is the single worst thing I need to make amends for the rest of my life. I didn't deserve any of this shit. She certainly doesn't.

So many guys who suffered sexual abuse have been lost in this boat in the middle of the Pacific, all by themselves all these years. I met a guy who was seventy years old, and this was the first time he had talked about it. He didn't want to be helpless or act out any more. I believe if you have all these sexual violations you're gonna act out till you act to heal it. You have to tell the truth. Otherwise, a guy gets isolated, and turns into a fucking nut. Your heart just breaks.

For the most part, every survivor is absolutely awe-inspiring. At the same time, we can be very, "I want what I want when I want it." Like terrible twos. Maybe because we didn't get to have our terrible twos? To me, the bottom line is having patience. Express what you need to release. Say it all. Keep expressing until you can't express anymore. But then, there's a point where you have to move forward.

People will say put it behind you! Everything you *do* is to put it behind you. Reprogramming your unconscious consciously takes as long as it takes. There is no map or path. It's like walking in the snow. I feel we're all just out there making our way the best we can. Being in our lives as freely as we can.

In incest groups, the level of stuckness is profound. We all get stuck. I just keep trying like everyone else. Some of the most beautiful stories are from people who have been stuck for ten years and, finally, they do yet another act of faith and this time, after millions of knocks on the door, something opens. They let go in a group—somehow allowing air in, allowing change. It's a miracle. Like they are breathing correctly, the way their bodies were meant to, for the first time. And they glow and glow. The thing that scares me the most is, these miracle men and women, after the workshop so many of them go back home. They're back in that boat, nothing but thousands of miles of water surrounding them, and they're completely alone again.

I would like these guys to know there is a prison—the prison of not being able to be in your life because your survival system is overriding everything. It kept you alive and it's still there, and that's why you put in the time and you pray every day. You don't get freedom from finding the answers. *The work itself is the freedom.* It's like you survived the baking of the cake, so you'll survive the remembering of the baking. The survival systems that kept you alive will kill you now. Everything that you're right about, you're 100% wrong about. Everything that feels natural and normal probably is not a good thing. Any kind of self-righteousness, any kind of reactionary thing—those are little flags telling you something needs to be loved, to be cared for, to be healed.

I've learned that I have to love the most unattractive, darkest, most repulsive aspects of me. That's the only thing that's going to give me freedom. I can't hide them. I can't bury them. I can't go, "It didn't happen." I've got to just sit there and love the unlovable parts. Like forgiveness, it's a process. You're going to forgive hundreds of times, over and over again. It's a lot of work. You're going to have to forgive yourself that you're having to forgive. But the truth is, each time it's less and less. You put your arm around the most painful, emotionally violating moment, and then you have to love that part of you. Bottom line, there's all this love in this world, all this happiness, all this peace, all this paradise and, it's not going to be the way I want it and it's not going to be when I want it. And it's not that way for anybody.

I made a discovery recently. I realized that, to that little boy in me, I won. Because even when my brother was torturing me and trying to drown me in the tub and it was so bad I wanted to go, I wanted to breathe the water, I didn't. I fought.

I don't have the answers, but I need to believe that I kept the faith. I need to believe that I fought the good fight, that I've done well on my time on this earth. Everyone has the same cross. It weighs the same for everybody. The only way out is, you walk the path. You talk, you journal, you pray, fucking bloody knee prayers. Do you *really* want peace of mind? That's when the universe shifts.

≈

When my grandmother died, I did not stand on a mountain and go, "I fuckin' love my grandma." I didn't know I could. After her funeral, it ached for years that I had kept silent. So when my mom died, I knew I had to say something. I didn't know what, but I was going to talk.

Before the funeral, I'm with her third husband. He is a really decent man and took amazing care of my mom. I literally have ten bucks to my name, and I'm completely vulnerable. We're having breakfast, and I asked him if he was going to say anything at the funeral. He says no. "Well, I am," I tell him, like it was a fact. He asks me what, and I have no idea. He reacts, but I'm in grief, and slow on the uptake. I don't get that they're *not* wanting me to speak. I don't care. I'm going to speak. It's my mom's funeral. I am not gonna live with the feeling I had with my grandmother.

It's weird. All these people just kept coming up to me, saying, "Your mother was a wonderful, wonderful, wonderful woman." And I'm like, "Thank you." I don't know who these people are or who her best friend was or anything, but these people loved my mom in whatever way and I'm grateful to be here and now. The minister gets up there, and starts the funeral. It's bad, a canned thing, like, "We all loved . . ." He stops. And then he looks down at his notes and says her name. Just the kind of thing my mom would have dug. It makes my teeth hurt.

Soon the minister looks at me and says, "Now, she wasn't perfect," I'm profoundly offended. Why the fuck would he say something like that? I tell myself, "Just let it go, let it go." He starts going into stuff like how she might have lost the battle but won the war. Who the fuck are you talking about? My mom doesn't use or appreciate war analogies. And then he says it again — "She wasn't perfect." I'm barely holding on. Who the fuck is perfect? We know she was human. The third time he says it, I'm literally like, "Oh!" Everybody stops and looks at me. I'm looking at him, letting him know, "Do not say it again. *Do not.*"

But then he calls up this dude who was in her Bible group and this guy is blubbering, and it's all about him, okay? Absolutely nothing to do with my mom. But he's honest, and just his honesty is so freaking appealing to me. He ends with this poem, and he's just crying his ass off. I love this man. I fucking love this dude 'cause he's real. Don't stop talking. Don't make that other motherfucker get back up here again. But then the minister gets back up, and again he brings up the war analogy, I am just wanting to cry. I am grieving my mom and he's talking nonsense. Then he says, "Now her son wants to speak."

I get up there, and I'm just in the zone. I stand at the podium, and the minister stands literally right on top of me, his head pressed against my shoulder. The dude keeps his hand on the base of the mic. I am too in grief to understand what he is doing. I smell his breath, look at him and then out to the crowd, and start talking about my mom.

"My mom had my brother when she was a straight-A student, honor roll, scholarships to five colleges. Cheerleader, glee club, the whole bit. My grandmother told her not to date this one particular boy, but she did. She got pregnant. She put all her dreams aside to take care of my brother. By the time she's twenty, she has me. This was before single mothers were called single mothers. She's working at a job that, when she leaves, they hire three people to do what she does, getting paid half of what a man would make. She wears the same five outfits to work for eight years."

In this way, I talk about the stuff that was my mom. I tell a joke like her, punch line first. And then—"No wait. It's supposed to go like . . . I'll start over." She made incredible spaghetti sauce. The time she drove on the circular highway that surrounds Atlanta from noon until eleven at night, and we drove and drove and drove, looking for the exit, the end of that highway." The people at the funeral were screaming in laughter and sobbing, and I just talked and talked until I didn't have anything else to say. I talked about how everything in my life, everything that I see is because of my mother. Everything I value, everything I hold sacred, how I see the world, everything that I owe, everything that I am is because of my mother.

I end with a poem by e. e. cummings that begins:

> i thank You God for most this amazing day:
> for the leaping greenly spirits of tree
> and a blue true dream of sky; and for everything
> which is natural which is infinite which is yes . . .

I start walking away when the minister speaks, and I realize what has been happening. He was there to turn the mic off on me, to defend my mom against this evil son. All I know is I spoke from my heart as best I could. So I look out into the congregation and say, "My mom will never stop teaching me things, and this is just a new phase, and thank you for letting me speak." I said what I needed to say. If she heard me, she heard me. I was very blessed to have her as a mom. The most important thing to her was to be a good mother and she got lost profoundly, but the who of who I am and the who of who she is—absolutely astounding. Just no skills and no help.

In essence, there's nothing that can't be forgiven. For our own sanity. It's a process. It's a lot of work. There will be a place where you can find forgiveness for anything, but it's not all at once. It's little slices at a time.

III

Don't Know

"There is a teaching that says that behind all hardening and tightening and rigidity of the heart, there's always fear. But if you touch fear, behind fear there is a soft spot. And if you touch that soft spot, you find the vast blue sky. You find that which is ineffable, ungraspable, and unbiased, and that which can support and awaken us at any time."

"If we can stay with the soft spot and stay with the tender heart, then we are cultivating the seeds of peace."

—PEMA CHÖDRÖN

I don't know how men do their lives.

My heart was heavy. With all the violence, abuse and trauma so many boys are growing up with, I'm not surprised they often feel angry and want to be in control! It's a wonder they have *any* access to their vulnerability.

I was missing that boy.

There's something I want to say and I'm not sure how to say it. It seems to me that so many of these guys are hurting, and they need time out to grieve.

What if, from an early age, when you felt pain or feelings of fear or sadness, you were told (in the words of the men I interviewed):

> Man up
> Suck it up
> Shrug it off
> Walk it off
> Wear it, kid
> Tough it out
> Buck up
> Don't be a crybaby (sissy, wuss, wimp, pussy, faggot etc.)
> It doesn't hurt
> Forget about it
> Wipe it off
> You'll feel better later
> Park the pain

Park it *where?*

~

After I had been interviewing for a while, just listening and taking notes, I finally bought a tiny digital audio recorder. I opened up the manual to read it and felt immediately overwhelmed. That same thing happens when I try to figure out how to operate the DVD player and the remote. I mean, *really*, who needs all those buttons and what on earth are they for? Something in me shuts down. I can't take it all in. I wonder if this might be how many men feel when they're faced with an emotional situation? I know I often do. Where would any of us have learned the skills we need?

~

When I began to see so much of the behavior of men that had puzzled me as simply *not knowing how*, something in me softened. The world seemed suddenly more understandable. The man yelling in traffic, the sullen, withdrawn spouse, the death row inmate, the abusive boyfriend, the teenager not giving a straight answer, the adolescent starving or cutting himself, the approach and avoidance guy, the deer in headlights guy, the stonewalling boss, the disappearing lover, the numb nerd — all doing the very best they can, in that moment, with what they've been given.

I saw more clearly that my frustration was with the men's conditioning, not with them as human beings. The daily violence of not being allowed to be who you are. "There's just a lot of ways the life force gets beaten down in a man," a 51-year-old told me.

When I was growing up, my mother used to say, whenever someone was "upset" or being "unpleasant" — "They're probably either tired or hungry." What once seemed to me hopelessly naïve and simplistic now feels wisely true. Tired and hungry in the deepest sense. And often, not a lot of help. Now my wise adult kids remind me, in a fiercely kind way, "Don't inject your fear into our lives." Bringing me back, in the reliable uncertainty of life, to the real work of being a parent — to wake up, trusting.

I Didn't Know What to Do with My Feelings

"Men are angry because . . .
they don't know why."

Underneath all the stories, I was hearing so much fear and sadness. When I was talking with a man who practices psychotherapy, I asked about this and our conversation turned into a mini interview.

The expectation is that men should know, so guys try to be the guy who knows, or acts like he knows. How can you be a man in this culture and survive if you don't know? Do you think that men, in general, believe that they can be lovable to a woman if they don't know? They're afraid if they don't know, the woman's going to go for the guy who acts like he does.

In my practice, I see a lack of vitality in the eyes of the young people I work with. It's a hunger to have a relation or connection. The fear and sadness. They won't lead with it, but it's in their posture. The story of his life is he wants to belong. Girls have more permission for that. I see it with my daughter and her friends. There's all this huggy stuff. They're falling all over each other. They sleep in the same beds, they're so glad to see each other and envelop each other. And so many men who are having affairs, they're not in love with the affair. They're in love with the fantasy of how they want to belong.

Human beings come wired for attachment. I don't think we ever lose that. But boys and men start losing touch with it. Guys get so lost, so deformed, so misplaced. This belonging attachment is, I think, what the fear and sadness is all about.

So I asked these boys and men about fear and sadness—and what they learned to do with it.

~

FEAR OF CRIPPLING FEAR

If I feel afraid, I either run or I go play with my friends at their house and do stuff. If I'm at home, I go in my bedroom. That's where I feel the most safety. When I'm really in a bad mood, I just cut loose and get really mad, and I don't want to talk to anyone for a while. I don't want to be in this moment right now. I take a nap or something, and I talk in my sleep. That's one of my secrets.

(9 yr.)

Whenever I have a bad dream, my eye is like this superpower. I just blink three times and it's suddenly like changing the channel on TV. Just like it goes to another whole dream.

(9 yr.)

I don't really get scared very often. It's kind of like—boys don't really get scared. We're not supposed to.

(13 yr.)

I'm really scared of, like, losing my family. It's weird. I've known so many people who have died.

(13 yr.)

There's an enormous fear of not being accepted. That fear, that discomfort quickly goes to anger because it's a safer feeling—and sometimes, if we don't know how to manage it, to violence. It feels more like a position of strength.

(17 yr.)

It keeps you mysterious if you don't share too much. You know what I'm say-ing? If you share too much, it makes you vulnerable. And what's bad about being vulnerable is I think it has to do with the power in the relationship. You got the power. If you get vulnerable she might see you as a punk and may not be attracted to you no more. Even though she says I want a man to be open.

(20s)

For me, because of having been abused, to have somebody touch me sexually is both an extraordinarily warm and comforting feeling, but also the worst kind of terror I could possibly experience. It's very hard for me to not be aware of both sensations. And it makes it very difficult, at times, to be comfortable with being sexual. Combine that with the fear of getting close to somebody, opening myself up and then having the possibility of being ripped to shreds, metaphorically speaking—I'm always scared that that's going to happen. There are people, I'm told, for whom sex is a natural, beautiful, warm and open act; it's fantastic. I don't know what that's like.

I called up my old girlfriend from college to ask her if we had even had sex back then. I was so disconnected from my sexuality I didn't remember. She was incredulous. "Have sex?—Gregg, we had sex every night!" I had no memory of it. Sex is pretty much a reflex of the body. And I guess I just left my body.

I think the hardest thing for my wife is my not being able to fully reciprocate what she gives. I didn't know how frightened she was that I didn't love her. I struggle with receiving the daily compliments and I love yous. From a partner's perspective, I think its very difficult to understand how somebody could be comfortable and safe in your arms, but if you're standing an inch apart, feel terror. Other survivors probably totally understand that.

(30s)

Fear was something to be dealt with, just like any other emotion. Just because you were afraid to do something, there was no reason to talk about it, no reason to bring it into the open. You just dealt with it and went on, 'cause, you know, just 'cause you were scared of something didn't mean you didn't have to do it. So what good did being scared do ya?

(30s)

I think to be exposed as a coward is the worst. It's much worse than the pain ultimately. The fear of crippling fear.

(40s)

When I don't feel loved, I feel scared shitless. I'm afraid of not being loved. It feels like death, like I don't exist, and I don't know what to do next.

(40s)

I grew up in the Cold War and then the very beginning of the Vietnam War, when there was a draft. I can remember lying in my bunk bed somewhere between the ages of probably five and ten and being terrified of having to be a soldier and going off and being shot in some far-off land and not getting to live my life for something I had no idea about. Because of some idiot's idea of what we're supposed to be doing.

I had terror, literally terror, lying in bed.

(50s)

The dreams of men while we're awake are about being rejected. They're about fearing that our penises aren't good enough, big enough, strong enough to hold the woman to fulfillment. The story is the same, whether it's on the top or underneath.

Men are scared shitless, and they destroy what they can't control. They think they can control it, because that is the lesson we were all given. Don't get vulnerable; don't allow it; don't go there. To the intimacy, to the deeper realms, to opening the gate to the relaxation stage or relatedness.

Men have a common story. We are totally locked up in a genital world and we don't have anything else going. Seventy percent, a genital world. And we wish it wasn't and we don't know how.

(50s)

There is this fear of what men can do to each other, because we know that we all have that capacity to be pretty violent. And women, too. Oh my God, I've seen women go off the charts. I mean, I have the same feeling a woman does when a man is drunk and being really belligerent. I just immediately feel, "Get away from this guy. He is not trustworthy. You know, he can't trust himself." It's a red flag—if they're totally aware of only their own feelings, they're unlikely to include you. So I just back off and exit.

(50s)

Having dealt with abuse as a child, I notice now I tend to choose much younger women, usually of slight build. I need to feel in charge. I don't want to be hurt. And, if it came to it, it helps to feel that, especially in the bedroom, if anything happened, I could throw them off. I feel safer.

(50s)

In my men's group, a guy made a joke about the idea of having sex with an under-age girl. At the time, I had a daughter who was twelve. Shit, theoretically, he's talking about Amy. It took me a week or two to say I'm having trouble with this. You're talking about my daughter? You want to have sex with her? You think this is funny? The fact it took me so long, that's the point. I was afraid I'd be rejected, be alone, and if I'm alone that feels like shit—the fear of being ostracized, not feeling like you belong. You're going to be left hanging there by yourself, which feels like death.

(60s)

I wanted to be married first before I was willing to share certain things. So she won't reject me.

(60s)

I have a strong need to have privacy when processing something emotionally. It feels almost like a life and death thing to me. If somebody is trying to invade that space and they don't honor my request not to, it feels very threatening.

So if your boss gets mad at you and your reaction is really deep then—I'm not a likable or worthy person and I might get fired, I won't have any income, I won't be able to provide for my family and I won't survive. I'm gonna die. And that chain is actually what we are experiencing emotionally, so a seemingly small sense of rejection or invalidation, silly as it may sound, can *feel* like a bottomless life and death threat.

If I'm in a critical situation like that, physical or emotional, I can sense the tremendous power in myself and wanting to go into the cave. I actually want to make sure that I'm using that power in a way that's not only safe for me but safe for whoever is around. I've been in the process of unlearning that I always have to handle that kind of thing alone first.

(60s)

When I was growing up, the only way I had of dealing with fear was to override it. Just conquer it by pushing on. Take a lot of risks. You know, ride motorcycles fast. Climb mountains. Cross glaciers barefooted.

(60s)

The hardest thing for me to do was say that I was afraid. I don't get afraid, I get mad. If I have to, I'll get sad, but I will not get afraid because real men aren't afraid. God, it is such an incredible double standard. The truth is, every real man, every actual man is scared shitless, every single one of us every day of our lives. There's a lot of fear and sadness in men. But I think men are acculturated to absolutely 100% deny it.

(60s)

I didn't know what to do with fear. To externalize it, I wrote. That allowed me to give form to things. I feel the most safety when I'm writing. I am most in touch with being a human being. It's a timeless place. The left side of my brain is turned off. The last thing I think of is being afraid.

(60s)

Especially for those of us with abuse, I still see myself at work doing things that are reactions to my father. I'm treating the world like it's my father, right? You're constantly trying to figure out, as everything comes at you, how can I make this okay so that I don't get whacked? Fear.

On Sunday mornings, if my sister and I woke either of my parents up, there was just hell to pay. Bad, bad, stuff. Sandy and I knew every floorboard that had a squeak. We had exact paths how to get to each other's rooms. All this stuff was just so mapped out. And you don't drop those habits, really. They're very ingrained. So, at work now, I'm constantly trying to spin stuff to look as good as possible, to make it perfect. Because in your own brain, pathways get laid down. You're just tip-toeing. They're still alive. I'm still doing the floorboards.

(60s)

Intimacy — that's my biggest fear. And yet, it's what I want more than anything.

(60s)

~

A HUGE SORROW

I like to be alone when I feel sad, for like five minutes. I don't cry. I just hold in all the stuff that hurts. And then I usually just go into a corner for a short period of time. Just to be by myself. Or I just don't do anything about it. Or I like to be with my mom or dad. I like to be hugged. I just feel sad and then it goes away.

(10 yr.)

When I feel sad, I just cry. When I lost Sierra, my dog, I didn't stop crying 'til the next day. Still sometimes, when I see like a tuft of Sierra's dog fur in the shower or something, I just start crying because I miss her. My friend's little sister said that once their two cats die, she wants to, she actually said this, she wants to replace them. You can never replace an animal. You can always get another one to add to the family. But you can never replace an animal.

(11 yr.)

My first memory of sadness was when my cat got run over. Hercules. I think it was so traumatic to me that I didn't know what to do with my feelings. My mom told me, "You know, you were never allergic to cats until your cat died." There's never going to be another Hercules. I think I was about three or four. I'm sure unprocessed feelings like that have to do with a lot of allergies. It just gets stored in the body.

(20s)

Sadness is a snowball. I try not to run from it. If I keep pushing it away, it gets bigger. More denial, the worse it gets. I like to get out in nature, or snowboarding, hiking, biking. My wife is the only person I feel safe to fall apart with.

(30s)

In general, I don't experience sadness yet as a normal emotion that just sort of flows. When I get right down to it—every emotion is scary to me. But, it's strange, I don't get sad unless I'm in a place where it's safe for me to do it or I'm supported. Sadness doesn't come out in me. I think it very quickly turns to anger—not anger at other people but anger at myself. I either compartmentalize it or it turns very quickly into something I use to attack myself.

(30s)

I don't think men know how to be sad, in general. I don't think we're taught how to do it or encouraged to do it. I think when you look at the examples in popular culture, when men are emotional, they're always extreme moments. It's not a normal, everyday occurrence—like the hero cries when his one true love dies in his arms. There has to be some overwhelming, life-shattering drama to bring a tear to his eye. Otherwise, you're just being a sissy. That's kind of the stereotype.

(30s)

After my parents divorced, I was a very sad boy. My brother and I felt we were going to be abandoned. And I was picked on at school. That's why I think the one thing I did like to do was go and play sports. The physical outlet felt good. And the sense of mastery and positive reinforcement.

I guess I felt from a fairly early age that I had hardships, things were unfair. And I saw my purpose as trying to make the world a fairer place. I feel a sense of righteous anger and it's a positive, motivating force—like there's a battle going on in our world and I want *my side* to win! Anger feels like an easier or stronger way to express fear. My wife has a hard time with that.

(40s)

Often I'll find that I'm just feeling sad, and it'll take me a while to figure out why. As boys, we were not given skills to be reflective, to understand what the cause of our feelings are. We're not taught to put ourselves in someone else's shoes. It's not fancy. It's not sexy. It's just really basic, like understanding the emotional consequences of actual actions. We find ourselves feeling a certain way and don't know why. It's training to be unaware.

(40s)

Sadness is the emotion I have the hardest time with. I hate it. It's like the lights go out.

(50s)

We wanna make somebody wrong rather than just feel the sadness, or any fear that's there. If you have gotten into an accident, everybody's adrenaline kicks in, you face death in some way and it's scary. Tears might naturally come or you feel, "Well, this is scary. I might have died." Instead, people will yell at somebody, "That asshole! How did he ever do that?" You know? Because it's scary to feel scared, to feel that open and that vulnerable that we are.

(50s)

We'd have a lot less crazy people if there was a place for grief. A place for people to go crazy and come back. With no place for grief you can't even take a day off from your job. There's no place except for Prozac in the world. Prozac is about un-worked-out grief. And anger is there, too. Grief's before that. Because I'm telling you, when someone you loved passes and this or that has happened, the only way to channel it is to turn toward it. That turns into grief. I mean, two to three times during a person's life we need to be allotted time for a nervous breakdown. Just have a nervous breakdown. See you in a year. See you in a year and a half. See you in two years. And when you come back, we'll be there.

(50s)

It is a huge sorrow. I don't think we don't feel those feelings of fear and sadness. In a way, it's something worse than that. You're trying to control something that's inherently uncontrollable. This is why men have heart attacks. In order to control these feelings, you have to so tighten your chest as to keep that sobbing thing from happening. A double whammy—you're feeling it, but you're trying so hard not to feel it that you're out of touch with it.

(60s)

When I feel sad I go into my cave. I don't want to face the world. Or I work. Or go for a walk in nature. I feel the most safety in my office alone.

(60s)

There's a lot to feel sad about. I feel sadness every day about what's going on in the world. I feel sadness at the end of every week about the pain that I've just experienced with a lot of different clients. Question is—how do I get some of that sadness, that grief to move out of my body? I have some practices, but that's a big question on how to do that. I mean, sadness, if you don't feel it, if you push it down, then you get depressed. Sadness and grief are allied, really, breaks the heart open.

(60s)

After such a profound loss—the loss of my daughter—it's hard to even think you're a "together" human being, never mind "being a man." I'm glad I can grieve, because it gets me back into a place of being *human*. I can wade through the world, and maybe be more of a team member. When you're with people, you have to pretend you're not fucked-up. To go from being taught to not feel, to suffering an immense loss—that is hard. I'm not sure I want to get over it—not feel sadness and grief—because that means to forget the person you lost. I mean, you're not supposed to feel good when you feel grief, but I sort of do, because it makes me feel I'm not the shallow Southern Californian kid that I sometimes think I am. It's kind of weird because I'll be biking, and I'll feel sadness. I'll start to cry and miss my daughter. Then I'll look at myself, and feel, 'God, it's so cool that you still remember her, and can cry about it.

(60s)

I never saw anybody in my family cry. My grandmother from Jamaica was the strongest person I have ever met. She brought her seven daughters over a few at a time by ship. They were all seamstresses in New York City. She was strong, loving and warm. She would hug you and kiss you, but I never saw her cry. I never saw my mother cry. I never saw my father cry. I saw them argue, but they didn't cry. The life of an immigrant is challenging, because you have to make it. It's almost like you don't have time to cry. Kind of like when I was in Vietnam.

Once a month I go to lunch at a Mexican restaurant with four guys. We've known each other twenty years from a former corporate environment. If somebody dies in our family, we can say we're sad. You still can't share true sadness with each other though. I can tear up. But it's hard to cry. I tear up a lot now. I've never been able to sob.

For a long while in my life, I was very unemotional, very reasonable. My mind was working but my emotions were not. My wife's brother died in our house. We had him here for two weeks with us under hospice care while he was dying of lung cancer. I cried. Everyone cried. It was permissible to cry. Finally, I can now express sadness. It feels wonderful to cry, it really does. It feels free. I just wish I had been this way in my 20s and 30s. I'm starting to get to the point at 75 where I'm probably crying a bit too much. I mean, I get overwhelmed by — well, I don't really know if there's too much.

(70s)

Men have less access to sadness because of all the things that are on top of it. If we aren't allowed to feel this fundamental sorrow, how to feel the sorrow of our current situation, and hold the planet as sacred?

(70s)

Dennis (30s)

"That's what growing up street is—no fear."

I grew up in a rougher city environment. I was five years old when we moved to the United States from El Salvador, so I was caught in between. Because I was young, I grew up very Americanized. My parents were separated. I was raised by a single mom. I had three older brothers, so my ideas were influenced by them. The youngest was ten years older than me, so when I was a child, it was just me and my mom, and I realized we'd have to stick together. Now I can see that a lot of the things I learned were B.S. Being brave enough to accept that I can start over with new ideas doesn't make me less of a man.

My older brothers would hit me when I was a kid just because I didn't have my dad around. If I did something wrong, I'd get the belt. So I think I got in fights with other kids because I was already violent. I hear mothers say, "If he hits you, hit him back." Horrible advice. They don't say that to a girl. That's how moms collude, too.

My new awareness came a lot from education. I was highly educated. I got a scholarship to Campbell Hall, a private school here in Los Angeles. I took women's studies courses at UCLA. Then, ultimately, in a men's group, I reconciled my beliefs and truth.

I was a football player, a quarterback. Typical young man. Friends were enlisting. The group thing. I got more brainwashed than socialized, and strayed from loving women. This was at the beginning of my college career. By the end of it, I'd already been in the Marine Corps Reserves. I realized this experience had definitely detached me further from my feminine. Although, in an odd way, it also propelled and developed my ideas about my own manhood.

I finished my Bachelor degree in December of 2001. My last semester, I already had orders to mobilize. I did homeland defense for a year, then participated in the invasion of Iraq with the Marines as a corporal. I was 24 years old, and I'm now 30, so it's been over six years. Hard truth awakenings. It was hurtful toward my relationships with girlfriends, with my mother and just women in general. It took a lot of personal effort and spirituality to free myself from everything I had learned.

There's a certain harmony that occurs between a man and a woman. At a young age, I started to seek the truth. What interfered were the pre-beliefs. They're so ingrained, it's hard to let them go. You adapt because it's what the group believes, and nobody wants to feel alienated or that they're doing things differently, especially if you're young. We have to trust children's emotional intelligence. We treat them like they don't know. If people would have explained things to me differently I think I would have completely absorbed that, for the better. The training from my family and from the Marine Corps completely enforced traditional male roles and ideas about being tough and strong and emotionally detached, which obviously is not the way to live, or be.

In the Marine Corps, you're physically and psychologically pushed to the extreme to see how strong of a man you are, how you overcome obstacles and survive. There's a very strong bond. It's unusual because it's not a typical male bond. Marines who have been in combat are more open to hugging each other and saying, "I love you," or, "How are you?" We're brothers. We see each other like that, and ironically, as tough as Marines are—or just men, in general—it's contradictory to everything we've learned. One of my best friends, a Marine, just called. I haven't talked to him in about a year, and I was very happy. I want to call him back and tell him I'm going to be a father. I feel a real natural love towards him.

With him, I think I would downplay the other things I've been involved in—women's studies, emotional release body work, men's meditation group, and so on. Definitely not things we speak about. I'm sure if our commanders found out that we love each other and that we see each other as brothers, they would understand it, but they'd probably think it's a little soft or un-Marine-like. Ninety percent of the time, that's not how you're socialized in the Marine Corps. Just because he and I experienced the phenomenon of war, we've transcended the usual ways of relating. For the good, I think. It's real love.

I guess that's an extreme example, but we're fortunate because not many relationships are built like that, especially among men. My father will never have a close relationship with another man, not even myself as his son, and not with my older brothers, either. I just traveled with him, and our conversations are pretty dry. It's heartbreaking for me because my consciousness has changed, but you can't teach an old dog new tricks. So I just accept my father, and am compassionate. I know, somewhere deep in there, he loves me, but he'll never express it. Sad.

When I was a boy, I flew to New York every summer to see him. Although I didn't talk much with him, I did have a strong relationship with my two half sisters, who are closer in age with me. Especially one sister, who was very influential in molding my ideas about womanhood and my own manhood.

≈

I grew up in a strong gang culture. Love amongst men is strong in gang culture, or in an urban, tough environment. I've had the same friends since I was five years old, and we're all tough, but there's trust and we stand by each other. These guys open up to the different ideas that I now have about what manhood is, even though they're older than me and more socialized into certain beliefs. When I say, "Look, you're wrong, this is not manhood," it's defying them, because they're the one's who taught me manhood. But they're open to it because I think they somehow realize that the old way wasn't harmonious.

Most people don't understand gang culture. When you realize how powerful that bond is, then you understand why kids join gangs. Very similar to the Marine Corps, where a lot of guys have never had much family support or any bond to another man. The new friendship bond is filling the gap, so they feel completely justified being in the gang. It's family. If you don't have that, because of cultural reasons, you're lost.

I think I pursued these avenues of opening my consciousness and changing my perceptions about women because I admired them so much, starting with my mother, my girlfriends or just girls that I hung out with. Women are so amazing.

I had a good mom, and that might be a key. If you go to these Latin American countries, a lot of men believe in the macho way and the women accept this as the status quo, so nothing changes. My mom was not very educated. Having to raise four boys on her own, she was pushed to face the harsh realities of life. At that point, psychologically, I guess you've got to dismiss all the bullshit. So my manhood comes from my mother. The manhood she taught me is different than what my older brothers learned. They were more influenced by the Latin country and culture we came from.

I decided to take women's studies courses because I realized I didn't know anything about women. Since I was a child, if there were ten kids around me, I was the leader, the alpha male in a group. That may have given me the confidence to enroll in those classes, where, ironically, I learned the most about manhood. I realized, "Wow, my mother has to put up with all this bullshit just because she's a woman." There were very few other men in the class, maybe about ten percent. Obviously, if I told most of my friends, they would probably have laughed at me.

～

Tony, the leader of the men's meditation group, is the most important man in my life right now. There was before Tony, and after Tony. I was always searching for that harmony and balance and answers, that connection with women, and the group gave me some perspective on those things. The guys in the group were open and honest with each other, at the highest levels of spiritual consciousness. I'm still friends with most of them, and they all definitely see the group as a turning point in their lives. I was the youngest. The others were late thirties up to early seventies. We met weekly. We usually talked for about fifteen-twenty minutes, then we meditated. After that, we would talk about the ego and how it develops, and about how these ideas are formed.

When I came back from the war, I didn't really have any success with women. I was very unhappy and traumatized. I was soul searching. In the group, I realized that these older men were soul searching, too, so I felt kind of lucky. Everything was clear as to how I'd been programmed.

I grew up religious, Catholic. As a young adult you realize that some things in the Bible don't make sense, or are kind of ridiculous. You stray away. After Tony and the meditation class, I returned to my connection with God. It helped my sadness. I felt like a child again. When you're a child, you genuinely talk to God, and feel like God is there helping.

~

Fear is what dominates most human beings — primary, animalistic emotions. I don't know if I have let it go yet. It takes a lot of energy to deal with it on a daily basis. The message I received about fear when I was a young boy was, "Man up." My mother would say something more like, "Man up, but not so abrupt. You've got to have faith." No matter how aware I am, I can always feel fear within my body. Instead of it controlling you or transforming itself into anger, I use it in my meditation, and I expose it in my creative work as a writer. I think that women experience the exact same thing, so it's not inherently a man thing.

I feel fear in relation to women. It looks like a wall. I close off, and don't express myself. It's a relatively new thing I'm doing to be able to talk like this. It's very difficult. The best thing a woman could do is share the vulnerability. Then I can tell her, "I love you so much, and I want you to know I have this tremendous, crazy fear that takes over my body." Just by expressing that, it's almost enough. Before I dealt with my anger and the fear behind it, I needed to be more controlling in relationships because I felt more insecure.

Now that I'm going to be a father, I'm sharing my soul with a woman, because I know she feels fear, also. We're concentrating on saying, "We can't let fear dominate our existence and our love for each other, and the child that we're bringing into this world." It's faith. Trusting life.

We both have a strong belief in God. Most of the men in her life haven't treated her so well. Maybe they weren't as brave as she is to let go of that fear. I tell her, "Look, I'm so, so scared right now, I have this knot in my throat." I guess coming to the source of that is probably a good thing. If you're not even trying, then you're completely lost. Therein lies the problem that we're socialized into: "We don't have to know, because we're men."

Being in a relationship is a very vulnerable place to be, I think, 'cause you really are putting all your eggs in one basket. So it's scary. Really scary. Being on a cliff. Still, I'm willing to push through the fear, that's for sure.

Upholding the family, you forget that it's a union. My wife is pregnant. We're equally competent and all that, but *she's* having a baby. I'm the one who's got to carry this thing, because who's going to protect and provide? Bottom line, the strength to carry the family forward is in my hands, and that's pretty huge. It doesn't even make sense in nature. Female lions are the strongest in the family, and she's the feeder. My partner's pretty feminist and open-minded, but I think at the end of the day she looks to me. I don't know why. I hope it's not fear.

In Iraq, I realized, "Look, you could die at any second." You're so tired physically, emotionally, so tired of worrying about it that you get to the point where you're like, "Screw it. If I die right now, fuck it. I die right now." That realization, ironically, is very liberating. All of a sudden, you're not afraid anymore.

They say fear of death is the biggest fear that all humans feel. It guided all my curiosity, and I'm just now coming to terms with it. I think a lot of guys sign up for the military because of curiosity about death. It's what my gang friends that died faced. They had no fear. These were the sharpest of my friends, the most charismatic. I admired them because they stood up to death. But then it made me more fearful. In a way, that's what growing up street and growing up tough is — no fear. Standing up to death is powerful, almost like a drug. I channeled it differently.

I was in Iraq about seven months for the invasion, so I was in some pretty heavy-duty combat. 30 to 50 combat missions in less than four months. I saw and participated in some pretty rough stuff.

When I came back home, I went directly to film school. I was lost, sad and impulsive. "This is the only thing I can do right now. I can't work. I can't do academics." I was very close to taking my own life. It was good, because I wrote screenplays and made a film, channeling all that energy into a place where it wouldn't kill me. I was really aware that if I don't do something productive, I would self-destruct.

The fear I feel in relation to my wife is a similar feeling — of the unknown, and of being hurt. When you commit to someone for the rest of your life, it's like saying I'm only going to live once. I'm only going to have one family and one woman to love, so if this doesn't go right, then . . . It's the same thing as fear of death because you're fearing that time will run out.

No matter how aware I am, that fear is there. I can feel it within my body. Something natural, physiological maybe, like the fear of not being able to grasp the fear, if that makes any sense. The fear of the fear.

~

Before I met Tony, I was a very sad person. It wasn't depression or anger. I used to hold it in, and it tore me apart—sadness from experiencing war. Quiet hopelessness. It was hard to find anyone who could meet me there. After Tony and the group, I felt there was a safe place to share it. If it's hard for men to be in touch with emotion, something as subtle as sadness is even more difficult. You don't have permission to feel it. I would just suck it up and be quiet, very isolated, detached from myself. They used to call me Sergeant Silence. I was trained that way from my early life, and also from the Marine Corps. Show no pain, not even physically. "I'm a man, I can take pain. So ride it out." You don't really ride it out, you suppress it.

I did Emotional Release Therapy with Tony, which is a kind of bodywork. Spilled my guts, especially around the post-traumatic stress. It's amazing how all these negative emotions are stuck in your stomach. What came out was just energy, bad energy, pretty intense. So much was released that it affected Tony to the point he almost had to stop. During the therapy, I was able to confront a lot of the events in the war in Iraq that caused trauma. It was almost like an exorcism. I felt so light. I've learned to heal myself.

It's weird. When I first met Tony, I felt like, "Who is this man? Is he trying to hurt me? Deceive me? There's no way this man is trying to help me." This went on for a like a year, but I kept going to the group. Now I realize, "Wow, that was really my ego and my fear." Now I'm just like, "Oh, he's a beautiful man."

Now, when I'm in pain, I'm more apt to communicate it to those I love who are around me. Knowing I can is a powerful tool.

I'm on the path to that place where truth is, where peace is. Saying the truth is liberating. I feel that knot in my throat because it's not easy all the time. I must have learned it somewhere.

I think power is another one of those things that we're socialized into as men. Like boys getting into pissing contests and girls working together to avoid conflict. In my past relationships, I was very controlling. I didn't feel at ease unless I was the one with the power. It's a very negative way to be in a relationship, obviously.

My first love was the strongest physiologically. I wish somebody had told me, "Look, you're not going to get it right the first time. Maybe not even the second time." It was traumatic and definitely affected me. I held onto regret, even until now. When you're so innocent and young, you don't have fear.

An older person, a kind of free-spirited hippie, told me, "You know, it's about love." I don't think most boys realize you're going to be having sex with *another human being*. As simple as that may sound, we don't make the connection. It's more like, "We're going to have sex!" Or, "You need to lose your virginity." I held onto the idea that "it's about love." I expected it would be with someone who I'm friends with, and would be something higher than our physical bodies. It's funny. Now as an adult, I realize that's exactly what it is—much higher than our bodies and everything in the world: a spiritual connection, first and foremost, which is actually what's missing in most relationships.

When my partner tells me I'm not as affectionate as she would like, I communicate to her that I'm working on it. I don't just put it away somewhere. Since most people have had some negative experiences with love, it's hard to realize that love is what balances the entire universe. How do you say that to someone who's been crushed? Some people just substitute it with their children. My mother never got remarried, so she devoted all the love to us, her sons, and religiously to God.

~

In the environment that I grew up in, either you die young or you wake up and smell the coffee. I have been exposed to so much that's broken down: being in Iraq, growing up with a single mom, gangs, violence. So much breakdown. You get to the point where if someone tells you, "Do you want be free from this pain?"

you're not going to deny it. Two of my best friends died by the time I was twenty-one. Best, best friends. One robbing a bank, the other in a gang-related thing. I had that same energy. Fortunately, I was able to turn it around. If I could share the knowledge that I have now with my friends who passed away, it would be, "You guys were worried about the wrong things."

Whatever It Takes to Survive

"Anything to avoid feeling the pain"

Already wedged into the middle seat, I looked down the aisle at the stream of boarding passengers, and saw among them a very large man. A former football player, no doubt. Well over 200 pounds, well over six feet. "Please don't sit next to me, please don't sit next to me," my tiny mind chanted, certain he would take up all the space—figuratively and literally. Closer and closer this huge man came becoming huger and huger and, sure enough, sat down next to me. It was to be a five-hour flight. I let out an inaudible groan.

And then, I remembered this project I'd embarked on and began to inquire. Five hours flew by and so did all those assumptions I was making. I had a delightful time getting to know this man about whom I knew nothing but my preconceptions. A truly lovely, open-hearted human being who had been through a lot. He was lucky, he told me. He had a family who loved him enough to leave him, until he woke up and had the courage to get help and do the work of looking at what was underneath his addictive behaviors. And, I learned a thing or two about football along the way.

If you're trained to compete, oppose, even to kill—what does that do to a heart? During these interviews, I often heard a sense of "something missing," a feeling of lack, a disconnection with the aliveness of who they are. And a longing to reclaim their wild. Awake. What array of strategies might anyone manufacture to temporarily escape a very real and deep-rooted sorrow, and this sense of a too-small identity they've been asked to shrink down into?

It's easy to see how boys could get hooked on approval, praise and rewards, trying to know, figure it out, be in control, trying to be this thing that's impossible to be—"be a man." What do any of us do with the pain of not being who we truly are?

Many of the men talked about various kinds of addictions as one of those ways of coping. I heard a longing for empathetic love—to bond with someone or some-*thing*. The usuals—alcohol, drugs, sex and love, food, gambling, power, fame. And the sneakier ones—like intense experiences, perpetual busyness, buying stuff, self-criticism, self-improvement, compulsive exercise, media, video games, watching violent sports, internet pornography—any kind of screens and devices!

Like the rest of us, they do what they feel they have to do. Sometimes that includes strategies that try to flip the discomfort onto others—like blaming and judging, being "right," justifying, withdrawing or stonewalling, cutting off, running away, and feeling entitled. Subtle, and not so subtle. Passive-aggressive ways like condescension, disregard, ignoring, talking over, interrupting, not listening, taking credit for others' ideas and efforts. I now understand all of these responses as frightened efforts to avoid feeling pain; cruelty as the most extreme of these. And we live in a culture that supports and sometimes even makes a virtue of an over-blown sense of self-importance—a loneliness we have come to call narcissism, self-deception. All were becoming more understandable as ways of dealing with pain.

Even addiction began to make sense as a way to construct a refuge from what feel like intolerable feelings. An anesthetic to mute the pain. It seems to be our persistent human habit to divide up the world into ideas of race, gender, class, religion, sexual preference, etc. for some imagined safety of hierarchy. A ruckus of thoughts streaming though our heads. And we tend to believe them! So many different ways to pad our hearts and call it "me"—looking for a way to forget the discomfort and rawness of reality, and protect ourselves from feeling vulnerable with one another.

What gets any of us through?

And what gets through to any of us?

These stories touched my heart. When do boys and men just get to be human beings?

~

I was tough, but I hate violence. It makes me feel sick in my stomach, so I always avoided it. I watched a lot of fights and I broke up a lot of fights. My main survival skill was to be friendly, getting along with people. But then my friendliness became a pressure, a different kind of armor I couldn't let down.

I ingrained into myself such a need to be liked that I wouldn't want to be disliked by anyone. Definitely, absolutely I compromise my authenticity, even still to this day.

(20s)

My body has so much shrapnel in it from Iraq I have to work out two to three hours every day just to keep alive for my two young daughters.

I come from a military heritage. My dad, my uncles — all of them were in the military. I was a Navy seal. My dad taught me that it's a violent world out there. There are people who will hurt you. Avoid fights if you can, but if you get in a fight, make sure you get the other guy first.

When I was in kindergarten, or maybe it was first grade, a kid punched me. I got a pencil and broke it in two and stabbed him in the neck. This was at Catholic school!

I was trained to kill when I was in the military. Having to kill people makes me more aware of how important life is. Guys have an instinct to prove themselves worthy. We want intensity. I know I won't be a victim, and if I have to fight, I'll kill. But I learned how to read situations, and now I'm more apt to just walk away because I realize how fragile life is.

My view is that there are two classes: warrior and non-warrior. The non-warriors are living in a bubble and I feel like the kindest thing I can do for them is burst that bubble. Because the warriors are basically protecting the non-warriors. And the non-warriors don't seem to recognize or acknowledge it.

(30s)

We give up part of our humanity to go to war. It allows us to survive. Getting it back is the hard part.

(30s)

Some days I think I have a unique vantage point as a person who spent half his life so far in the world of ideas and intellectual pursuits, and the other half schlepping, grunting, and pushing to get a job done. I've dined with brilliant scholars who wouldn't know how to use a screwdriver and shared smoke breaks with crusty bigots who can build anything you want, but have no time for questions about truth or self-reflection. Who is a stronger man? Who, ultimately, has a greater impact on the world around them? And who, at the end of it all, do I find myself wanting to be?

(30s)

Pretending to be something that I'm not—how could I not feel depressed or angry, mostly at myself, for buying into it? Depression is a rational response!

(40s)

Having gone through abuse, you wonder, "Why work on my shit?" You're never going to get your childhood back. You'll never get that innocence back. You'll never get back those eyeballs or that skin or the freedom or the dreams, all that stuff. So why do the work? You stand in that void, and you go through that body memory of the abuse for whatever time it takes, until finally you make it your own. Before, you didn't know what your favorite color was. But when you get through that, when you have your favorite color, it's yours. So that's why you do it. In finding your favorite colors, you rediscovered who you are. Honesty, open-mindedness, willing-ness. What matters is that every day is these amazing miracles.

All these different people were like stakes on the cliff of my life. They changed my life. Like my grandmother. All the different people in your life that stand to love the unlovable. You know? They're hurting, they're this or that, but they freely can give these things and they don't need anything back and don't allow any of that nonsense to spill onto them. These amazing, amazing people.

(40s)

The best way for me to lighten up is to get on an animated storytelling jag about my life, engage with a responsive person, and find the humor. There's that fool element, laughing at myself and my situation. Men have a tendency to take so many things seriously. You hear guys debating seriously about rating the best guitarist. Why put it under this scrutiny? We're trying to have mastery or trying to be right. Humor is all about being wrong or not having mastery. Having even one supportive parent or sibling, or being around liberated people — you need *some* way to feel the courage to answer that call within yourself rather than to suppress it.

Service has the potential to be humanizing, but in our culture the identity of service is narrow. What about service to get excited about? Like, "Let's do something cool together. I don't have to take all the credit." Collaborating, helping others to gain independence or pleasure.

(40s)

I was being a self-deprecating fool as a way to control. One upsmanship. It was a superiority thing, not a clown.

(50s)

Guys get younger and younger girlfriends because they themselves are emotionally immature and undeveloped. I tried it. It didn't work. The sex was great, but after a while, I got bored.

(50s)

Maybe it's because of the abuse, but I feel safer with a younger woman. She looks up to me. I like being adored. I get strokes for being more experienced in life. She says, "Younger men don't know how to make love. They don't have their financial life together." I have more control.

(50s)

When you live your life in separateness, you don't know how it is all affecting you. You keep so busy that you can't have the stillness to feel it. A new business, a new girlfriend, anything new. I like the excitement. Meditation is one of the ways I try to structure my days now to maintain integration.

(50s)

As more and more men have jobs that don't require brute force, don't require aggression, in fact may require more and more being able to interact with people, being able to read emotions, and being able to connect with people, well, it kind of culturally opens up more images of what's possible. What being a man can be.

(50s)

I'm small. I had to address the fear. I had to know I was bigger than what perception was given me. So I became a little fierce guy, growling a bit more than what I really am. And it worked. Every boy has to fight, and learn how to be tough. The more tender part that every boy also has — well, it doesn't get used. And then he may have a job finding it. I don't think I lost it as much as some boys because I was always very artistic. I would paint and spend a lot of time by myself. I was a happy kid so I was always playing. I never lost my sense of play.

I couldn't be belittled, so I had to win on many levels — have a winning persona, a winning attitude, a winning something. When you're small, you're either overlooked or you're picked on. If you're careful, you can miss a lot of the violence because you're insignificant in their view. I had big guys that would do my work for me because everybody liked me. I was very likeable. Whatever it takes.

(60s)

I got good at being passive-aggressive. Blaming everything and everyone else. It's how I gave myself permission to be angry. I didn't even know how angry I was. Not exactly a way to heal a disturbingly dysfunctional childhood, but it was all I knew for a long while, so I clung to it.

(60s)

I was always being criticized, so I hear criticism in the least little things. So sometimes I will answer in a very sharp way, which is my strategy for dealing with that. What I noted is that hurts people. It is not what they intended, or even if it is, there's no reason for me to respond like that. I can just slow down a little bit. So basically, I saw how it affected other people. The other thing that I've noticed is often there's an underlying agenda that I wasn't even aware of until they would ask me about it. I learn more from women I'm intimate with than anybody else.

(60s)

I have to really work to not be dominating in my interactions with women, because that's how I was trained. Even when I'm talking with my partner about wanting to learn from her and not being so dominating, I dominate!

(60s)

When I was a younger man and not feeling good about myself, I wanted lots of women to like me so I could tell myself, "Well, at least *they* like me." If months went by and I didn't have a sexual connection with a woman, then I was afraid it would be years. If not for them, I felt I would have lost *all* connection and been irretrievably isolated. I'm ashamed to say it. I never really saw who those women were.

Now, I think it would be just being connected with people, not necessarily sexually. Today, I look at my nephew, who is living alone right now and is very happy and content. I was never happy and content.

At this point, what I'd tell younger men is, it's important to be alone and be still and understand who you are yourself before you can move out and fully embrace another human being. And be authentic about who you are instead of using women to reflect back that you feel good about yourself. If I really know who I am I don't need to use people that way.

What I've observed with my female friends, who are in similar situations, is they seem to be so much better at self-soothing or connecting with their girlfriends or doing things that are very good for them, but don't necessarily have anything to do with finding another human to make themselves feel like they're whole again. Many men, and I'm including myself in this one, feel incomplete without a female in their lives, so they will do whatever it takes to get one.

(60s)

I lied to survive as a child. It's hard to undo the habit. A lot of the time I don't even know I'm doing it. I don't want to be that guy. So I lie.

(60s)

I came from a family of alcoholics, and I prided myself on the fact I didn't drink or take drugs. Recently, I've begun to look at how I use work and women in the same way. It's painful to admit. My whole life was built on a lie.

(60s)

For many years in my life, I slept with an automatic pistol underneath my pillow. With a round in the chamber. The hammer back and the safety on. So that all I had to do was flick the safety down and it was ready to fire. There were times in the night when I had to hold that pistol in order to be able to sleep. The time I slept best was when I was in the Marine Corps in a barracks full of men. My abuser was a woman, so I think that it made a difference being amongst all those men.

I don't know whether it was related to the abuse or not, but I was almost priapic until I was about 28 or so. I could maintain an erection for hours, up to five, six hours. Continuously. That moment, when, if a man's making love to a woman, especially if she has vaginal orgasms, in the moment of that orgasm, when her arms and legs come up around you and hold you so tightly, that sure feels like love. It sure feels like acceptance. And if I was able to do that repeatedly — especially if she was having an orgasm, I felt that illusion of love. Soon as the intercourse was over, soon as we got out of bed, these women were like my mother. Then I had to try just that much harder to maintain the relationship and figure out, what is it now that they want, what do you need me to do now, and how soon can we get back in bed? So that I can get that feeling again that you love me? Most of the women I hooked up with left me. I recreated the same type of abandonment and betrayal. I kept doing this over and over. When survivors haven't done their recovery work yet, we tend to pick unsuitable mates. So much of my sexuality was about trying to get what I didn't get from my mother.

So many men don't want to do the work of recovery. Because when you start to deal with the pain, you really don't know whether you're gonna survive it or not. That's how hard it is. God damn! It's tough to take a step into a world that you don't even see yet.

What I want to tell others is — there'll always be things that will trigger the pain, but it will be momentary and then you'll be back on your feet and doing whatever it is that you want to do, not because you cowboyed up, because you've really *human-beinged up.* You've discovered how to feel grief and yet still function and do good.

(60s)

We're all addicts. Trying to block out the pain of not being able to be this idealized self that we can't be anyway, right? So you just blot out experience.

The trick is just to move to higher quality addictions, ones that don't numb me to things. Right now, it's the gym.

(60s)

I believed that when people spoke to me in a kind way and were nice to me, they were doing it because they felt sorry for me, because I was somehow pathetic. For many years, all my actions and relationships with women and men were framed around trying to get love, to somehow be lovable, rather than authentic.

I made an altar, and on the altar I folded a little paper door that said NOLO for "not lovable." I could open that door, and so whenever the feeling of not being loveable came up, I would bow with the feeling and say, "You're not true, and you're not useful in my life. So I'll give you this space behind the NOLO door," with the understanding that you can't get rid of things by denying them or by saying they don't exist. I did this for about two years.

I mean, boy, I can see that door so clearly. It was about this tall. It was on a piece of paper in the corner of the altar, and I remember being in places where I didn't feel like I was loveable and I wasn't at my altar, but I could just imagine saying it and I called him NOLOV, not lovable — NOLO.

(60s)

To survive a dysfunctional family like mine, you had to be able to anticipate and read what was going on. You got very perceptive, out of self-defense.

I found that very useful in being a committee chairman and interviewing applicants for medial school admission. Boy — I could tell you in short order whether they were suitable applicants or not, many times in the first five minutes.

(70s)

Paul (40s)

"It comes back to strength in vulnerability. If you just speak your truth, that's powerful."

I always felt more comfortable around girls, and *liked* doing girl things more than boy things. I was never into sports. I was into music and art and drama and dance, and I loved dolls. When I was almost four, I wanted a doll for Christmas—a specific doll, and I wanted it more than anything. My dad was opposed. My mom said to him, "He's three and if he wants a doll, we're giving him a doll." My favorite picture of myself is Christmas morning and I'm hugging that doll, holding it to my chest with the biggest smile on my face. It says a lot that my mom, in 1968, was willing to buy a doll for her son.

I grew up in the Mormon Church, a very conservative, patriarchal religion with rigid rules for men and women. If you don't fit into the prescribed roles, then the problem is with you. I believe there's a reason that Utah has the highest per capita use of anti-depressants of any state in the country. In the '90s and well into the 2000s, a large percentage of young women between the ages of eighteen and thirty were leaving the church in droves, because they couldn't have a voice.

In the religious culture of the Mormon Church, women have always played a secondary role to men. They play a huge role in the raising of the future generation and all it takes to keep a home, but they haven't had any voice in the governing of the church. I think some of this has to do with the whole polygamy thing, which was there from the founding of the church, and is a very touchy subject. Officially, they stopped polygamy in 1890. Otherwise, Utah wasn't going to be allowed to enter the Union as a new state. "Miraculously," the leader of the church got a vision from God that it was no longer the chosen way.

From the age of four or five, I remember thinking that something was wrong with me. I felt inside the way girls feel, and I knew I was different. I didn't know what that meant. I just knew it. I also knew instinctively that I should hide it and not let people know. I had already picked up on the cues from the church that it was a bad thing.

When a Mormon boy turns twelve, he gets ordained into what they call the priesthood, and enters the ascending levels of authority in the church, none of which involve women. Before boys reach twelve, women can be in charge of them and the primary education they receive in Sunday school. After they turn twelve, though, there is no instance in the Mormon Church where a woman is an authority figure over boys, whether in the home or the congregation.

I remember sitting in a Sunday meeting—just boys—talking about the role of women. I started feeling really bad for women, because they were not valued as much as men. That was about as far as it went at that time. I felt I was completely alone with those feelings. I never told anybody about them. I grew up in the heart of the church—Utah County, probably 80% Mormon. I knew very few people who weren't Mormon.

I could not have asked for a better mother. I adore my mom. Honestly, both my parents are wonderful. I had eight years alone with my parents before my little sister came along. Almost like being an only child. When my parents first got married, they were very poor. My dad was a schoolteacher, and my mom taught piano. At twenty-five, she was diagnosed with rheumatoid arthritis, so they didn't know if she would be able to have another kid. Then she got pregnant with me, and they were really happy. Even though my dad is much more of the regular guy's guy kind of a man, he's very much in touch with his feelings, and never had a problem telling us he loved us and showing us physical affection. I didn't realize how uncommon that was growing up, because that's just the way our family was. We always hugged and kissed each other, and said we loved each other. A little older, around junior high, I heard other kids talk about their families, and realized how lucky I was. Every night before bed, I would hug both of my parents, and give them a kiss and tell them I loved them. That was just what we did.

When I came out in my twenties, the first thing my parents said was, "We love you. There's nothing you can say to us that would ever change that." I knew that would be the case, because there was never any question in my mind that they would always love me. That didn't mean they were happy that I came out as gay, and that I left the church, but the bottom line is, they loved their son more than they loved their church, and they never stopped showing me that.

I think my coming-out really widened their world. I don't think my parents knew any gay people back then. That was just not part of their world. They had a very specific belief, shaped by their church, that being gay was a sin, a lifestyle choice, and people could un-choose it. When I came out, it was another year before they were comfortable enough to actually talk about it with other people. If I hadn't done it, they wouldn't have questioned what they were taught or believed. That's why I think it's so important for gay people to come out. It really did shift my parents' paradigm. It's been a journey for all of us.

I left the church in my early twenties, and I haven't been back. My dad's ever the optimist, and he has this hope that someday maybe—but, it's never going to happen. Even if the Mormon Church got a revelation that I could take my partner to the temple and get married for time and all eternity. I just don't believe in organized religion. I've evolved out of that.

If there are a lot of voices in your world, loud voices saying, "You're doing it wrong, you're going to go to hell, something's wrong with you," then it is difficult to find your own way. It's difficult to say, "No, I'm going to trust my gut and forge my own path, and find what's right for me."

~

My older brother is a really good guy, a successful physician and a devout Mormon and he believes everything the Church teaches, which in some ways dumbfounds me. Nothing about his life has ever contradicted anything that he's been taught. Except for me. He has one son, his youngest child, and they doted on him. My brother's wife was terrified their son would turn out to be gay if he had much contact with me, so I hardly ever saw him.

Well, it turns out he is gay. They did everything they could to try to make him not be gay, short of putting him in therapy. Now he's in his twenties. He's graduated from college, and he has come out to them, and he wants nothing to do with the church.

Not long ago, this nephew reached out to me. I hadn't seen him since he was twelve years old. We caught up, and talked about our family and the whole church thing. It's helped to repair my relationship with his parents, too. Now his mom, who had been standoffish to my former partner, is much more open to my current partner and acts like he's part of the family. It's still evolving.

I'm so glad I had the courage to come out. It's not easy being the first one in your family. There are many people in the Mormon Church who just kind of disappear from the family. They move far away, and the family is left in the dark. I'm lucky I get to talk to my family about everything in our lives. They know my partner, and they treat him no differently than my sisters' husbands. I credit them for being great people. Not every family does that. Some people disown their kids. My family doesn't let a rigid belief system get in the way of loving. They demonstrate true Christian love, and it's ironic because it was actually their church that taught them to be that way.

I hear about kids coming out younger and younger. In high school, I didn't know any out gay people. Now there are some who are courageous enough to do that—living their lives, forming gay/straight clubs, being who they are—and I applaud them. People realize being gay is not that weird. We're no different from anybody else, and that will give more and more courage to others. In an ideal world, just as little girls who are attracted to little boys are allowed to express their crushes in elementary school and junior high, I think gay kids will be allowed to express those same feelings. Then they can go through adolescence, when it's appropriate to have those feelings, not suppressing them until they're adults and finally come out.

Many who come out later in life, at least in the gay male population, go wild, and are really promiscuous and do crazy things. I think they're going through their adolescence as adults, because they didn't get to experience it when they were actual adolescents.

When I first started questioning the church, I thought, "If they're wrong about homosexuality, what else are they wrong about?" I started drinking and smoking and going to bars every weekend. I wasn't too promiscuous, though, because I was afraid, which saved me from catching a disease. I was just as miserable and unhappy in that lifestyle as I was in the religious lifestyle. I thought, "There has to be something else. What's the middle ground?"

I was lucky enough to find a support group that some people had just started in Provo, Utah of all places. It was people just dealing with coming out. It turned out to be life changing for me. We had discussions about things like spirituality versus religion and the role of gender. I was twenty-five, so it was before I came out officially. I was out to myself, but not out to the world at large.

The group was started by a gay man. He enlisted a straight woman co-worker of his to be part of the group leadership. Her presence somehow legitimized the group and made it so we weren't just a bunch of gay people trying to pat ourselves on the back kind of thing. It seemed to make it okay and legit in the eyes of straight people. I learned so much from that woman about femininity and the feminist movement. She said something once that was mind-blowing. She said the Mormon Church will never accept gay people until they accept women as full equals, and give women the priesthood. Prejudice against gays, she said, was really about gender. Gay men are seen as feminine, and it's the devaluing of the female and the feminine that is where most gay prejudice comes from.

I attended meetings for over a year there. I found out I wasn't alone. I got support, I felt safe, and learned some tools and skills. We were able to be ourselves.

At the time, I had been leery of regular men's groups, which usually consisted of just straight men. I was invited to one once. They were learning to get in touch with and express their feelings, and be more well-rounded individual people. They felt more comfortable letting their guard down with a group of men who were doing the same thing. It was okay to be vulnerable there, which helped them be more vulnerable in their lives and relationships, with their wives or their girl-friends. I thought, "How interesting. We need more men like this."

~

Men have been running this whole system for a few thousand years now, and it's not working, so why do we want a woman to do it like a man? I think men just don't want to relinquish control. It's amazing to me that our society values a CEO of a company who makes money over a teacher who is shaping the life of an entire country. Or a mother!

There was a time when I wondered if I had low testosterone, because so many gay men that I know—and I think it's stereotypical—were very sexual, and very sexually motivated. I like sex as much as the next person, but it's not the primary motivator for me. When I wasn't with a partner, I could go long stretches with-out sex and I didn't even think about it. "Maybe something's wrong with me," I thought. "Maybe I'm supposed to feel randy all the time." I actually went and got tested, just because I was curious. The doctor said my testosterone was in the nor-mal range.

What I would like men to understand is that their true strength lies in their vulnerability. I don't know how to say it better than that. If they can access their vulnerability and own it, that's when they can be strong people. That's when they can make the most difference in the lives of the people that they're in a relation-ship with. It doesn't make them weak, it really makes them strong.

When I was growing up, I had very few male friends. The ones I had were good friends, but I didn't have a gang of guys to hang out with the way most guys did. I had lots of girlfriends. In particular, I was very uncomfortable in large groups of gay men. I don't know if I was afraid of my own attractions or what, but I found gay men to be some of the most misogynistic men around. Maybe that was a backlash because of the way they were treated growing up. I don't know. It used to really bother me, so I didn't spend time around men who said negative things about women. I know it's a stereotype, but I don't have room in my life for men who put down women. Fortunately, the gay men in my life now aren't like that. In fact, I now have straight male friends and gay male friends and gay women friends and straight women friends. Part of that is thanks to my partner.

In the gay community, there's a kind of stratifying of roles, too. I think part of that stems from wanting to play the game like the straight world. It's like, "See, I'm just as successful as they are." Then you've got other people who are like, "Fuck the world and what they think. I'm just going to be myself and be crazy." In a way, they cut off their nose to spite their face. I don't know if that's limited to the gay culture. It's probably true of everyone.

Any person who is the sexual object of a man, whether it's a straight woman or a gay man, seems to have a disproportionate amount of body issues or body shame. I don't hear a lot of straight men saying, "Oh, I feel bad about my gut or my body or whatever." But in the gay community you hear that a lot. There's this body shame. You have to have the perfect body and be slender, or you have to be well-built and muscle-y. They're ashamed about their body, which you hear a lot from women, too. Their body isn't good enough—too fat, too this, too that. It's objectifying. The whole culture is a blame and shame culture, and you're not okay. I mean, the concept of original sin is terrible—"It's nothing you did, but you're flawed. You came in flawed." Sorry, that's just ridiculous.

≈

I take great delight in lots of little things. I guess the flip side of not doing that typically successful career path thing is that I didn't ever feel the need to suppress the spontaneous side of myself. Just being myself and being happy—that's more important to me than accumulating stuff.

It's fascinating to me to watch men who can put on different hats and play different roles. I'm kind of one-size-fits-all. Wherever I go, it is what it is.

I think my worst fear might have to do with things that are happening in our government, with the rise of the extreme right, the wanting to take away people's civil liberties and legislate morality and enforce a narrow percentage of the population's views on the larger percentage. The recent decision of the Supreme Court regarding the defense of marriage act and prop 8 has been so hopeful. My partner and I are going to be able to have a life I've always wanted to have. But *my* life, not a straight life. But what if all that gets taken away? If something would happen to my partner and I would be denied access to him in the hospital, or the life we're building together would be taken away, with no recourse legally—*that's* my worst fear.

I think the best thing that I can do to have an effect on this is, number one, to vote. And, number two, to talk to people about it, sort of like coming out, but on different topics. Talk about how political things affect people you love. It's not about one-upmanship or beating the other person down. You approach it from a respectful place. Again, it comes back to strength in vulnerability—being vulnerable to open yourself up to their criticism or lashing back at you. If you just speak your truth and be open about it, that's powerful.

I had an experience once right out of college when I worked at a record store, and I was still in the process of the whole coming-out thing. A girl came in and wanted to return a CD. I asked her why. She said, "Look at the guy on the cover. He looks like a fag." I told her, "Wow, you know what? As a gay person, that really offends me."

I was kind of taken aback she would say that to someone she didn't know. She assumed I would agree with her, and was shocked by what I said. I wasn't mean or rude. I just told her it was offensive, and I was proud of myself for speaking up. She kind of turned red, and slunk out. The interesting thing was, she did come back another time to buy something else. Of course I remembered her face. She specifically came to my line, and was so friendly and warm to me. I was like, wow, she has clearly thought about this, and now she wants me to know, without saying it, that she's okay with me being gay.

So that's what I mean about the power of speaking up—little things like that, when so many times it's just easier to let things pass. It's hard to tell the truth, but it's always the right thing to do. Always. I realized the power of that by coming out. More than anything, that is what has transformed my life, and it can be extrapolated to every other area of life, whether it's coming out as an artist or coming out as somebody who likes Justin Bieber. Whoever you are, come out about it. Be that. Be proud of that.

Love is the most important thing. I got that from my upbringing, from my parents. The big thing for Jesus was love. Oftentimes, people say the opposite of love is hate. I believe the opposite of love is fear. Either we act out of love or fear. I'm just grateful that I had a safe, solid foundation from which to build. It was always modeled for me from an early age that you love people, and you take care of people.

I did a one-man show about my coming-out. It was well received, and I was super pleased. What people mentioned again and again was how universal they found the theme of learning to trust yourself, no matter what, and finding your voice. For me, it was being gay and also being an artist, and being able to trust that and put that out there in the world. For other people it might be a different issue, but it was still about learning to trust yourself.

After awhile, though, I didn't want to keep doing the show. It put the emphasis on being gay. I didn't want that to be my identity. It's too small. I'm a human being who happens to be gay.

The Tenderness of These Men

"Human qualities, like empathy, listening, nurturing, gentleness, softness — things that we all have, but don't necessarily develop."

Women have the habit of talk. We share about our heartaches and losses even in the check-out line. It could be with complete strangers. A number of men talked about the learning and wisdom they absorbed from women, as boys, playing around the kitchen table. Almost invisible to the women, the boys could freely observe in a way that grown men can't.

> There's a lot of "male" stuff I don't know how to do. But there's a whole lot of anxiety around the "feminine" stuff, as well. How to sort out all these feelings? No one to tell me. No male role model to teach me. Women seem to do it differently. I can't do it like them, so how to do it? Then boys say it's not cool to feel, so why bother? Why learn if it's "queer"? I give up.
>
> (50s)

It could be that a big part of the "not knowing how," is not knowing how to do the things that, traditionally, women do. Be in touch with feelings, work through problems in relationships, listen, be tender, nurturing, empathetic, compassionate.

Collaborate instead of compete. A whole half of human development that boys and men have often been required to renounce when, at four years old, if not before, the culture asks them to go underground and hide their song. An 80-year-old told me, "Boys have divine feminine, but we're asked to abandon it." And a 69-year-old, "After four, everything in my life was conditional."

If a boy grows up in a situation where the caregivers are in chaos, it's often not safe to feel empathy and so this innate ability gets covered over. Abuse, like privilege, can cut off access to vulnerable feelings and make it hard to feel remorse. Remorse and apology are the beginning of healing and recovering our full humanity.

As I listened to story after story, I began to see how the struggle to "produce a male identity" is as unnatural to men as extreme femininity is to women. Feeling what a challenge it must be and hearing a wish—not to be just like women, but to reclaim these aspects of *themselves* and have them valued, I asked "How do you keep your 'feminine' qualities alive?"

Some guys talked about how having older sisters or girl cousins or really good female friends helped them keep in touch with these "feminine" aspects. One man spoke of reading classics like *Anne of Green Gables* and *Little Women* when he was a boy. Books don't care about their readers' gender. Others spoke of watching films as a way to access feeling.

I noticed that there was a handful of men who had been either ill or had a serious accident when they were young. It had stopped them and given them time out. Most often, in the company of nurturing, supportive women—mothers, nurses, caregivers. They experienced it as a reprieve from the male world.

And yet, one of the most moving experiences I had took place right in the middle of their very male world. I was invited to a court-ordered support group for men who had been convicted of domestic violence. The men sat in a circle. The only hierarchy was one of experience. The ones who had been there longer were helping the newcomer, sitting nearest the door, his hoodie pulled up over his head, gaze fixed on the floor. I was touched by the tenderness of these men reaching out to one another. Over time, honesty replaced shame, which showed up in their body posture and language, becoming progressively more at ease as I looked around the circle. The group sometimes included men who had murdered their wives.

≈

Women are their own alpha male now, so we have to widen our game. Wear more hats, be more complex, have more patience and understanding. We also get a chance to explore more of our feminine side. It's a dance now. When I let go of my machismo, my bravado, and just put myself out there, it makes it easier for other men to do the same. You almost have to learn and then unlearn, and then continue to learn. As a man, you just have to be open to that.

(20s)

I think, as a guy, we need to find stories and explanations of those things that we don't ask or were never exposed to. When you read a book it's kind of like you're spying. Someone is telling you a secret, you know. It's like guys who read girls' magazines. They're trying to find out a secret. They don't want to get caught dead with them, but they're interesting to us because we're not aware and we want to learn.

(30s)

Empathy for other people, and a feeling for victims, I think I got that from my grandmother. That's not the same as letting your little child look around with joy and curiosity and wonder and anticipation at the universe around them. The way that I could do that when I was a child was by reading a lot of science fiction and fantasy. Books were my escape from my chaotic household, a very safe way to do it. You can take your book, you can go somewhere, get in the corner. Nobody's around, you can read your book. You can go anywhere in the universe, past, future—books are wonderful. I think my little boy was able to stay alive that way.

(40s)

I was a sickly child, in the hospital a lot. I almost died a couple of times. Having people feeling sorry for me was sort of the theme of my life until I was probably fifteen. My mother saved all the get-well notes. I still have them—boxes of them. And every grownup that I came into contact with—nurses, doctors, family friends—was nice and kind and wonderful.

I went into a coma when I was five. My appendix ruptured—infection, peritonitis. Penicillin saved me. But I was just about dead. Four and a half years later, I got a streptococcus infection that went into my kidneys and caused nephritis. My kidneys basically stopped working. Again, penicillin saved me. And then I cut my Achilles tendon in my left foot severely, twice. All this sickliness definitely protected me from the pressures of being a little boy.

In the children's hospital during my kidney thing, I was put in isolation. The priest was at the end of my bed every day for I don't know how long. My whole body got filled with fluids, and I turned into a balloon. So I'd lie there and look at myself in the mirror at the foot of my bed on the opposite wall — ugh! I was really alone, feeling that I could be dying. I was ten years old. I went through lots of soul searching.

I was just looking at a painting by Velasquez of a club-footed boy, and he's obviously not well. I looked into this boy's face and I could see myself. He's looking at the viewer because people feel sorry for him. You're looking at a child's face that is open and completely willing to accept the care and concern and alms and whatever of others. This poor little kid gets love and kindness from grownups, wherever he goes. At least, that's what I read into this painting, this beautiful painting. I had that as a kid, I trusted everyone and I think I still do on some level, because that was my indoctrination. I trusted everybody because I knew everyone loved me and felt sorry for me. My intention really is to respond as an innocent to what happens in the world, so it doesn't seem inconsistent that I get sad quickly. I just let myself feel it all.

(50s)

From a jump off a garage, probably trying to fly, I jammed my hipbone into my hip, which cut off the blood supply. My left hip deteriorated. On an x-ray, it was mush, so for two years I had to wear a brace from the waist down. Strapping this thing on every morning, I had to pay attention in a way that kids usually don't. Never, never taking a single step without it on. It dropped me out of the usual thing. I was the umpire, not the player. I had the support of my grandparents and that whole community. The gift of life became pretty obvious. It was just a very painful two years. And in the summertime in Minnesota, it was sweaty and my crotch hurt from where it rubbed. Everybody empathized with me. There was no negative. When other kids were playing, I read three encyclopedias, cover to cover. That's what I got a kick out of. I had more time to develop a life of the mind and, from having the kind of grandparents that I did, an inner life. It was a break from the pressures of being a boy.

(60s)

I missed fourth grade because I had rheumatic fever. I had a lot of out of body and near death experiences that I think I was very fortunate to have. So, in that high school period when guys are just incredibly awkward geeks and it's really bad, since I had experienced something that most of the other guys hadn't, I just had more girlfriends than you could name. I mean girls who were friends. I think it was related to the rheumatic fever. It was an opening. I think it gave me more empathy. That part of me probably hadn't been quite as shut down as for most guys.

Although I have to say, in high school, I spent so much time hanging out with women, I thought that from sort of 8th grade on, and maybe it's earlier, that in some ways the women had it tougher than men. The cliqueish stuff and the verbal stuff and lack of directness. I'd rather just punch each other out.

(60s)

My boyhood was hard. I missed a lot of boy-ness. When I was four and a half, I was sick off and on for a couple of years. I got rheumatic fever. I almost died on the operating table with ruptured appendicitis; then, it was tonsillitis. I didn't go back to school until I was in the third grade. I was a teacher's pet, nerdy, lonely, very smart, geeky kid. The boys scared me because I was so physically uncoordinated. Recess scared me. I wanted to stay in and do extra credit.

Imagine having a fever of 105 degrees off and on for weeks. I'm on fire. I'm on a couch that was turned so that my little sister couldn't come and torment me. I'm so weak I couldn't walk to the bathroom to pee. And, you know, I learned how to pray. I was four to six years old. I went back to space, way, way back in, and would have these little talks with God about getting to live this time around. Asking God, hoping I would get to live, asking for help.

So, yeah, I was afraid of dying. That was my big fear.

It really wasn't until 7th grade when I looked around and said, "You know, I wanna have friends, I wanna connect with people. I'm gonna do this little thing where I'll learn people's names and stop in the hall and greet them and I'm just gonna do it with everybody. I don't care who they are, whatever race, because we were mixed, we had a lot of Hispanic kids and African-American kids, a big junior high, 1400 kids. So I did that. I just stopped and greeted people and learned their names. Of course, it totally changed my life.

I really got this in junior high, certainly in high school. I'm never gonna be cool. I can just give up on that. I'm gonna really like people and people genuinely like me. I'm not gonna fit in any clique, I'm not gonna be cool and I'm not gonna worry about it. It just worked totally. People let me get away with high fives. I could come up and embrace people, say things that are really acknowledging. I learned how to turn ridicule into relaxation and connection. I had to.

It really wasn't until I was a teenager that I caught up in my coordination and became a pretty good athlete. It was a catch up job to become a guy's guy. I had no idea, having not experienced that as natural, it wasn't given to me, how much it meant to me to be fully able and be accepted. And, because it was so hard to get there, I've made a practice of keeping that space of the boy and the playful young man alive.

(60s)

Butch (50s)

"If only in schools kids learned about breathing . . .
they'd have access to themselves in a different way."

I present very masculine—I'm big, and I'm athletic, so that kind of lets me in the club, so to speak. I can teach about how we can connect with our feminine self to connect better with our feminine partners. What do I mean by our feminine self? I think it has a listening quality and a curiosity. Learning to listen from the point of view of the woman, to be present to a woman's kind of perception. I mean, I'm a big, black male, so I can be threatening. Just hugging a woman could appear threatening to her and you never know what her experience has been. So I've learned to step back, to leave some space, to avoid an aggressive or a forward movement even if what I am doing, like a hug, is not overtly sexual.

Five years old, I wander down the hall, I open the door and I see my parents having sex. I'm looking at them, trying to figure it out, wondering what's going on, and are they hurting each other? Then they see me, they stop and sit up in bed nude. My father invites me to come sit at the edge of the bed and he says, "We're making love, Butchie, and one day you'll really be interested in this. We really care about you, both of us, very much. Could you leave and close the door?" "Oh, okay." I'm glad I was in there. I'm glad I know what's going on. I'm glad it's okay. And I leave.

So I had honesty and openness about sex from an early age. I hear a lot of young fathers say, "I never even thought I could say that to my kid, if they came in on me." I hear stories about kids getting slapped—"What are you, some kind of peeping Tom?" or being told, "Oh we're wrestling." Lies and beatings.

There was very clear conversation with my father about everything else, too. I had this wonderful stepmom. We talked and spent a lot of time. So there was a real open experience for me around the sexual. And that, I think, plays a big role in how I live my life today and have lived my whole life, and why I've been able to keep the feminine alive.

My mom, after I was born, had this disconnect. She just didn't want to have anything to do with me for two years. My father was a young psychiatrist, so they hired a nanny that kind of raised me for my first two years. So there was no tit for me. I know where my stuff exists around attachment in relationship, and jealously and all that. I've done enough work with myself that I can recognize it and step away—not have it totally consume me and run me. And yet, I see it. You know, these aspects of myself that I see—it's like, they never go away. They just kind of flatten, and I can step away. Befriend it a little bit.

I remember there was a time when it felt really good—Dad was around, and he and I just hit it off. I'd sit on his lap and we'd read the funny papers. He never beat me. My mom was like, "Hey, if they get out of line, they're gettin' a whoopin'." Pops never hit us, and told her never to. He didn't believe in spanking kids. They had this big fight one night. I guess I was probably about four. Pops grabbed his bags and left. That was the beginning of their separation, and then their divorce. It was a really crazy time for me. My mom and I aren't really connected and now I'm stuck with her, and he's gone. Pfffttt. I mean, there was a real loss there. I was just confused. I felt really alone. And then, when I was seven, my mom and I were fighting. I said I wanted to go live with my dad, and they let me do it. If I could say something to that four-year-old Butchie I'd like to tell him, "It's okay, it's gonna be all right."

What really allowed me to stay whole was my father staying connected after the divorce, and there was the re-alivening of the woman relationship with my stepmom. She was the sweetest. A pretty lady. She felt safe, she listened to me and I could kind of reconnect with the feminine part of myself. She shared a lot of things about the woman's perspective. As a young kid I was able to glean a lot from her sharing that helped me to understand how a woman sees things. And I'm not putting anything against my mom. I think just, at the time, it wasn't possible for her to take care of us kids, given who she was. But for me, there was this loving and supportive stepmom and my father who took me in. So I wasn't just lost forever. I was able to be supported again, at seven years old. That's what saved me.

~

My mom used to try to beat me, but I would run. So there was that little bit of violence, but not a lot with her. And then, fighting with my friends, you know. Because of my father I was exposed to academics; because of where we lived, I was exposed to ghetto people. There was one guy who was a Ph.D. psychologist who carried a switchblade. In L.A. we lived in a place that was right on the edge—you go north, you were in multi-million dollar homes; you go south a block, you were in the ghetto. I had friends in both camps. A lot of shit happened when I was ten. The tens were heavy. My buddy, a ghetto guy, had an older friend, maybe seventeen years old, who was sniffing glue and he put a knife to my throat trying to steal my motorbike. I outsmarted him, but that was the scariest thing I remember.

Another time, I was with the same buddy. It was about the time of the Watts riots. We were eating at this lunch counter. We left and went out into the parking lot, and there was this white kid, probably about seventeen—big kid. I was just this little scrawny ten-year-old. He starts calling me nigger, grabs me, and punches me in the face. I said, "Wait here, motherfucker." We lived right around the corner. I went and got my father's .38, and I was gonna kill him. I was livid. I got the gun, and I'm walking with my buddy. He says, "Man, don't do it. Don't, please don't do it." We got right back to the thing, and the guy was standing over there. I sat down on the curb with my buddy, and again he said, "Don't do it, man, don't do it." I knew how to use that gun. My father taught me to shoot. I was gonna kill the guy, at ten years old. But I didn't do it. What stopped me? Well, I think I just came to my senses. By the time I went home, got the gun, came back, sat at the curb, my buddy's telling me to cool down. I trusted him. I was breathing, I was calming down, thanks to my friend—because by then it would have just been a forced thing to do it. The passion of it had gone. I didn't do it. But that was the most violent thing I remember.

When I was fifteen my father gave me a book to read about tantra. I started learning about using my breathing. I loved the whole idea of integrating meditation with my sexual orgasm, and extending it, and moving it, and all of that. And, at fifteen, you're just full of sex anyway. "Hey, one more thing to play with. Give me a reason." You know what I mean?

When I was in high school I lived in Hawaii, which was a very natural, feminine place. There were banana and coconut and lychee nut trees in our front yard. Life was good. I went to school in flip-flops.

I kept reading and doing tantra workshops through college, and applying it in my personal relationships and in athletics. I never thought I'd teach it. After college, I taught school for a couple years. I did music professionally for a few years. And then I got married, took a job in corporate America, and did that for a lot of years. Never had kids. Got close a couple times, but never did. We divorced and I stayed in corporate America.

The first ten years were cool, but the last five or six years of it, I was just miserable. I was in San Francisco, and had everything going—a great car, great space, the money was good. Then I took a job with a company in Chicago, doing the same thing, and that's where I met my partner. I was forty-four at the time. She was a very successful international business consultant and tantra practitioner. We pooled our resources and started to teach what we had been learning about tantra. We've been together fifteen years now.

~

When I was a kid, there were several buddies that I hung out and did stuff with. I don't have many buddies now. I have a lot of people that know me. And hundreds of people that I know, and people I work with. I could probably count my friends on one hand. They're few and far between. I mean, they kind of fall through the cracks.

The bottom line is guys don't trust themselves, much less each other. And that's where the whole thing about not trusting women begins—they don't trust themselves. "Oh, I can't leave my wife with so-and-so, because I know he's gonna try and screw her." Well that's all in your head. Nobody said that but you. You thought of that, and you don't know what they're thinkin', so it's you thinking about that. You know what I mean? And see, guys would be out screwing holes in trees if there weren't women. So until we bring some mastery around that sexual self, we are doomed.

You know, you have a five-year-old son, you're driving in the car, and he's in the back seat. He gets an erection, and he says, "Oh, my God, Mommy, it's hard, it's hard." And he gets all crazy and excited. "I don't know what to—I'm not going to—" He can be a little crazy, and she gets a little crazy, and he gets crazier. You don't know what to say. But you can start teaching meditation around it. Say, "Oh, great, son. So what I want you to do now is take a deep breath in your belly, shwwww. And I want you to visualize sending the energy in your penis, and your belly, down into the floor and into the earth, and now exhale shwwww. And visualize sending it down." So now he's learning some meditation, and mastery. He's comfortable. And she's comfortable, 'cause he's probably doing that with her because he sees the reaction he gets. He's got a little control now. He's paying attention to his breathing.

≈

The work that I do is one aspect of keeping the feminine alive because it's nurturing and helps people, especially men, become conscious of their sexuality. We're working with CEOs now, too. The guys who are running things. Teaching about working with their breath. Using the life force energy so we can experience pleasure as a wholeness within ourselves and each other. To be present with one another. That's the sexual energy, that creative spark of the divine that we are. That's what I teach, that's what I practice. I do this very intimate work with people, and it's like—what could prepare you for that? I think my whole life has been in preparation for it. I always felt like I was just hiding in corporate America, because no one can relate to any of my real experiences.

Kids coming into their puberty, they're curious about themselves. You can say, "Well, here's a book on masturbation. Go in your room." Be honest. But don't put yourself in it and become part of it with them. I think that's where it becomes confusing—for everybody. We naturally know how to feel ourselves, and procreate and have kids. And yet, there's all this social stuff, and guilt stuff, and emotional stuff that happens. How do we discern the difference between—this is a natural process, and how do I navigate through the emotional stuff? That's what we don't learn. We just don't. And when we're in that sexual energetic, we're so open, so vulnerable. And yet there's all this other unconsciousness heaped on top of that. So it becomes like the bastard thing. "I'll never fall in love again because. . ."—he didn't, or she didn't, or she did this or he did that. How can we, in that open vulnerability, honor it? It's either, "We're just in the dark, we're going to create a baby, because that's what we physically do." Or, "I'm lusting, and I'm guilty, and I'm jerking off every fifteen minutes to something on the internet." What about—"How can I bring my best awareness and consciousness to this energy?"

≈

I love sad. I experience a little sadness every day. I have this routine where I go and I work out at the club early in the morning, and then after my workout I sit in the sauna, and sometimes I cry, I weep in the sauna. About life and things and friends and people who died and hopes that have been lost, and new dreams—just everything. I let the energy come and I let it flow, and I don't get stuck in it, I don't have to shy from it. It's like, okay, great, I'm feeling something, you know? How fortunate am I to be born in the family I was born in, in the time I was born, in the country I was born, in the place I was born, and not born yesterday in some dirt hole with a tyrant running the city, crippled or blind or—it's just a stroke of luck. We're alive.

Sharing hurt, sharing things that have affected me deeply—with someone who's involved in it and would be willing and able to listen to whatever is there for me and not be defensive or get angry themselves—that's when I feel most vulnerable. Fear of not being loved, misunderstood, destroyed, attacked—yeah, those are probably some things that are there around my not saying everything about my personal life.

Men want to be loved, men want to love, and we want to be guided in a lot of ways, too. We get so confused with the woman's quickness from emotional to analytical. We can't make those changes so quickly, because when we get emotional—we want to fight, automatically, we fight. We don't go to the emotional part of listening, or feeling what someone's pain is. We get defensive. Especially, if we feel attacked.

There's an inability to move more smoothly through the emotional part because it's so unfamiliar to us, both innately and as the culture trains us. We don't listen internally as efficiently as a woman. A woman's made to listen, to have the baby, and she's just much calmer in a lot of ways. We are just denser. We can develop the meditation and ability to listen more deeply. We just have to work at it.

⁓

The sexual energy is a love energy. It's a life force. It's not about even doing anything to anybody. It's about getting this in a way that enlivens and connects us—it's the supportive energy. The joy is missing. It's gone. Or it's masked in an over-exuberance in lusting or porn addiction. That energy that never dies, in a way that is like that child, that creative energy, that aliveness—what's missing is for guys to tap into that. And we can. We can learn practices to keep that alive. That's the good news. We can learn how to separate orgasm from ejaculation. To squeeze and release and breathe the energy up into the heart space so we can open and connect. Using the sexual energy and breathing as a doorway. Freeing the energy up allows more creativity and pleasure and intimacy in our lives. When you're getting people in touch with their whole self, including their feminine aspect, there's gonna be less aggression.

That man stuff served its purpose when we needed to just be muscle to cut down the trees, and hone out some civilization. But now it's about integrating the feminine aspect and nurturing, seeing ourselves in each other. That's what's gonna continue our existence.

I know a lot of people who have died. And I'm very aware that death is gonna get me one day. Might be today, I don't know. I rode my motorcycle here. My biggest fear is not doing something that I really want to do and then dying before I did it. So I try to figure out ways to do it!

Without that fear? I would be my finest self. I have moments of that brilliance from time to time. What matters is living life, living life fully. When we bring consciousness to the sexual, the divine shows up, the divine being—just that still, quiet, no agenda, no opinion, just being, easy breaths, peace of being. And then from that place, creating what we will to create—"I want to create work that's fulfilling," or, "A place that's inspiring," or, "a beloved." Or whatever. From that nothingness, something starts to show up.

Listening and Language

"Many men go to the grave never telling their story
because there's not a listening in their world."

I heard this story from a female psychotherapist.

> I remember sitting with a young couple, and she kept turning to him and saying, "But I want to know what's *inside* you, I want to know what you *feel*." And he kept saying, "There's nothing there." He wasn't lamenting it. He'd sort of think and look and he'd say, "There's nothing there," over and over again. "Well, a feeling, how about a feeling?" And he'd look again. Nothing. He wasn't withholding. He really didn't know what it was she was asking for or how to give it to her.

He really didn't know. When I shared this story with a 30-year-old, he said:

> Well, therein lies the problem we're socialized into. *We don't have to know, we're men.*

Why is it so hard for men to listen? Especially, to women. Not all men, of course, but lots of them. And to acknowledge mistakes and apologize? Be accountable? Things that naturally come when you feel the pain and needs of others.

Maybe nobody listened to them as boys. Maybe no one gave them permission to not know and even be changed by what they hear. If they haven't been encouraged to listen to their own feelings, how could they listen to anyone else? All this already having to know, always being on guard, maintaining their position and this fictional self—doesn't leave a lot of room for whatever else might be going on. Traditional manhood seems to require so much defending! If you're angry or defensive, it's hard to listen. Listening is not knowing. And the beginning of collaboration.

One man I interviewed, when he realized there was a transgendered man in the book, said he didn't want to be included. He refused to consider him a man. Almost as if there were a contagion. I kept listening. Some of his story is now in the book. And he's writing his own book about his life.

Language brings a quality of attention to the world. Finding words to express what's going on inside is like turning on a light. What are boys asked to pay attention to? Are they being taught violence? Trained to be separate, to think themselves apart? Are they learning games of winning or games about keeping things in play? Are they learning to cultivate the imagination it takes to feel what someone else might feel—the opposite of violence. What are they being prepared *for*?

I've often wondered why many men feel a need to use harsh and dismissive language, even as small boys. When so much of male language is laced with brutality, how do they find words to express fear and vulnerability? Intimate language to speak of how they feel, what they've endured, to tell their sorrow. Who helps young men with heartache?

They don't seem to be getting much support from the cyber world and the hiding it allows from the beautiful, often messy vulnerability of face-to-face communication. When we look into someone's eyes it's hard to treat them like an object. And I wondered—who creates the media and how have they dealt with pain or trauma? Are they simply passing it on? I've noticed men sometimes being shy to use the word "love."

I've also been puzzled by the habit I've observed in many guys of speaking in the second or third person, a little distancing from the tenderness and truth of connection. And making assertions. As if there were a "right" way to do life! Or, bringing the conversation back to themselves. Where might they learn an ordinary, plain language of the heart that reveals and opens, repairs and restores connection and knows how to make amends? Peace-making language that says—Me, too.

~

I don't know why grown-ups don't listen to kids more. Like, we have a lot of interesting things to say.

(9 yr.)

My mom was always a hugger and a kisser and, "I love you." I'd tell my dad I loved
him even if he didn't say I love you back. I knew he did, but I would still say it, say
it, say it. So now, finally, he's saying it back.

(20s)

We're taught about assumptions. "This is how women are. Whoa, whoa, whoa.
This is what they want. This is how they act. Whoa, whoa, whoa. " So you go after
those assumptions and you fuck up. You don't see who's actually there.

(20s)

Sometimes the women in my life are very full and expressive of their emotions,
maybe crying. I don't express it in the same way, so they think I'm not feeling it. I
am definitely feeling a lot inside. I don't know if that's a personal thing, or something among other men, too. Oftentimes, when I try to express my emotions,
it comes out as more intellectual—basically talking *about*. It's hard to wrap the
mind and the bodily emotions together at the same time.

(20s)

For women, intimacy is a response to verbal communication about feelings. Having that knowledge as a young man would help a lot. I certainly didn't have it.

(30s)

I don't have a language for what's missing.

(30s)

I think it's an uphill battle for most of us being able to relax and be who we are.
Men are not, by and large, trained to listen. Because, if you're trained to be dominant and to see things in an hierarchical way, you're constantly vying for position

and you're missing a chance to listen. That openness we're born with starts to shut down.

(30s)

After my dad died, I noticed I didn't have very many peers besides my siblings that I felt could really get where I was. But I had a few, and the ones that jump out the most are girls. The girls hadn't necessarily had loss, but they were really good at just being there, not trying to know what I was feeling but just really comfortable around me feeling whatever I was feeling, which guys aren't as good at. I think a guy needs to have a personal experience with something to then feel like maybe they're an expert on the subject. Maybe I would have only benefited from talking to another guy who had also lost his father as a teenager.

If you're pushing away feelings that are uncomfortable, let's call them bad feelings, then you're muting good feelings too. You're just choosing to feel less in general. That will serve you at times, because when the hard stuff comes up you don't have to feel it as much. But when the good stuff comes you also don't get to feel it as much. So you miss a lot of life.

(30s)

Girls and women have tremendous experience and expertise in engaging, educating, and supporting the transformation of men and boys — male colleagues, bosses, brothers, fathers, nephews, sons and partners. They have a much longer history of doing that difficult work with men than men and boys in our communities do. I don't mean to put the weight back on women and girls. They have had to work so hard to get men to listen. We can learn a lot by listening to them.

That willingness to overlook women's experience is amplified by racism and colonization. We are far quicker to seek expertise in whiteness than to listen deeply to the leadership of women organizing for justice in marginalized communities. If we did listen, we would understand the work of uprooting male violence far more deeply than we have so far imagined in our efforts to engage men.

(30s)

It's difficult to find words for what's not going well.

(40s)

We're quick to get angry about losing the connection. So we go, "Fuck you."
We come out with aggression, because if we come out vulnerably, "Oh, I'm so
scared," now I'm the bitch. So we need to move out of, "You hurt me, therefore I
have to pull away," and into, "You hurt me. Can we talk about that?" Inquiry.

Fear of intimacy for men, I think, is connected to shame and a feeling of
powerlessness.

(50s)

I grew up trying to be good, so it was harder to enlarge my scope into the realm
of "bad" or "dark." Those were languages I had to learn through pain. If I had had
more music, art and drama in my growing-up, I think I would have learned more
languages for different kinds of feelings.

I shudder at the ignorance with which I hurt some girls in my teens and twenties; at how little I really understood the female experience of life.

(60s)

I would like to learn how to talk more like women do.

(60s)

It's hard to find men that are so loose that they can just go off into verbal meditation, where they'll just use words not just for describing things, but to *play*. You
know, use words for communicating with the heart and not with the head. Instead
of for announcing themselves over and over.

When they get interestingly talking, it's usually about something that they do.
And then they will go on forever. You realize you've just turned down a cul-de-
sac and the car won't turn around. I don't find much genuine curiosity about each
other. Or the habit of really listening.

(60s)

For guys there's so much that's unspeakable. We need to not be ashamed of shame. We need a different kind of training. If I had had that kind of training in junior high, I'd be a different person. When guys learn the tools it's contagious. So the guys who get them need to really be able to share them.

Where would guys get trained to listen? All the things that it takes to be a "successful guy" are almost the opposite. All the stuff that I do at work in talent development and leadership, that is the single most important and hardest thing for people to get. Listening. It's all about listening. We don't know how.

Women have a culture of talking back and forth and — well, just think of it. If you're a man, and you know you're an imposter, and you're not really a man, but you're trying to prove to everybody — hey, you know what? I really am a man, then, whenever anyone else is talking, you're just trying as fast as hell to figure out what you're going to say back, to prove that you're okay. You're preparing your case. There's no time for listening.

My wife and I saw a therapist who gave us language that helped us move into painful things rather than blocking them out. In the midst of doing my habitual defending against her accusations of affairs, and trying to prove I'm this man it's impossible to be, he would stop me, so there was a gap between that stream of thoughts. He asked what my response would be if none of the other stuff mattered? I just turned to my wife and said, "I love you." Right to the heart of the matter. Addressing her fear, instead of defending my shame and proving I'm right.

I was trying to be the big guy and solve every problem. I was angry so deep. It was a habit. Just his pointing it out that it wasn't very helpful helped me let go of it. Having a witness. And permission. I learned that if men understood how fear works in woman and women understood how shame works in men, a lot of the problems around compatibility and connectivity shift. We're basically telling the truth. Now we start to go down some bad road and I'll just say I'm really feeling shame here. We have a name and language for it.

The idea of being a man and failing at it is huge. When you go into shame or fear, you are chemically a reptile. Having just had a cortisol dump in your brain, it's not the time to talk things through. It's not personal. We all trigger each other's habitual patterns. We're doing this crap to each other all the time. If we can just name it, it's amazing what it does. But it's not part of the handbook on how to be a man.

Everything that's made you successful at what you've been doing is exactly what's holding you back from being successful at this stuff. Leadership 101. What got you here won't get you there, right? And it's really hard in the men's canon to deal with that.

(60s)

Men bullshit. This is what we do. We do it so long that we don't know we're bullshitting. We're bullshitting ourselves as well. It's a whole identity. To stop this requires unlearning a learned behavior. If I don't like me and don't even know I don't like me, and I've been bullshitting for fifty years, then I don't know anything else. Unless a man gets taken amongst a group of men who have addressed all this in their lives — been confronted by it, been pushed to their limits — the chances are the guy is going to go to his grave not knowing who he is, being afraid he won't be accepted, won't be loved, won't be able to have sex.

What happens to the aliveness of boys is they watch the men in their lives and innately know that they're bullshitting. So they learn to bullshit, and boyhood dies at that point. Complete trauma. They haven't even had any trauma yet. And then, of course, at five, six, seven years old, they start bumping into the traumas of life, and shut down. Watch the light go out of their eyes.

I don't think all the bullshit got knocked out of me by any one experience. I do think that a lot got knocked out of me in the Los Angeles County Jail when I was waiting for the verdict of my murder case. There were six of us in that cell. A big black man put a physical beating on me like I never, ever had before. I knew I couldn't go anywhere for help. I was 100% alone. I knew I was going to be convicted of this murder, and that I was going to head on from that County Jail into a life of prison. To take with me up to the prison the experience of getting a beating, no matter how severe, was better than asking the guards for help. And in fact, four or five years later, a man in my cell in San Quentin shook my hand for that.

I was in San Quentin almost nine years. Intent to kill, but no malice and aforethought — that's what I was convicted of. It's probably about average time for a young man who is not a career criminal. Last April was the first time I went back. The feelings were all over the place — excitement and fear. Sometimes I felt like I was going home. I walked across the exercise yard, and it looked exactly as it had forty years ago. The black men were in one corner, the white men in the other, the brown men in a third. As I headed for the room where I would talk, I saw the sweat lodge — a huge lodge and a huge pile of stones. I was blown away. Then I walked into a room full of men, hundred-and-fifty strong. The racial separation didn't exist there. It was a haven, this place where, hey, it's like the main shot-caller of the prison stood in the doorway and said, "We don't play that shit in here. You want to play that? Fine, but out there in the yard."

I just sat there in awe, and felt rubber legs. There were men in there that seriously wanted something different. The same path of recovery from drugs that I've been walking all these years. Thirty-seven years of being clean — thirty-eight in April, if I don't get stupid between now and then. Getting clean from drugs was what gave me the key. The bullshit meter was refining itself. Somebody reached through the gate into hell, and handed me the key. They said, "Come on out, lock the gate behind you, and then you're going to hand it back in to someone else." I have spent a lifetime now handing the key back in. It's what I do.

I loved doing it. Almost makes me want to move to the Bay Area, so I could do it on a regular basis. I love convicts. They're honest, and real, and direct. No bullshit. It was like a homecoming, too.

I never felt so at home as in those meetings. No room for dogma of any sort. No rights, no wrongs. There are two driving forces of life that are positive: loving and giving. That's how I've lived my life, focused on loving and giving — a new concept for me. I hadn't seen it anywhere. I believe it's human nature to recognize kindness and feel it when it's genuine, but we can be so twisted that we don't even begin to see it. God gave me a job when I retired as a motherfucker. My job now is to love, encourage and support. I'm way, way overpaid — and I don't have enough work.

On the emotional side, I wish John Wayne had cried just one tear for us. Then the men of America could say, "Well, John Wayne shed one, so I can too."

I love nine- and ten-year-olds. They're not masters at bullshitting yet. Not afraid to tell you the truth. Yet. Most guys, they'll weave a web around the question you ask. They do it in such a wonderful way, and it has nothing to do with what you asked. That's what bullshit is. Older guys begin to want to share their wisdom, but their wisdom is all bullshit. If you're trying to share your wisdom, you don't have any.

(60s)

There's an outer directedness that a lot of men have growing up. We're looking to find out what do they want of me? What's expected of me? You're not listening to yourself. You're not talking about what you feel or what your reactions are. The lack of awareness robs a certain spontaneity, a certain kind of spiritual honesty that you have to rediscover. There is something in the testosterone-driven part of the man that doesn't listen *by nature*. Because it's your task to accomplish, figure it out, scope it out, do your duty, *act*.

In the cocoon of being listened to I can access tenderness, which is immediately covered up when a man steps out into the world. I had to learn to listen because I wanted my marriage to survive. We both had to learn. After 43 years of marriage I can attest that what it distills to is *listening*.

Men don't have a lot of places to be listened to. Many men go to the grave never telling their story because there's not a listening in their world.

(60s)

We need a map to get out, to find things we've never been allowed to say to, or about, ourselves, instead of only being known through the lens of how other people want us to be known. And take our place in the magnificence of the universe.

(70s)

William (60s)

I walked across almost half of the United States. I am a black man and I just had to let go of all the fears of what people said might happen to me.

I was born in an East Coast town. My father, an electrician, and his parents, had gone to find work building the Panama Canal. Like so many, he immigrated to the U.S. from the Caribbean with his family when he was still a little boy. My mother was from Philadelphia. She could trace her roots back to Native Americans and North Carolina slaves.

In 1971, at the age of twenty-four, I witnessed a river catch on fire from all the pollution. It was my first experience of a major environmental insult, and I felt some responsibility for the mess. Nearly a year afterwards, still feeling this responsibility, I gave up the use of motorized vehicles and started walking.

Inspired by something I read, I stopped speaking and spent a day in silence. My life altered. As that day of silence stretched out before me, I realized I had begun a pilgrimage, an outer and inner journey, walking and sailing around the world as part of my education, dedicated to raise environmental consciousness and promote earth stewardship and world peace.

I had to stop talking, because I was arguing too much with the people who said my giving up automobiles wouldn't make a difference. Honestly, I didn't know how it would make any difference, except mean more gasoline for them, but I knew I had to do it.

Later, I learned there were other issues that demanded attention. Environment is also about human and civil rights, equity, gender equality. From the standpoint of a pilgrim on the road, it is also about how we treat each other.

Keeping silent was a vow I made one year at a time. Every year on my birthday, I would ask myself, "Are you ready to keep this up? Are you going to keep miming and acting out, walking and not talking?" Revisiting the vow, I kept it alive and fresh.

On my forty-fourth birthday, after seventeen years of silence, I decided to speak for the first time. I was with a small gathering of family and friends in Washington, D.C. In my mind, each word presented itself to me for brief inspection. I willed them into the existence of sound, and spoke. "Hallelujah!" was the shout that went up from aunts and cousins and others around the table. "Billy's talking!"

I kept up my walking for another five years without the use of motorized vehicles.

~

There is no one moment when I felt I became a man. It keeps happening. I am and I'm not, and it goes away again and then it comes back. One concept of manhood I got was—you've got to be strong and handsome and have a lot of money. From my mom, it was, "Just treat women with respect and be a good boy."

When I wrote my mother and said I'm not riding in cars and I'm not talking, she said, "Your dad will be on the next plane." Wow, my father is going to come all the way out here to find me. So he joined me on my silent walk in places like Montana and North Dakota, and he would say things like, "You can't do this. You got to do something different." He worried if I was going to make it in the world that he knew. My father kept being surprised by what I was up to, but his time with me on the road was nice. It opened me up to the fact my dad would always be there for me, no matter what he said. That's one of the most important things. You got to show up. Be yourself, and show up.

When I was five or six, I wanted to sail around the world. I would go down in the basement and try to build a boat. Ships were part of my consciousness. My grandfather was a cook on whaling ships that went all over the world. After I finished college, I worked for a boat builder. Sailing ships are a wonderful metaphor for escape.

The first love I had was when I was in fourth grade. It happened when my parents sent me to a sanitarium because of an epidemic of tuberculosis in Philadelphia. There was a little girl in there with me, and we fell in love. She was a white girl, and her parents called my parents and said that their daughter wanted to see me. A few months later her parents brought her over to our house and we played all day. I can't remember her name, but I have never forgotten her.

I had my first experience of anger while living in an integrated neighborhood. I went to play with a little girl one day, and her mother said I couldn't because I was colored. I went home, and I was like, "What is this colored business?" My parents tried to explain to me about being colored and white.

One time, my dad took me down to Virginia on a bus. We left Philadelphia, and when we got to Maryland, across the Mason-Dickson Line, the bus stopped at a Howard Johnson's—beautiful. I wanted to go inside to use the bathroom, but my dad said we had to follow a sign that said "Colored." So we went around the back of the Howard Johnson's where there was this rusty tin building, and a line of people. That was the bathroom, at the end of a long line of colored folks. There was another building next to it where there was some rotisserie thing with hotdogs on it, and that was the restaurant. There were no water fountains, just a rusty pipe outside the bathroom that came out of the ground with a faucet.

After that, I got on the bus and someone said, "Oh, no, you have to sit back there." I was furious. What does a child even make of that? There was a white woman on that bus, and she gave me a red Life Saver. She said, "Here, you have this."

In reaction to such experiences, you wonder how you're going to fit in. Who do you want to be? Well, I thought to myself I sure don't want to be Colored. So what can I be? That's where the lies begin. At first, I thought it was just Colored folk who got caught up in that. But, no, it's everybody—white men, white women, native people, everyone.

After I shut up and started walking, I learned to listen. And the first thing I learned from listening was that I hadn't been listening at all, because I thought

I knew everything. What I had been missing all that time was everybody else's wisdom. Also, I discovered that when I talked, I was capable of lying. There was a person I was trying to be for everybody else, a false person who wasn't me. The problem is that after living that person awhile, you lose touch with the person you really are. You're afraid somebody is going to find you out—find out you're not you. To make things worse, you don't know who you are because you need to take the time to do that, and who has time?

As an African-American growing up Colored in the 50s, there weren't a lot of models to look up to. I tried to be anyone but who I was—always pretending. The silence allowed me to rediscover the person I was. I learned a lot about my mind. I learned to listen.

~

What really interests me is being able to break out of prison—the prison that keeps us from the person we're trying to become. For that, we have to stop being the person we are, break free and let that person go, and become the next person. Trouble is, that's scary. It's comfortable in prison, and we want to stay there.

I had an epiphany about this as I was walking through a prison town one day. I began to think I was in that prison, because I was literally in prison inside myself. I believed I would just remain the same person on the walk. I had no idea who I was going to become. As the green man walking, I had a larger responsibility. I had a message to get out, so eventually I would have to leave the green guy behind. He only walks. That was scary, because it was who I had been.

~

As an adolescent, I was very emotional, very high, very low, very high, very low—pretty much suicidal. I was a spiritual person, too, raised Protestant, converted to Catholicism. At one time I thought about becoming a monk. Then I learned that this particular order of monks didn't speak. They took a vow of silence, so I gave that up. I liked the robes, but I didn't want to not speak. It was funny how that worked out.

In high school, I did medical research under the guidance of the surgeon, Dr. Perlman, the most important man in my life growing up, after my dad. He gave me the part of the equation, the white part, the Jewish part that my parents couldn't give me. He did things like heart transplants on animals at the Cardiovascular Institute, which was across the street from my high school. There also was a college dropout program, so I got to be with very bright kids who were mentored by the surgeon as well. I got into medicine in a big way. If you became a doctor, that was success, so that's where I was going. I really didn't want to, but I was trying to please my parents by becoming what they wanted me to be, or what I thought they wanted.

When I first left home and went to Catholic school, I thought, "I can't do this. I'm an impostor." Back then as a Colored boy in a Catholic high school, I was told by the counselor that I shouldn't think about going to college, that I might have a better aptitude to do something like being a street cleaner or a garbage man. I thought, "Well, there isn't anything wrong with that, but that's not what I want to do." But for that person to tell me that, you know what I'm saying?

There's nobody to blame. I mean, I *could* blame somebody, but I'm not going to shoot myself in the foot over it. The society was just saying that a rare person could do that, but not you. Next thing I know, I am looking at going to college, only now I am not speaking and not riding in motorized vehicles. I told myself, "You can't do this. You're not smart enough." That's when I got to see me in action, the part of me that shoots myself in the foot.

So I'm listening to myself, and I'm looking at where I am. It took awhile to realize that the people around me thought I could be successful in whatever I was doing, so I stepped up to the plate. Even went on to get advanced degrees. I thank walking for that. When you only walk, you can't just get in your car, and run away. You can't say, "Oh, I'm over here, and I am going to get over there." I'm rarely in that mind-set now. I'm *being here now*.

Go to college and not drive a car and not talk? People ask me how I did that. One step at a time, I say. Other people hear my story, and say, "Oh, that took so much courage." I tell them I was just being who I was. One thing that helped was going back to my childhood to find the kid, to find little Billy, so that I could be the person I am today.

～

Anger, like fear, is something that points you in a direction. You can't just go, "I'm angry," or "I'm afraid." When I was walking and I felt those things, I would ask, "Is this something I have to look at now?" Anger and fear are messages. My anger about the war is making me refine myself, refine how I feel about my environment, about myself, about people. Now I tell people that the environment is about how we treat each other. We can't kill thousands over there for some resource like oil, like water, then wonder why we have an environmental mess here.

"So what are you going to do to help?" I ask myself. Yes, I can vote. I can run for office, but the most I can do is understand my part in it. And my part in it is my inability to live with the person next to me, to respect the person behind me and each person beside me. The biggest challenge in being a good person, is to be good to each other, and walk through life in that way. I think that is just common sense. Maybe as people say, "Common sense is not so common, but it's taught in every major religion."

We are the environment, and how we treat each other is how we're treating the environment. We're talking about saving the planet. We can send our troops over to Afghanistan and wherever in the world, and we can kill each other and be killed. But to save the planet, really all we need to do—those who feel called to it—is just get out of our cars and start caring for each other.

～

In my marriage, the best thing for me is watching my wife grow and become who she is, and trying not to influence her too much. It is a practice. We're getting good at that. I let her be how she needs to be, and she pretty much lets me be how I need to be, and do what I need to do, given that when she started out with me, I was a strange duck.

It's about mutual respect and caring. Often when she and I have our differences, we're really looking at the same thing through testosterone versus estrogen. It's chemical, and we all have to deal with it. Essentially, we're all dealing with the same thing, so there's no blame in it. We just have to look at each other, and accept each other.

I want to leave my sons and daughter something, but while I'm still here. While I'm here, I'm here—that's my legacy. After my body falls away, I'll keep going. When one son was in kindergarten, they asked him, "What's your favorite thing? "He goes, "Walking with my dad. Walking down Deer Valley with my dad." That was it for him.

It's the funniest thing. I like to say, "Look, you want to go walking with me tomorrow at 6:30?" And he'll say, "Yeah!" He's just into it. He'll walk ten miles with me, up and down and over mountains without complaining.

What I'd say to young people is, I can't tell you to give up riding in a car. I can't tell you to stop talking. But there is something that you can do, that you want to do—to be who you are. If you can't find it, begin by treating yourself with honor and respect, and others the same way. Then you'll be on your path.

To other people out there, I would say, think about walking. Think about stepping outside the machine that is the industrial complex zipping us around. I know you can do it. I've done it, and I know others who have done it as well. When one person does it, look at all the people who are affected by it. Just say, "That's how I'm going to live."

It's not only the human to nature relationship, but the human-to-human relationship that will determine ecological success, or even survival, as the planet changes. We're hurting ourselves so badly. We need to use our time in this relative calm to get together as the people of the planet and figure out how we can work together.

I know how vulnerable we are and how fragile this planet is. I'm vulnerable all the time, so I feel I've got to live this moment now. As we walk upon the road, we meet ourselves. At the end, perhaps we'll find there are no sides to take, no enemies of state, no arguments against the other. There's only death that waits. But on this tiny planet, and in this precious moment, we have the chance to live in peace together. If only we all would take a walk . . . and listen.

Some Wisdoms

"There's a lot more that we don't know . . ."

I noticed that as the men I interviewed neared seventy, they seemed to become softer, more easily moved, and perhaps even more honest. Accepting of things as they are. More light-hearted. A 60-something man told me, speaking from his own hard-won wisdom: "Start to tell the truth together and that's where laughter and humor begin."

When I asked the older men, "If you could say something to younger men what would you say?" what I heard was: "Lighten up; don't take it so seriously" "No healing without telling the truth." "You've got to realize this self you've created is a creation, it's a fiction, it's a story that has its roots in the past. What you are in the present, nobody knows."

I learned that in old age, the body begins to put out more oxytocin, the hormone of nursing women and the newly in love. As the body is slowing down, there's more room to be a better listener. Weary of all the proving and winning, there's an openness to affection and sentiment—the tenderness of human existence. More chance to be themselves and wear that mantle of manhood a little more lightly. "We can put down the burden of self-importance and experience the joy of losing our carefully constructed selves for a moment," said a 73-year-old, wishing he had done so sooner.

There is often more time and space for what I had referred to as feminine qualities until one man gently corrected me saying, "No, it's *human qualities*. Compassion, empathy, kindness, listening—those aren't feminine, those are human."

My own father was a privileged white man. He stuttered as a boy. Then he grew up to have pretty much everything everyone thinks they want. He was "on top." In his mid-40s he developed Parkinson's disease. For the next twenty years, little by little, he was undressed of the roles and many of the ideas and beliefs he had acquired. As he navigated the challenge of an illness he couldn't control, he softened, gentled, and strengthened. His body crippled and bent over, his heart and mind opened. With very little left of the protective walls of "identity," he knew immediately the pain and suffering of others. He said he could feel, hunched over in his wheelchair, head nearly touching the table, the minute somebody walked in the door where their heart was. Trained as a lawyer, he stopped fighting—all sense of opposition gone—and lived in gratitude and awkward grace. He learned how to ask. He listened more deeply. He let himself sob. Freed of the mantle of manhood, he became more of who he truly was. And after decades of living with his illness, he died quickly with a heart attack on his way to take a bath.

∾

Viagra was great in my eighties, but now I just sit in the hot tub with my old friends and tell dirty jokes.

(90s)

My treatment for prostate cancer includes the hormone blocker Lupron to suppress testosterone which "feeds" the cancer. One side effect of Lupron is the complete loss of sexual drive. But to my great surprise and delight, the emotional intimacy between my wife and I has never been better.

(80s)

I was searching really for what a man would be, could be, should be for me. I'd read novels 'cause I wanted to find out what life was like. I had a heart operation when I was sixty. That changed a lot of things for me. I don't try to make up my mind any more. I just take it as it comes.

In my drinking years, I thought a lot about where I stood in my work — any kind of standing you can think of. Was I a good enough tennis player? Measuring and comparing. The hell with it, you know? I've enjoyed life a lot more since then. Age is a relief from competition.

(80s)

I have this internal reality that has sustained me, and kept fresh — a sense of wonder and awe. It's hard to say. I don't do much with "the spirit world," as some others do, or communicate with some entity. I have my "quiet time" all the time. It just is there. It was always with me — even when I ran a company and raised money on Wall Street. I really believe everything is mysterious, and it's a wonderful mystery! There's a lot more that we don't know about than we do know. And I trusted that from the time I was a little boy.

(80s)

I'm in the checkout line at my local grocery story, and the checkout girl is just diddling around. I don't know what she's doing. Diddling around, you know? I say something like, "C'mon, you know I don't have *all day*. . ." Then I look. For the first time, I really *look* at her, and I see that the muscles on her neck sort of grabbed up a little bit — a little hurt. Suddenly, I realize what I've done. It's a little cruelty. I've treated her like a thing, like a machine that's not working. I said, "I'm sorry. I'm just grouchy today." And she said, "I know. I kind of feel that way myself."

There's nothing very mysterious about it. I just looked and listened. At first, I felt empathy. And then, I felt sympathy. That takes paying attention and being open. To live in the presence of the sacred requires a thousand thousand acts in any given week. Little tiny things like that, whether you're dealing with yourself, your child, whatever else. Stop, look, listen, remember. Remember what a wondrous place you are in and how you have no idea how you got here or where you're going but, by golly, you got this. Life is a gift! It was given to you.

Instead of going first to her suffering and compassion I went to using "the girl" as a target for my own daily frustrations.

So often, we don't know how to take care of the wounds we've caused. We don't have a lot of notion of how to repair. It's not usually what men were trained for. Any wisdom I've gained, I'm sad to say, has been at other people's expense.

SOME WISDOMS

311

The major challenges that face us in terms of our survival as a civilization are not genderly based at all. We are *equally* challenged. I don't want a men's movement. *Forget* a men's movement. We need a movement for *people*, not for men or women. Find out how to help people get into those kinds of situations where they can do a lot of good. And where it takes a lot of courage and sacrifice to do it. Enemy psychology is outdated. Obsolete. The real "heroes" confront the challenges of their day (social, environmental, economic), work anonymously and give their lives.

There was a time when wisdom and compassion were what made a "real" man. In some parts of the world "not knowing" was considered an advanced state.

(80s)

I remember the first years of the '60s. I would go to these parties with hippies around the Haight Ashbury. I was involved with the Tribe, and one day I was stoned and with a bunch of people. There was this 16-year-old girl sitting next to me. She started asking me questions about myself. I told her something, I don't even know what it was, and she said, "Oh wow, you sure have a lot to unlearn." Out of the mouths of babes. She nailed me like I'd never been nailed in my life.

(80s)

Everybody has something to hide. Now, I feel "there's nothing to hide." It just seems silly. I got tired of judging myself and accepting other people's judgment. So, to hell with it.

(80s)

I loved to sing, and had a good voice. I've sung all my life. In 1964, I sang at a wedding, and it was the worst I'd ever sung — so embarrassing I never sang a solo again. This year, when my great-grandson was baptized, they sang the Hallelujah Chorus at the end of Easter Mass, and I joined in. I found my voice, and it was better than ever — a kind of miracle!

(80s)

Boy isn't immature, irresponsible. Boy is what it is to be *alive*. A lot of people do the so-called grown-up things of being a man, and they feel dead inside, because that's the cost, that boy they traded in.

(80s)

After seventy, I think people start to get wiser generally. They've either made their mark or haven't, but in any case they're not the young bucks any more, they can't compete in the same way. There's a decrease in testosterone and we're more obviously closer to our own death. And those three things kind of bring you into the present.

In the men's group I was in, they were all achieving men. We started in our thirties, and we all thought we were going to rise to the top of our field — law, journalism, real estate, etc.. Ten years later, some of the ones who did reach the zenith left. I think they saw the rest of us as losers. Finally, we sat around, and said, "Let's face facts. Very few men rise to the top of their field. And the ones who do, sometimes they're pretty lonely, pretty messed-up. We're somewhere in the middle."

(70s)

When we're young, for boys it's pretty much all about sex. It would help if girls knew this. And we have a lot of fears. Homophobia is a big one. I had a guru for thirty years, trying to find the love that I felt was missing, looking outside myself until one day I looked into my guru's eyes and realized that that love I felt from him was me. That I was looking into my own eyes. All fear is fear of death. I had a heart attack when I was sixty and had to face that in a more bodily way. Life's more precious now. Simpler, slower. Peaceful. I need to pay attention to my body more. Inevitably, it's women I'm learning from about how to take care of myself.

(70s)

I don't feel any fear in relation to women anymore. I used to feel they were sort of aliens from another planet, and I didn't know what to expect from them. What changed was my attitude about people as I allowed in more of my *human* qualities like empathy, nurturing, gentleness, softness — things that we all have, but don't necessarily develop. At this point in my life, power is the quality of being present.

(70s)

I feel different since turning seventy, more at peace with myself. I feel I understand myself. On the other side of the coin, even though I always considered myself a very calm person, I find I'm quicker to anger now. I don't know why. My weapon was silence. Now I'm quicker to say something, but it tends to be over quicker, too. I no longer do slow burns. I don't believe in silences anymore either. You don't have to be insulting, but you can say what you have to say and get it out.

There were decades when I was all about career. I chased money for many years, and I was successful at it. I chased power. I chased position, and ended up a senior vice-president before I retired. Society says that's a good thing. Is it true? No, I don't think so, but it's better than being poor. Being poor has no value, as far as I'm concerned. Zero value. What matters to me now is family and relationships, more than ever before.

(70s)

Does crap happen during the day? You betcha. I do kind of a balancing at night before I go to bed. You always get to choose your perception. For me, whatever's happened, it's been a very good day.

I enjoy the night. I go and sit out on the bench on the deck at night. I'll sit there for hours, looking at the stars and wondering what's beyond. It makes all the other problems kind of walk away. Hurts get diluted. My wife has had M.S. for forty years, the last twenty in a wheelchair, and it's really difficult. I'm her caregiver. Watching the stars helps.

(70s)

At a certain time in a baseball season, there's a game where you would predict the top hitters and pitchers. It was something my dad enjoyed doing a lot. We talked about it and worked on it a lot together and submitted our entry. One day, he called me into their bedroom and announced that we had won third prize in the whole country. I was so excited that I just went running over to him and jumped up on him and gave him a hug. He just froze up — went stiff and cold and got really awkward. I didn't know what was going on. I felt like I had done something wrong. I remember turning around and leaving the room and being really sad and confused about it. I was maybe twelve.

Later on in life, after I had gone to some workshops and done some work with it, I got a huge liberation inside myself. I got on a plane and flew home to just be with my dad and share some of what was going on with me. He really listened intently. At one point, I said, "What I've really gotten in touch with out of this is how much I love you and I really haven't said that to you." He went cold again, and he gives a roar, with mocking laughter, "I guess they say that kind of thing a lot in California."

That's when I would've clamped up before. I could see myself doing it again and I thought, I'm not going to do that this time. So I was able to actually kind of chuckle. I looked at him and said, "Dad, you know, I'm not going to let you get away with that anymore. I really want you to hear me." At which point, he started to weep and he let it in . . . and then we had the first real genuine hug probably since I was an infant. We were really close from that time on. We could talk about anything. There was this sense that we had come together on a different level. Later on, he came to me and apologized for having treated me that way, for spanking me, for having tried to make me eat certain foods that made me throw up. It felt so good to have that reconciliation.

He said, "I was doing the best I could. This is what my dad showed me and I never thought about it. I just thought I was supposed to pass it on."

(60s)

I got very badly burned in a fire, and I had an out-of-body experience. I looked back at my body, and said, "Oh, was that it?" A voice said, "No, no, you are going to go back." Once I was back, I looked at my life, and said, "I just don't want to do it anymore. It's too phony, the whole thing." I was a commercial photographer. I was twenty-nine. I quit my job and dropped out for nine years with a girl I met. It was good. Nothing really happened except that we let everything fall away. I bored myself with all my boring parts. We bought ourselves time, the best thing anybody can ever buy. I recovered myself.

I think most people carry a lot of fear and sadness around. And the cure for it, well it may not be the cure, but it will sure go a long way — we can't be human beings until we're willing to sit with ourselves and be nobody and be content. The rest is all fear, fear of death.

(60s)

The biggest turning point in my life, in my mid-twenties, was my first Aikido class. I went home and threw up. I was not sick. I had thrown up a knot of tension I'd been carrying since third grade, this, "Oh, my God! How can I be who I want to be while having to be the toughest I can possibly be? How can I be gentle and strong at the same time?"

I'll never forget the first time — it was a *kote gaeishi* — where the teacher was lowering me to the ground — and I had no fight-back to make. He was just smiling lovingly in my face. I thought, "Uh-huh, this is something different." A gentle power that was beyond me against you, or I have to be stronger or higher than you.

(60s)

The advice my spiritual friend gave me was very, very useful. He said what you're going through is like going on the biggest, fastest rollercoaster of your life. Don't try to hang on to the rails to slow it down. And second, know that life has chapters, and these chapters have beginnings and middles and ends, and that's fine, that's how life works. That's actually how you develop and grow in life and prepare for death. It's all going to go — so let it go. It's nothing to be afraid of. I'd like my son to know that.

It helps a lot to be able to know that you're not alone in this, that there's nothing wrong with you. Other people have been through it, and knowing what their experiences were in going through it at least it gives you a sense that the weather's likely to be turbulent.

(60s)

In my late 30s I just decided to throw out all the things from my parents I didn't like and that weren't me. In Jamaica I learned to live like a Jamaican, which means the biggest problem you've got is what's for dinner. Sometimes you have to work to see the humor, but it's there. Never uptight. Nothing serious.

(60s)

I was a single "dad-mom." Having to care for a baby by myself changed my life for five, six years. I relied on my mom a lot, but I had the whole experience. Part of the message that came out of the '60s was that men have the capacity to be different. We can be emotionally expressive. We can be physically affectionate. We can be really devoted, hands-on parents. We can have lots and lots of best friends.

(60s)

One of my sons is so brilliant he went from 10th grade into college and aced everything. He never has suffered fools gladly and knows everything, and his daughters have transformed him into this doting father. He was lucky, that's what he got. He was so hard and so rigid and knew all the answers to everything. Now he's just like oh, what can I get you? Soft and serving.

(60s)

I watch my grandkids. They're busy all the time. They've got athletic schedules, music lessons, video games. Maybe it's a generational thing, but when do they just sit and do nothing? Having nothing to do is really good. It's horrifying to me that we could have whole generations now that have no idea about silence.

(60s)

At his Bar Mitzvah, the boy's parents got up to talk about his achievements and so forth. The main thing they talked about was how his life was a series of all these acts of kindness. That becomes the family expectation, rather than the other. The kids respond. The kids I see are way better than my generation. They're being allowed to be more who they are.

(60s)

I trust the scary thing most of all. I think it stems back from being in London, without money, in an aggressive environment. I mean, business and the world in general. It's not very compassionate. They'll let you starve. They'll let you be homeless. And all those things are the bottom lines of where fear really mingles. I've been there and, you know, I survived. From that comes enormous confidence and trust in the higher wisdom in us. I saw that I was nowhere *near* the bottom, and I could still help people.

(60s)

When I was a senior in high school, I saw a psychiatrist. He conveyed to me, "You're not crazy. You're in the middle of insanity, you're in a lot of pain, but there's nothing wrong with you." Just having a man who was emotionally astute, unlike my father, say to me, "You're okay"—he saved my little keister.

I've had men throw me a lifeline my whole life. Men who saw that I needed something to sustain myself, my heart, and offered to help. They were coming from *their* hearts, so I felt, oh, okay. That goes a long way for a kid. They somehow saw me before I could see myself. It made all the difference.

(60s)

In the old days, when I reverted into my tightness, my brain would leave me and I would freeze up. All my wisdom, all my insight into myself, gone. My wife would call them uh-oh moments. As I'm becoming more mindful, what I notice is a smaller gap between the freezing up and my going, "Oh, that's what hap- pened. I was feeling defensive. I was feeling threatened." That kind of awareness was nowhere in my many years of formal education. If boys were allowed to be incompetent, to be vulnerable, to not know the answers—and not have the world implode—I believe it would make a huge difference.

(60s)

There is a natural mellowing that occurs in men, I think. The testosterone does start dropping off. I work at having more compassion for people rather than anger at them. Anger might be one of the things I still go to, but I'm smart enough now so that I look at that and go, "Well, what's the second thing I need to do now besides get mad?"

(60s)

Hard—That's the image of man. That's kind of it in a nutshell. We were raised to be hard thinking, have a hard penis, a hard attitude, a hard everything, you know, it's just hard. And then I found, as I was aging, that I felt more in touch with humanity and myself when I softened. I encourage boys and young men to lighten up, soften up. Hard is not good.

(60s)

I think I was basically numb because I had no idea how to handle all the feelings that come with looking down at your newborn child. And I wasn't there for my grandchildren either. So when my great granddaughter, Olive, was born, after all this recovery work I've been doing about abuse, I could finally feel it! I could feel the feeling that I would've had for my little boy, and for my grandchildren, that was still in there. It all hit me. God—it was really overwhelming. I remember looking at Olive and thinking, this is it. This is what they feel. It's wonderful. It's wonderful. I am so lucky.

(60s)

I'm 67, and you know, you don't outgrow your need for your mother. I think there are many men who live secret lives, maintaining an identification with their mothers. The fear is, you don't want to be a mama's boy. Well, I *was* a mama's boy. I loved my mother, and I didn't feel I had to somehow protect myself from that. I never went through this thing of believing the masculine is the negation of the feminine. I experience myself as a human being.

(60s)

My father was one of the most miserable people I've ever met. It was interesting to learn later on, that his father was even more abusive than he was. There's this chain. My sister was an ally that I went through the wars with. I don't have that bond with anyone else in the world. My wife's amazed how close we are. So my sister and I had a pact that we're going to break this cycle with our kids. No violence. That's actually my biggest accomplishment in my life, truthfully. It's huge, and the thing about it is, if you can stop it, it's like ripples in a pond.

(60s)

Glenn

"I was a woods colt."

At 80, my path has become short. I can pretty much see the end of it. It could be pleasant if I go in my sleep, but I may just crap out in the middle of the road. In any case, I can't complain. I've had an incredible life. Whatever happens now, it's just like cream in your coffee. Most days, I'm pretty good until noon, but then in the afternoon the aches and pains get a little tough. I have to force myself to move. Stagnant water goes bad. Only moving water has life, and we're mostly water.

Growing up in Kentucky, I was what the hillbillies called a woods colt, a kid that doesn't have parents and pretty much runs wild. In those days, if you cut school, you went to the woods or to the river—swimming in the creek, playing with frogs and snakes and little critters, stuff like that. You stayed off the roads.

The earliest memory I have of my childhood is walking on a gravel road with my grandmother, my father's mother. I was four years old, and we were on the way to my mother's funeral. There was wild mint growing on the side of the road. I picked a leaf, dusted it off against my leg, and chewed it. I remember walking into the room where they had her casket laid out between straight-back chairs. All these people weeping, and I was wondering why, not realizing it was my mother. That's the very first memory I have of my life.

I have no memory whatsoever of being with my mother. She was ill with pneumonia and the complications killed her. The only thing I know about her life is what my grandmother told me—that she liked to party. At the funeral, she was mostly just a body. I didn't get to know her, and I have just had to accept that. It didn't bother me at all at the time. I was too busy eating mint leaves.

After that, my dad moved to Arizona. I went to see him when I was nine. We spent three or four months together. I remember a darkened bedroom. He was sick, and died within six months.

I was raised by my grandmother, who was awesome. This big, burly woman, part Cherokee, and very intelligent. She'd raised eleven kids and all she wanted was her rocking chair. I remember holding onto her apron, and staying close to her. She taught school. Her and I lived in the old home place, the pine tree farm, by ourselves in one room. Family life with my mom and dad? It never happened. That's the way it went down. My grandfather seemed to have zoned out—a stroke or whatever. He just sat on the porch. Nobody talked to him, and he didn't talk to anybody. No role model there.

All the adults around me were already old. Poor, but kind. I was never spanked. The only thing I ever had to do in the way of chores was help my grandmother in the garden. We grew most all of our own food. She was highly educated, but she only put shoes on when winter came. During the summertime, she went barefooted. Because of her education, a lot of people, especially women, came to her for advice. She never told me nothing. She just kept giving me books to read, all kind of books.

In those early days, I had one good friend three miles away by the dirt roads and cow paths—Eugene Creek. He came from a real poor family, Creek Indians who lived way back in the woods. He and I would get in the creek beds and walk for hours. The river bottoms are cut into the land, so people up on the roads and in the fields can't see you. All the little wild critters are there. We played, but it wasn't about winning. A little world, a universe all its own, only for children.

One time, I built a little stone hut on a bluff overlooking the river in the woods. That was my first meditation place. No one ever found it. Eugene and I would walk fourteen miles to town and fourteen miles back. With a one-dollar bill, we'd buy a twelve-cent pack of Camel cigarettes and a cone of sherbet ice cream. We'd smoke those cigarettes all the way home. Man, we felt so big and mature and rich having those tailor-made cigarettes instead of the homemade rolling tobacco everyone else was smoking.

We had nature back then, and nature teaches you a lot. If you're young and there's a void there, nature will fill it. I worry about kids these days growing up with computers and no affectionate parents. It's dehumanizing.

My first dog was named Tinker. When I was seven or eight, he got all tore up by these wild dogs that came running through the hills. My grandma figured they probably had rabies, and that Tinker had to be put down. For some strange reason, I had this idea that I couldn't let somebody else do that. I had to do it. I took a maddock, which is like a hoe, and slipped the big heavy handle out from the head. I took Tinker back in the woods and had him sit down, and hit him right on top of the head as hard as I could. I cried. Then I covered him up, and went home. That was my first experience of violence. Quick. Physical. I felt sadness mixed with awe and mystery. I went into a zone. It was traumatic.

~

When my grandmother died, my Aunt May scooped me up and decided she would get me an education, and that I should be a doctor because doctors made a lot of money. I was eleven, twelve, something like that. She had married an older man, a German banker in Cincinnati, Ohio who was rich—three-story home, indoor and outdoor pools, a billiard room, da-da-da. Okay, she didn't take me to live there, she just put me in a series of expensive boarding schools. Catholic, all kinds. As I got older I went to be with different uncles and aunts on the summer vacations from these boarding schools. Their kids sat on the couch and read comic books, and I did the chores because I had to earn my way—the token hired hand. The parents didn't realize their kids were spoiled. That's how I remember it.

In the Catholic boarding school—boys and priests and brothers—they were all mean, and sick, sick, sick about religion. I ran away, and got kicked out. So my aunt took me out, and let me try to live with them in Los Angeles. She had remarried by then. I think she married seven times in all, most of it for money. She was a beautiful woman, beautiful. They had an apartment with a large walk-in closet. They put a bunk in there, and that was my room. So that's how I started going to public school.

When I turned sixteen, the bully of the school decided that since I was such a big kid, kind of goofy and clumsy, he would whack me up and earn a notch on his gun. So he did, he whacked me a couple of times. Then I proceeded to clean his clock. The authorities told me, you're going to reformatory for this. So I went to my aunt, and I did a little psychology on her. I said, "Look, if they put me in the reform school, it'll seem you didn't take care of me, and you'll get a bad reputation. But if you let me go into the Army, it won't look so bad." She signed the papers, and at sixteen I went off to the Army, to the Airborne. I never finished high school.

In the Airborne, I jumped out of airplanes. Never landed in an airplane for years. I always jumped out of them. It was during the Korean conflict and I don't . . . I don't go there at all. Bad memories, so let's just say I was in the Airborne. For about a year and a half, two years. I was an angry young man. I wouldn't think twice about shooting somebody.

When I came out of the Army, my anger was at circumstances, not at any person. I was angry over the fact I didn't get to grow up with parents, I didn't get to have a bicycle, I didn't get to have siblings, I didn't get to have a home. My other grandmother was illiterate, but she was the only one who let me know, just by everything she did, that she actually cared for me and loved me. Without that, it would have been hard to know the emotion. I was just generally pissed off at circumstances, which meant I was a dangerous guy because I had no conscience. I was in my late thirties or forties before I understood that a lot of the stuff I did was because of my anger.

Anyway, I rented an apartment in L.A., got a job, and went to work. I sent my aunt some money, and bought myself a convertible car, a yellow one. Chasing girls, dating pretty girls, was a big part of my life at that point. My first love, Patty, didn't love me. I sat in front of her house and cried. Eventually, I got into trouble and went to prison.

The way it came down was, I wanted more money than I could make at a nine-to-five job—eighty bucks a week take-home, about average for a labor-type dude in those days. I wanted all the good stuff, the toys, so I got a pistol and started doing some armed robberies. Liquor stores, supermarkets, places that always had cash. I could rationalize it by telling myself, "Their insurance will cover the loss. As long as I don't hurt anybody seriously, I'll be all right."

The first time I did that, I was helping a friend who was going to lose his car.

I found out robbery wasn't that difficult, and it was nice to have a whole stack of hundreds on your table. Then my friend got in trouble, turned state's witness and gave me up. When I got out of prison, the first guy that met me was his dad, saying, "Please don't kill my son." That was it for that friendship.

~

I was in prison almost three years. I got a job in the hospital where I could help people. I worked my way up to being the pharmacist. I had some disability checks from the Army for messing up my back, so I bought books. I figure I averaged almost a book a day. During that time, I got interested in yoga and Buddhism. Paramahansa Yogananda was one of the first, and the *Dhammapada*. I read Emerson and the Transcendentalists, and all of the psychologists I could get my hands on. I liked Carl Gustav Jung the best. He's one of the guys that got me going on Buddhism. When he was dying, he read *The Tibetan Book of the Dead*.

In prison, you have to be politic and pay off people with cigarettes and things like that in order to get the privacy of a cell. At first, you're in a dormitory. From there, if you're fortunate, you can get in a cell with somebody else. Then, if you've got enough cigarettes or enough ducats, the form of money, you end up with a single cell. Nobody is going to take care of you, so you have to take care of yourself. We ate a whole lot of shit on a shingle, ground beef with gravy on cold toast. In the food line, somebody may be getting their throat cut or a knife shoved in their kidney right in front of you.

You learn how to be kind of invisible in prison. They call it, "doing your own time." That means you don't snivel to somebody else. Nobody wants to hear your problems, how you feel or how your family's doing. They don't want to hear that shit. They'll look at you and say, "Hey, man, do your own time." And that's how it goes. Nobody's allowed to be friends.

Prison doesn't deter people from crime. That's bullshit, especially with career criminals. It's like a vacation for them. They get fresh clothes, fresh linen, three meals a day, a library, a free room, free medical care. Sending all these people to prison is just another business. That's why prisons have become privately owned. It's the money involved.

I learned to sit in prison. Having been in a Catholic boarding school, I didn't want to have anything to do with Christianity or organized religion. I'd seen too much hypocrisy in the preachers I'd met. When they showed me a way that I could expand my mind and become happier without any of that, I went, right on! I sat *zazen*. I took a pen and I made a dot the size of a dime, a perfect black circle on a white wall in my cell. Then I sat on my bunk, and stared at that circle until it went away. Hardly anyone else was doing this kind of thing, so I was kind of a freak. But people didn't make fun of it, because I was the pharmacist and I could hide their stash.

I'm just a fictitious character, but what I'm telling you is the truth. This is my life. That's why I'm so grateful. I've had a good life. Given all the foolish things I did, I should have been killed several times over. It's all just a story. As Carl Jung said, "You are as you see yourself." I would add, "You are as each person sees you." In that sense, who can know? And what does it matter?

≈

When I got out of prison, I went to work at a shipping and packaging place the parole officer had helped me find. I met a guy on the job who wanted me to be a wrassler, an amateur wrassler. I told him, "No, no, no, I don't want to hurt people any more." He said, "Well, I really like you, so if you don't want to do this, I'm going to talk to my brother at the Hollywood Teamsters."

The union is really tight. If you can get in, you work. That was the first decent job I had. It paid good. I drove the stars. Got to be good friends with a few. One of them, Warren Oates, found out that we grew up about forty miles from each other in Kentucky. Then I met the director Sam Peckinpah, who says, "I'll make you a star." I says, "No, you won't. I'm not doing that."

I was still making less than a hundred dollars take-home a week at the studios, when this friend of mine said he wanted to sail to Mexico. There was a lot of money involved. I said I'm in for that. As hard to believe as it might seem, I didn't do it for the money. Sure, I was concerned about going back to prison, but when in hell was a little hillbilly like me going to get a chance to sail down the Pacific in a 59-foot schooner? Ain't gonna happen. That's why I did it, for the excitement, for the thrill. I'm not advising kids to smuggle in order to have a wonderful experience, but that's what happened to me.

The owner of the boat was one of the youngest guys ever in the Rand Think Tank. Really smart, but neither of us had ever sailed a big boat. So I got a book called *Seamanship & Small Boat Handling*, and he bought the boat, and we took off for Mexico. With the first load we brought back, we paid off the boat. After that, we went again. By then we had a suitcase full of hundreds, and I said, "It's going to raise a flag." He made the third trip without me, and got busted. I lost my share of the boat, but maintained my freedom. I spent the money, of course.

After I got out of prison, I met a young woman, Lila. Totally wild, really beautiful. She had far more experience in life than I had. She lived with her mother in the middle of Hollywood, and had taken LSD, and was just a swinger. So she and I became fruitarians, and I'm going around dipping my head in doorways of any kind of Buddhist thing I can find in L.A. I read an article that the San Francisco Zen Center was going to start a monastery in Big Sur.

I wanted to get some structure to my meditation practice, and I had enough sense to know that I didn't know everything. The only Zen master I'd ever heard of, Suzuki Roshi, was opening a new place near San Francisco, so away we went, Lila and me, in my old '51 Chevy pickup truck with a camper. We got there before it opened, and were among the first five people — two caretakers, another guy, Lila and I. We stayed there for a year and a half.

When I met Suzuki Roshi at Tassajara, I was down in this old foundation with a pick and shovel, digging a ditch. I looked up, and there were his shoes. I looked up a little further, and there's this little guy in brown robes, smiling big at me, and I'm smiling big at him from out the hole. I said, "Well, I've waited a long time to meet a Zen master, and here you are, and I can't think of a thing to say." Suzuki Roshi thought that was hilarious.

You had to write a letter saying why you wanted to be there. I said I came to practice Buddhism in harmony with other people. I stressed the harmony part. They said, "Okay, you can stay." I had read D.T. Suzuki, and the few things I could get my hands on in prison. Not much literature about it in those days, and not a lot of Zen places opening up. Everything was just new. I didn't know what was going on from moment to moment.

At Tassajara, we were encouraged not to talk to each other, and definitely not talk about our practice, and definitely, definitely not talk about *dokusan*, the formal private meeting with the teacher, who gave everybody the medicine that they needed. He didn't have no stock thing. That's the way dharma is — not something you can get out of a book. You can prepare with books, and you can study it with books, but when the action happens, there's no language involved. Psychedelics made me aware of many other dimensions and want to explore my mind. I've sat and had the room fill up with billowing clouds and have a heavy incense smell. What did that, my imagination? What do I know? Psychedelics gave me a tongue tip taste, but sitting zazen gives you a full belly.

Then the bullshit started at Tassajara. That happens when you have a lot of people practicing together. Little groups of people would split off and say that we don't like this guy or that guy, and we think this should be done this way and that way. I saw a lot of stuff I didn't like, so I told the teacher, "I'm out of here."

There was a young monk there from Japan, Kobun, who was the one was really available to us. He and Suzuki Roshi translated the Heart Sutra into English, the one that everybody chants. He was like a mom to many of those guys. He planted, cultivated, nurtured and brought it all to harvest, and then stepped back and stood in the back row. Didn't say a word. That's one of the reasons I love him so much. He became a teacher and friend to me for the rest of his life.

≈

I had relationships with a lot of women in my life, incredibly beautiful women, but I don't believe any of them ever cared much about me. It was more about them. Except for Lila. Lila actually cared about me and many other people more than she did herself. Very touching. She took an enormous amount of LSD, so she was blissed out half the time. Everybody would say she's gaga, she laughs too much, always saying how pretty everything is. The only thing Lila was interested in was doing a little yoga with me. She was happier than most of the people, and they condemned her. Bless her for that.

Many years later, we were living in a temple in the mountains. Lila didn't want to be living there. It's such a public life, sort of a fishbowl. Anyway, our love survived all that. We don't seem to be able to live together, but we still love each other after all these years. Still talk on the phone. She still sends me coffee. We were together twenty-two years. It's difficult living with me, I can see that now. She's definitely happier. She loves the ocean, and loves Hawaii, where she lives now. If you love somebody, the best of all worlds is that they be happy, even if it means they're not with you. So that's where that is.

≈

The philosophy of Buddhism is what saved my proverbial ass. Suzuki Roshi was the first one that really talked seriously to me about compassion wisdom. He said it was like your hand. One side of your hand is compassion, the other is wisdom. Just opposite sides of the same thing. Compassion is the better part of wisdom. It's the root of wisdom. Then I learned about caring. It's taken years and years for it to grow and mature in me—the caring for other people, the bad people, the uncaring people, the nasty, mean people, and all the rest, down to and including insects. They're all just part of what I am.

I learned impermanence early. If you go to your mom's funeral when you're four, you get it straight. What I saw at Tassajara, and in the world generally, was not harmony but disharmony. People couldn't agree on anything. If you got three people together, you couldn't screw in a light bulb. The world doesn't look any different to me today. A lot of waste. Like the Dalai Lama keeps saying, you don't need this, you don't need that. Don't get me started.

Practicing means being what we really are. Embodying the understanding of emptiness. Nothing to attain! You just help people. Most people just want someone to listen and know that someone cares. My buddy Dale, who I live next door to, is the most compassionate person I know. He'll do anything for anybody. He's never read a word of Buddhism. He cares for people, truly. He doesn't close the door on anyone. He doesn't judge. Just keeps on giving it up.

Dying. I hope it's an interesting adventure. I've taken more than a few hallucinogens, so I've been here and there. I pretty much go with the *Shunyata** thing, so I think it's probably going to be a little hum and a click and bye-bye. I'm not freaked out about it. I know something's going to kill me—you don't get out of here alive—but so far I've been lucky. I've seen people go out in several ways. Screaming, moaning, groaning, or just with a desperate glance. I'm going to try to remember to breathe, and be aware for as much of it as I can. In case there's something there, I don't want to miss it. I've thought several times that if things got rough, I'd pull the plug on myself. Take a long walk off a short pier. If somebody says, you're going to die in a month or six weeks, I'd be all right with that. But if they say you're going to live for a year, but you're going to suffer incredibly—oh, yeah? Watch this.

At eighty, though, it's a little late to start worrying about it. About any of it.

We're going around in a circle anyway. You don't have to worry about "getting older." Your body/mind is going to make it easy to become like a child again anyway. So it's something else that everybody spends a lot of time worrying about that you don't have to worry about!

Most people would say I've been totally unsuccessful. I was living for the experience of it, not for the rewards. I've had such a good life. The only emotion I have or want to have now is gratitude. The most fortunate thing that happened to me in my life has been people. It wasn't anything that I did or know about. I just have known some of the most beautiful people. One of my teachers said, "People are the flowers of life." And I've had a bouquet on my table most of my life.

---

* *Shunyata* (Sanskrit): Emptiness. Fullness that includes everything. A completely open and unbounded clarity of mind characterized by groundlessness and freedom from all conceptual frameworks.

What Would You Love Women to Understand?

> "A 90 lb. woman can fell a 300 lb. man
> in a single conversation."

Here I come back to the very first question I asked. I saved it for last: "What would you love women to understand?" I know there are some things I would like men to understand about women; I figured that the same might be true in reverse.

Some men were brimming with response and immediately had a lot to say, as if—phew!—finally someone's asking! Some paused, thoughtfully, and let the words find them. Several were stopped by the question altogether. Nothing came. I offered to come back to it later. In some cases we did, in others, we didn't. More than a few seemed surprised that anyone would ask. Especially, a woman.

≈

If women could understand us it would be awesome. If they asked more questions to the men, they'd know how they work their life.

Well, how men do is they stick to their ground and hold onto things for kind of a long time. Because they feel they have to be super strong. I don't know why. But then they just get tired of holding it. They don't want to have to deal with it anymore. Kind of a relief. Like with feelings, I throw them out so I don't have to have them.

I think it's kind of up to women to be helping men more because they have more tools. They're allowed to develop those tools better. Men should get a few more tools to understand. They don't have that many. Women have tools before they even know they have them. My mom has more tools and, if she could use them more it helps with my dad and with me, and that's how we're going to learn.

(9 yr.)

To not think that boys are disgusting. To not say things like "Girls rule and boys drool." Because we're just, different. Some boys like to do more dirtier things, but that doesn't make them disgusting.

(10 yr.)

If women could understand that it's not all easy and laid back for the men then they would start trusting the men more and maybe relax more.

(11 yr.)

I would like girls to understand that men and boys have some problems that the girls don't even know about. Like the peer pressure is different. Boys do a lot more dangerous stuff. They *want* to, but also, sometimes we feel *pressured* to because friends do it and if we don't, we'll be made fun of and then also be called a girl and stuff like that.

(12 yr.)

I want them to know I'm different than them, differently abled. Don't judge me by the outside. And just love me for who I am.

(14 yr.)

Guys wanna go and invite girls over to their house and have sex with them. What's the reason for that? It's really just about feeling loved. A part of you that wants to feel loved and accepted by the girls.

(17 yr.)

Guys have a lot of fear of being rejected. We get scarred by those rejections. The least comment can set us off. It's all we've got to go on.

(17 yr.)

I'd like women to understand that it takes a lot of work in this culture to not just be a guy who wants to get in fights and sleep with everybody and all that stuff. I get hassled, especially by partners, almost like they have to just pigeonhole me, as if I must be a "guy" even though I try so hard not to be a "man" in the negative sense. I think I've spent a lot more time trying to not be a "man" than actually learning how to be one.

I don't even know if using the word "man" is the right thing, because I think it's so beautiful to be a man and you can do it so well, and some of the masculine qualities are so needed and great. But there's a bad reputation, and I feel like it's hard for women to get past that, even when you're not really playing into it.

(20s)

I grew up in quiet mind and need more time alone. I'd like to have that be okay. What I'd want a woman to understand is that it's important to figure out how to coexist — be a friend or a partner with somebody, and not try to change them. Take 'em as they are. Accept them for who they are. If somebody needs somebody else to change so much, how are they feeling about themselves?

Also, I want to say to moms, "You gotta let me figure it out . . . You've got a whole lot of different things going on that us men won't understand either. Just, let go."

(20s)

In sex-ed classes, it'd be great if they taught more about communicating directly, about real love-making instead of just, "This is a penis, this is a vagina, don't get AIDS." They could show non-porno examples of couples just loving each other and talking about all the fears and doubts, pressures and anxieties. If women could get that guys have these feelings, too, then they wouldn't be so mystified or misled.

(20s)

If I'm romantically interested, I worry if she'll be interested in me and I revert back to shyness. But with women I'm not interested in — I can be myself. I wish the romantic ones could see me for who I am.

(20s)

That I show my love in little ways, throughout the day. Most go unrecognized.

(30s)

Something along the lines of — I'm sorry that I need you to reassure and comfort me, but I can't help it, I need it. And at the same time, I'm ashamed of that.

The potential to totally unseat me has solely belonged to women. I'm very aware that I've given that power, but I'm still a little fearful of it. I'm scared to acknowledge that I've failed to respect that power.

I'm really tired of the way men treat women. It's horse shit. I'm just really tired of men. I think we've been excusing ourselves. Women are still raped? How is that still so common? I don't know how to deal with that. I see men out on the prowl all the time in the bars and I just despise them — but I got 'em, I got all those desires too. I get it. I see it in myself. I disgust myself.

It's kind of funny to say, but I think a woman's sex is different than a man's. There's a little bit of the sacred in it.

(30s)

If a man and woman are co-creating a new kind of relationship, it can be very scary. And, very alive! If women turning thirty are obsessed with having a baby and pushing a man, then they're not co-creators. They're only seeing him in a limited way, as a solution, not for who he is. They put their fear as pressure on him, feeling anxious and in a hurry. Kind of takes the fun out of dating.

(30s)

We have nowhere to relax and just be ourselves. With all this armoring, of course we want to be touched.

(30s)

I've heard from women — "Oh, he's just a pushover. He'll get you whatever you want." Well, maybe he will, but it's not because he's a pushover. *It's his strength.* he really, genuinely wants you to be happy. It takes a lot of strength to go out of your comfort zone to please or accommodate you — to help provide happiness.

Another thing — there seems to be a notion that men just want sex. I think one thing that men really want and don't necessarily get is we do really want to *be touched*. Not necessarily sexual touch. But being touched is the most wonderful and relaxing and loving thing — it can just be patting your hair, rubbing your neck. It's magical. At least in my own life, the actual sex is secondary to that need. For men, physical intimacy is a gateway to emotional intimacy.

(30s)

Essentially, talking with each other about sex more. Especially as a teenager. It's totally taboo. We had co-ed sex classes, but it was like health education—like how to put a condom on a banana. It wasn't sex-ed *communication* classes. Like, "Here's what it's like to be a 16-year-old male in the society and here's what it's like to be a 16-year-old female." You know, "I hate being catcalled continuously, having my butt pinched, my boobs grabbed. That sucks. What the hell do you guys think you're doing?" I mean, you and I normally wouldn't talk about this, but there is a forum for it.

If it got down to a real level—"Well, actually, you know, I just want your attention. I want to be touched by you. I want to be close to you. I want to be able to talk with you in a real way. I think you are totally attractive and beautiful, and I want to have a closer connection with you."

(30s)

Male sexuality feels . . . there's a certain animal rawness, physical. It needs an acceptance, some sort of welcoming in, or else I can feel like I can't come out with it. It might be too intense for her.

(30s)

Well I wish someone had told me—look, you're not going to get it right the first time. Maybe, not even the second time.

(30s)

What matters is just simple, simple, simple. Gestures, touches, acknowledgements. Simple little things.

(30s)

When I share my vulnerability, reveal a piece of myself, I often lose the relationship. I'm no longer the guy she expects me to be. So I'm confused.

(30s)

Men are way more sensitive than women think we are—even the roughest, gruffest, you know, solitary loner figure. In fact, probably those people are even more sensitive than most.

I think women need to realize that the solution to many of their needs comes from within, from things that they haven't uncovered in their own lives or come to terms with. To expect a partner to make you happy is not only unfair, it's unrealistic. It's more fun to feel like you're a team, as opposed to being the coach all the time. I feel like many men just want to feel they can take care of a woman. That's what they're really looking for—to feel like he's protecting somebody, or fulfilling someone's needs. I'd like someone who isn't trying to change me, but that also challenges me.

(30s)

I wish men and women would be more honest with each other about what's really going on. When women want children they often don't think about what that's going to do to the man's life. If a woman isn't putting away money for a mortgage or a kid's education, she's not taking equal responsibility. It's a heavy expectation on men. Men's work is taken for granted. That's a big weight of responsibility. The feminist movement seems to have taught women that work gives them an identity and support, but *not* that it supports a *family.*

A man wants a safe place where he can let down and not be judged and made fun of. A haven. If a woman doesn't have that ground herself, a man doesn't feel safe enough, in a deep sense, to fall apart. Safe means that you can fall apart—which means you get to be creative. Not always be the one holding it all together.

(30s)

Men are looking for something to give their lives to. We want to know we're not a waste of time. We can't have babies, so we need to create. Make our mark somehow.

(30s)

Give me my space. Don't try to fix me. Sometimes I need to go away into my whatever, and I'll come back when I'm ready. Being non-judgmental is really important. A lot of women are attracted to jerks—an alcoholic, an addict, a partier, a womanizer—and they end up trying to change them. Then, when they get in over their heads, they realize they can't. I've changed in my relationship because I *wanted* to change. She's not trying to change me.

(30s)

The most important thing women should know about men is that we're not women. You know, you can sit there and work really hard at seeing someone, but it takes a long time to really get out of your way and really, truly see someone as they *are.*

Men will try to meet you half way. Give us something we can do, we'll do it. You have to put it in our world where we understand it. Then we'll gladly do it for you for nothing, because we're glad to make you happy. We like to make you happy. If you're really good friends, it'll all work out.

Just know that most of what you consider love is fantasy. It has nothing to do with the dude or who he is.

And oh, wait a minute. Know you use entirely too much toilet paper. It is an astounding thing for a guy to experience the amount of toilet paper usage — a lifetime supply in one month. Toilet paper is like the female duct tape; pretty much anything can be solved with it. Instead of having us agonize over where it goes and what you do with it, just buy the toilet paper yourself. Life will be better, I'm telling you.

(40s)

I've heard women complain that men don't listen, but when I start to share vulnerable feelings, it seems it's too much for them. They'd rather I go back to "being a man."

(40s)

It would be nice if women could understand that we're struggling to re-educate ourselves, and learning to be healthy partners.

(40s)

A woman has a lot of power in relation to a man. If she uses it negatively, she can really crush him.

(40s)

Almost all my girlfriends who were younger and got married, they all say about themselves, "I was gorgeous and didn't know it." No matter what age you are, what girls should know is they're perfect right now. Just enjoy the shit out of it.

(40s)

When the women in my office come to me with a problem, I often think, "Okay, I'm gonna need to fix this." But then, I realized, "Oh, they just wanna vent." If women could give a clue when they just need to process and let us know — "I'm not asking for anyone to fix this. I just need to say this," it would help.

(40s)

When the guy gets upset, girls assume it's something they did. But you know, most of the time the guy's going to tell you if it's about you. If they're not saying it's about you, then don't assume. Because, in reality, guys are more romantic in a lot of ways than girls are.

(40s)

I'd like women to understand how clueless most men are, or feel, about their fundamental lack of confidence about fulfilling what they assume a man should be. So you're always kind of skating on the thin ice of uncertainty about what you think your role, your job is.

If women would understand that men really are just little boys. We're expected to know what's going on and have it all together. We want to be held and told it's okay. We want tenderness.

(50s)

When I'm vulnerable, when that's accepted, I feel like there's room for me to be a man. If a woman can just join me where I am. I mean, sometimes I do need to be mothered. But if I don't need to be mothered and she goes there, then she's not seeing me. She's creating something herself or acting something out. And if she's doing it to protect herself, under the guise of holding me, like, "That's too much for me, so let me mother you." Then I say, "Wait, wait, stay away from me."

(50s)

When I'm anxious to please a woman and be loved by her, I want to answer her questions well, so I get into trouble. I invent answers to please. I'm not totally honest and forthright, which puts me in a compromising position. If I answer truthfully, saying, "I don't know," and that isn't good enough for her, then she'll go for the guy who's willing to lie, leaving me out in the cold. I'd love to tell the truth and be honored for that, be loved all the more for it.

(50s)

That all men aren't just out to get laid, you know. When you're younger, a lot of them are. But men should not just be judged by that. It's okay to be quiet and not talk at every minute of the day. Just because you're not speaking, doesn't mean there's anything wrong.

(50s)

I'm just a big hairy man and all that stuff, but I feel more like a sensitive woman most of the time. I'm loud and raucous, so it's perfectly understandable why people, women especially, would think that I don't understand their softer, more sensitive side, which is what I try to do. I want to be able to do that, that's sort of a reason for being. I don't want to be insensitive, even though I'm a typical boy most of the time. It belies this feeling inside of me.

(50s)

I would like first to understand myself. Then, maybe, a woman can understand me.

(50s)

If a woman is really open, I feel lust for her, *or* I feel intimidated because I'm afraid I can't match it. Especially if it's a woman I really care about.

(50s)

That all men want is sex is a fallacy. Yeah, I want sex, but deeper than that, I want to be loved unconditionally. We will give our last breath for that. Sex is just the entry point.

There is nothing more insecure than a man. Period. The bigger and badder we are, the more afraid we are. Oh, my God, especially around a woman. A 90 lb. woman can fell a 300 lb. man in a single conversation. It's called power.

Make it simple. Because we're wired. Watch the mechanical repetition of the maleness happen. Look at this mechanical man trying to respond to this watery woman who moves about in two directions at once — vertically and horizontally — slithering across the water. Making movements through areas that no man can possibly navigate — emotionally, psychically, physically, so on. This is not for men — these territories. We're stuck with this maleness.

(50s)

What would I love for women to understand? Sexual needs. The overrating of monogamy in long-term relationships. We need to appreciate the need and wants in other humans. If you have out-of-the-box fantasies and you tell your partner, she just kind of looks at you. She probably has fantasies herself, but totally different ones and they don't necessarily meld. I've been with my partner 30 years. She's the best friend I've ever had, mother of my children, supporter of all that I am . . . How do you keep it fresh and lively?

(50s)

Nothing to make the self breathe a little easier than the love of a woman. Not complicated. I don't need sex every day. I want love as many ways as I can get it. Get what? Just a brush. You know a little wind goes by. Something. It could be in a cup of tea. It could be in the dinner. It can be anywhere. I can find it. I am not blind. The whole world depends on it, and yet I don't know if it will or it won't happen.

(50s)

I think men are looking for some refuge. How great it would be to have someone who has seen all these pieces and knows how hard it's been, knows the lies you've had to tell, the compromises you've had to make, the things you've had to let go of, and the parts of yourself you couldn't claim, you had to disown, etc., etc. Because, everybody gets tired. I may be on the downward spiral of this worldly game, but maybe on the upward spiral into wisdom.

To have a woman who's there who will listen to you and hold your vulnerabilities and nurture you and unconditionally accept you — that's what men want. And not, in the most vulnerable times, for the woman to say, "Well, cowboy up," or, "Get back out there." "I'm counting on you."

(50s)

We love you, we respect you, we want you. We yearn for your acceptance, your love and understanding. We want to be a part of your life.

(50s)

I'd like women to understand more about what I do. The *value* of it. What my work is. Have more empathy, increased appreciation. I feel there's a rivalry with my wife because she resents that I know what I love to do. I love my work. She's supportive of what I do for *financial* reasons.

(50s)

Women stepping into their power, being authentically present and guiding men into a more harmonious way, because they have the skills and tools and practice. Men stepping back and learning to listen. That's what we need.

(50s)

I would love for women to be able to truly accept that I'm doing the best that I can in each moment. That doesn't mean that I can't do better, but that in any particular moment, I am actually doing my best, whatever it looks like. If I feel that acceptance and appreciation, then I tend to be not only open but am eager to learn from their input and especially from their example.

(60s)

Difference can be a benefit rather than an obstacle. I have a different perspective than a woman has because I have a different set of experiences that may or may not be gender-based. It's just difference. Maybe what I'm trying to get to is — acceptance and relishing difference and not letting it get in the way. Trusting that I am as sincere as she is about dealing with whatever the issues are in front of us.

(60s)

What would I like for women to understand? That we can't do it for you. We can't rescue you. We're all swimming in the same sea.

(60s)

How hard it is for me to get access to my emotional life and speak of it and how much I'd like to, but I don't know how. Be patient with me.

(60s)

I'd like women to understand that men are not as they seem to be. There's a very rich deep interior, emotional, often spiritual, certainly psychologically questing life that I find in men of almost all categories, walks of life, and classes, that often doesn't get seen because of the conditioning layers on top. And the way men and women play to each other's stereotype works both ways. It keeps those layers from emerging in relaxed and authentic ways with women when, in fact, they *can* often emerge with other men, depending upon the situation.

Because of hierarchal male culture, men are required to behave with each other a particular way and that then makes it hard to move out of that. The way men are required or conditioned to behave with each other is *profoundly* influenced by the presence of women. Whether it's carrying one's mother with them psychologically or one's wife, a few blocks away, or whether it's one's girlfriend who walks into the bar when you're having a conversation with the other guys. It's hooked into their relationship to and their sense of being perceived and being successful with women.

I think a lot of women, certainly young women, don't understand how much power they have over men. Men have been conditioned to sacrifice for the family, the tribe, the nation; and hopefully soon, for the planet. It's built into us. We want to be warriors. We *are* warriors, and we need acknowledgment. We need women to notice us, appreciate us, and put some of their fairy dust on us. The old knight thing — the woman gives her little scarf to the guy who goes off to risk his life — it's idiocy at one level, but it's been deeply ingrained.

Never assume that we know what you're talking about, and always do perception checks because we're just in our own movies.

(60s)

Men need their space away from women.

(60s)

All men really want is to be respected. Not because we're men, but to be respected simply for who we actually are. It's that simple. Respect and love, combo.

(60s)

I wish women would stop making themselves into something they're not. All that fashion and makeup. You're great just the way you are. And I don't understand those spike heels. What are they thinking?

(60s)

I don't have a misunderstanding of women. I have *no* understanding of women!

(60s)

I'd like women to understand there is hope for us. Therefore there is hope for the human race, for human beings, for what we can be together. And women are the primary reason. They started it with the feminist movement.

(60s)

Women come into the world knowing, but they are told they don't know. Men come into the world not knowing, but they are told they know. This creates insecurity.

(60s)

I just want to be seen and loved for who I *am*. Not as a provider. Not for my accomplishments. Not for what I can do for you.

(60s)

This may sound chauvinistic, and I don't want to offend you, but I think men should still have that final say. I know there's a lot of women wearing the pants in the family nowadays. My younger son is married to one. But I still think that last little bit should be for the man.

(70s)

I don't define myself by being a sports person who is associated with masculin-ity or a hunter or a male sex symbol or whatever. I just define myself as a human who has interests. When I no longer have to define myself, I don't find myself being defined by others. Like Popeye, I am what I am!

(70s)

If only women could understand that we're not the same. Why can't that be all right? Not try to change us and remake us. I think men fall into two classes — either they become subservient to women or they dominate them out of fear of being subservient.

(70s)

Don't separate us from our childhood friends. Let us be who we are. I like a woman who will sit down, look me in the eye and communicate on a deeper level.

(70s)

It's not always great to have to always be the leader. Sometimes it's nice to be led.

(70s)

Men feel inadequate. My feeling is it all stems from the fact that women can have multiple orgasms whereas we are pretty much "one and done." *And* we can't give birth. So, we feel inferior. Traditionally, feeling fear and wanting to feel safe, men have felt a need for control and domination.

(70s)

Well, this is a very complex question to answer. If I were twelve, I could do it.

(80s)

What would I like women to understand? Oh, my. They already know more than me. A *lot* more!

(90s)

I came from a different age. Don't try to change me. I may be wrong, but I think a lot of women think, when they marry, if there are bad points, they'll correct them. A man tries to stand by his beliefs, but if he wants to get along with the woman, he eventually has to become milquetoast. So, I will tell you my secret. Instead of arguing and slamming doors, yelling, just say, "Yes, dear." And do what you're going to do anyway.

(90s)

~

I like pink. It's just a color. It's actually one of my favorite colors, pink and purple. People say girl colors. They always say red is a boy color because it's blood and they say boys always love blood and girls always like happiness. Like some grown-ups, when someone wears pink, the other grown-up thinks he's gay. I know what it means because my older brother, he told me a lot of it, but how would he be gay if he was wearing pink? If he wants to wear pink, why not? Why not?

I've never tried wearing pink to school. No, but it's like I do just blurt out, there you go, like anybody who asks, I tell them I like pink and purple and I do crocheting and I have a pink crochet hook and I'm not gay and who cares anyway? Just because you're a boy doesn't mean you have to be the strongest person in the world. I can be whatever I want! It's a free country! It's a free world!

You know, the bully guy thinks there is a girl and a boy color. Also, he thinks a guy in our class, his name is Earl, a lot of people say he's a girl because he plays with a bunch of girls and he has fun. I'm telling everybody he's playing with the girls because he wants to play the game he wants. It's not like fairy time or anything. He likes Star Wars, so he wants to play it. And the girls are playing it.

I've got girl in me *and* boy in me. Of course I do.

(9 yr.)

In Common

"From the moment of birth every human being wants happiness and wants to avoid suffering. In this we are all the same."

— DALAI LAMA

Afterword

While I was interviewing these men and boys, there was no place else I'd rather be. There we were, human beings sitting together on the front porch of our lives, sharing stories. I loved getting to be with men in this way, just listening, without blame or judgment as best I could, wondering—Who is this? Like listening to a part of myself I hadn't yet fully included. I loved who it let me be. Most of the time, it felt like dancing.

Later though, finding a way to put together what I heard so that, as a male editor said, "it would be tolerable to males," was more like carrying a plate of water!

This inquiry was born of heartache. The sorrow of not knowing how to reach one another when this is so much our common human longing. I wanted to keep my heart and mind open. Especially at this time of life, that's what matters to me most. And it's what sustained me through this years' long journey, when some of my friends began to wonder about me. Sometimes, I began to wonder, too. But I had the encouragement of a few close friends and several of the guys who, when my spirit flagged, insisted, "You're onto something. Keep going." On one of the later drafts, when I was feeling close to giving up, a twenty-year-old man I'd never met who had just finished binding the manuscript, handed it across the counter, looked me in the eye and said: "I implore you to continue."

I wanted to learn to love well. I wanted to look into the violence in my own heart and not add to the aggression on the planet. "Everything included," a beloved older friend once said to me. "If you have any idea of 'us and them,' you're going the wrong way."

I got to practice listening and staying open. Whenever my heart clicked closed with thought, ideas of blame, judgment, making wrong, my own impatience or projection — reacting with the whole array of human habits — so did the exchange. When I took a breath and relaxed, suspended my beliefs long enough to put myself in their shoes, and let myself just listen and *not know*, the world lit up. It was like falling in love again and again with life ~

~

I was listening for that boy.

I was hearing the stories boys were told about "being a man" — the pressures and expectations, all the things they're "supposed to" know and be, how they have to hide their fears and their tears, listen *away* from the soft and wise voice of their own knowing and learn to cover their sensitivity with anger or blame, with shame or arrogance, the other side of the coin. This "misunderstanding of maleness," a 50-year-old called it. So many men scared away from the aliveness of the present moment. We are all complicit.

The most surprising thing to me was the pervasiveness of violence that boys are growing up with, the fear it inspires, and the fact that many men, when speaking about it, did not consider it "violence" or "abuse." A man would tell me he hadn't had any violence in his life and then, as we talked, the memories would begin to emerge and stories of the immense suffering caused by trauma, abuse and neglect.

All of the men I listened to had endured some kind of violence. Or, as a 67-year-old man added, the *fear* of violence, which is another form of violence. If it hadn't happened at home, by the time they got to school or camp, or were out on the street, they were initiated. Most boys had little help or guidance dealing with the feelings they were left with. Few felt permitted to talk about them. "We live in a violent culture of blame and shame," a man in his 40s told me, "and there's not a lot of help knowing what to do with it." This same man continued, "There's more cultural permission to be angry and violent than there is for men to be vulnerable."

I wasn't hearing support for the bravery it takes to feel the vulnerability in the anger, move into the pain and fear, and let it turn to a kind of gentle sadness. If you're scared away, as a boy, from innate empathy, and trained instead to dominate, it would be easy to get hooked on control. It's not natural, but for many, it becomes habitual. Some even create an identity based on their ability to control other people's lives.

If fear is off limits for a man, how can he ever get to know it and make friends with it? For a brief while, being really angry feels so alive! Listening helped me appreciate why so many men feel a need to be in control in order to feel safe; and how this need manifests in the privacy of their minds and homes, and shapes their world view.

Now when I find a situation challenging, my new mantra is "Oh, *they don't know how.*" Not to excuse or justify behavior I find difficult—like not listening, dominating, interrupting—or to condone any other forms of aggression, but to not add the aggression of my own reactivity. And, instead, make a little more space in my heart to listen more deeply.

~

I have never wept more than during the years of interviewing. These men are trying to hold onto something true. A whole part of their humanness that gets denied or covered over because we're all participating in saying, "No. Men can't have that gentleness, that tender-heartedness, that vulnerability."

Well, why not?

Who made up this story and what keeps us all passing it on? A stream of sorrow under the anger and violence.

The pain that boys have endured, when they are supported in feeling it, staying with the discomfort without getting caught up in it, *is* their reservoir of empathy and compassion—connecting them to everyone and everything. Seeds of peace.

I have a new appreciation for the courage of tenderness it takes for boys to be who they are in the midst of all the ideas about what it is to "be a man." These boys and men, even after trauma and betrayal, were willing to let me come and ask all these questions and share their experience with me.

They were *eager* to talk! The more they said, the more they wanted to say. Some men called back and wanted to do an update interview, or have me interview someone they knew. I often heard, "I've never said this before." A nine-year-old, who had stopped by the apartment where I was interviewing his best friend, joined right in. When I was getting ready to leave, he looked at me, eyes expectant, and said, "This is cool. So, are we gonna do this every week now?"

When I asked the question "Who do you feel is the most important man in your life?" many men felt they *should* say their dad, but they didn't. I was heartened to hear that, in general, the guys under twenty were finding more help navigating other ways to be a man. Sometimes from their fathers, and often from men who have already been living more gracefully and empathetically, from a more inclusive awareness of what it means to "be a man." And they're becoming the kind of fathers they wish they'd had.

Some men asked—"What's the way out?" More than a few men asked—"What are the other men saying?" They really wanted to know. Like me, they seemed to wonder—how do others do this mysterious life? And, what do we have in common?

I was stopped by this last question, finding it hard to imagine a woman asking this about other women. We would be more likely to know what we have in common. And, if not, we could more easily ask another woman. In this regard, the current culture has been kinder to us. We have each other to talk to.

Could it be that the traditional concept of "being a man" is one of the first traumas of a boy's life? And is it killing life?

≈

"I've been in recovery from being a man," a 63-year-old told me. There are a lot of stories of men who have done some kind of recovery work in these pages because often these are the ones who have found language for what they'd had no words for. I noticed several things they shared: In a place of safety, they told the truth. They found out they weren't alone. With honesty comes trust; with trust, intimacy. They felt support and connection and learned tools and skills to use in their daily lives. No one to blame; everyone 100% responsible. A big exhale.

Underneath all that learned "manhood," I heard an often frightened and confused boy, longing to recover the wonder and aliveness of a boy—*just being myself.* The freedom that comes from being what we are, as we are, right now. Back to the freshness—the joy of being a boy, ripened. The light in children's eyes.

Why would anyone ever give that up?

~

The more I listened, the more tenderness I felt and the more trust I heard. A kind of universal trust. Often too ordinary to notice and appreciate. It's very close to us. We use it all the time. The purr of the world, when we don't resist. Truly, we don't know what's going to happen on any given day. You know, we get up in the morning, swing our legs over the bed, put our feet on the floor and stand up to start our day. We're trusting that there's a floor to stand on, air to breathe; the sun comes up, our heart beats . . . and a whole day stretches out before us.

The trust is already here.

If we're lucky, something happens that lets us notice. A gap between the stories we're telling ourselves where the light of something larger shines through. A little opening, room to see what's here when we're not taking ourselves too seriously. As Wavy Gravy, a hero of mine, says, "If you don't have a sense of humor, it just isn't funny any more."

Hiking together up a trail in the Sangre de Cristo mountains, a former CEO of a Silicon Valley tech company, now in his early 70s, spoke to me about wanting a new kind of "warrior." He was tired, worn out from the role he'd been expected to play. He recited to me this stanza from a poem by Hafiz:

> *The warrior*
> *Wisely sits in a circle*
> *With other men*
> *Gathering the strength to unmask*
> *Himself.*

Out of openness, kindness comes. Ordinary as morning. It's just common sense. Like the hand feeding the mouth. We take care of what we love, what we let ourselves be touched by.

This is the most common voice I heard: weary of the facade, wanting to be real, be themselves—relaxing back into the spacious heart of the boy, already connected and so very alive.

≈

When I started this inquiry, I thought I might figure something out. What actually happened was simpler. I got to listen. Listening was its own answer, melting my heart and widening my sense of what it is to be alive on this earth at this exciting and dire time.

What if the intelligence of fear is bringing out the best of us? Waking us up to pay attention and question the world we've created, to *feel* our fear and sadness, our grief—human, not male or female—our *mutual* vulnerability. Such profound uncertainty and fear can open our hearts and imaginations to feel what another feels and enjoy the freedom of trying on different views. Not tilting off into hope, not wallowing in fear, but willing to look at what's *right here*, and so have the clarity to see and the energy to do what needs to be done

Aren't we all vulnerable all the time? All of us in a boat with a hole in it, headed out to sea. Climate change makes more obvious what has always been true. We don't know what's going to happen next. *That's* the aliveness! And the source of creativity. Listening can be an antidote to fear. "Maybe solutions come around when you're more empathetic," a man in his 70s said. "A profound change of heart may be our most important survival skill." A mind that knows no enemy.

Out of the decay of the patriarchal experiment, a wide array of seeds are sprouting — seeds of possibility, of something we've never seen before. This violence against ourselves and all forms of life that we call climate change is showing us how out of balance we've become. One Big Mis-Understanding. It's only natural, as women are learning to do the things that men have traditionally done, that men are beginning to learn the things that women have traditionally done. We have so much to learn from one another. We're each then free to choose who we want to be and how we want to live in equal partnership with life, treating all beings with respect and reverence.

For me, that means being the person I found I needed to be when I was listening. And now, speaking up. We need all of us and the boundless resourcefulness, resilience and creativity of that boy (and that girl!) — "that limitlessness" — more than ever. The wonder that comes from paying attention to the world as it is, not as we think it is.

"Tay appention! Tay appention!" My four-year-old daughter would shout at me whenever I seemed to her to be anywhere else. And when she had yanked me back from dreaming and wishing and hoping and was certain — stone sure — I would not wobble again, she'd smile that satisfied grin, turn on her toes, and merrily trot off with me, reeled in and blessed to be in her wake.

Maybe this is what children are asking of us often pre-occupied adults, lost in our own thoughts and stories. Be present. Join me *here* where the play of life is happening. Fresh, * A l i v e *

Joy—that most vulnerable of feelings—is available at any moment.

When I asked, "What are three words to describe women?" a man in his 40s responded—"Just like me." In the depths of our hearts, we all want the same things—to be *all* of ourselves, fully human, fully alive.

How we care for one another or not *is* climate change. In this ever more crowded boat, the only thing that makes sense is kindness.

≈

What have I learned? What do I know now? Mostly, how little I know. Nothing suddenly solved. Glorious, messy, unfigureoutable life!

For me, it's been more of an un-doing, an un-learning—a wearing out of a lot of my ideas and assumptions. Leaving more room for not knowing. And for seeing these beautiful boys and men freshly, *as they are*.

Everywhere I go now, I see men differently.

"To live is so startling it leaves little time for anything else."

— EMILY DICKINSON

ACKNOWLEDGEMENTS

BOY is completely a collaboration. Being new at this book-making business, I needed a lot of help!

My deep appreciation starts with all the brave and courageous boys and men who shared their stories with me. I continue to learn from all of you. Whether or not your specific story appears in this book, I hope you find some part of yourself in these pages. As the readers and editors will attest, the hardest part for me has been cutting any of the voices. From the bottom of my heart, thank you. I am forever grateful. Especially for the men who did not live to see this book in print.

When my neighbor, whom I had met only once, heard what I was up to, she called me up and asked if she could interview me about what I was learning. Thank you to Kim Chernin for her curiosity. She has truly midwifed this book with her patience, endurance, and seasoned skills, keeping me company throughout most of the journey—as listener and questioner, unflagging supporter, dear friend and finally, an editor.

Toby Campion, another friend and ally, listened again to my listening—with his playwright's ear, editor's eye and kind heart—and helped shape and give story to many of the voices.

So many hands and eyes have helped with different iterations of this manuscript, each adding their feedback and flavor: Hal Clifford, who started the whittling of what we affectionately called "The Heap," Ariane Conrad, Shams Kairys, Sam Scott, Kai Barry, Iris Campion, Julie Searle, Renate Stendhal, Tom Callanan, Linda Sparrow, Jim Keogh, Alison Owings, Suzanne Sherman. And those who generously helped by reading different versions or parts, questioning, encouraging or supporting: Cathy Scott, Mark Dowie, Tracy Gary, Yoshiko Chino, John Tarrant, Susan Tillett, Terry Boyer, Gail Jardine, Richard Kirschman, Mike Schwartzman, Doris Ober, Sura Hart, Albert Miller, Nick Slugocki.

Boundless thanks for inspiring and educating me and opening possibilities along the way: Mary Harper, Sonja Margulies, Carol Gilligan, Cheryl Strayed, Caroline Casey, Donna Garske, David Lisak, Kathy Barbini, Howard Fradkin, Richard Gartner. And offering support and quiet places to work: Craig & Heidi Schindler,

Michael Broome & Patty Kavaletti, Terry & Peter Boyer, Roxanne & Jerry & Sadie & Sydney Foley, Bruce Tobias, Dania Moss, Marjie Findlay & Geoff Freeman.

For friendship, support and gifts that played a part in the birthing of this book: Jim Gimian, Patty Clarke, Anna Lappé, Frankie Lappé, Pat & Larry Sargent, Carolyn Clebsch, Susan Berman, Cornelia Durrant, Peter Barnes, Carol Merrill, Lorraine Fisher-Smith, Carolyn Crosby, Leezie Borden, Ruby Fisher-Smith, Olivia Fisher-Smith. And for their kindness and help in keeping my spirit and body going: Teresa Black, Judi Reichart, Jeannie Kerrigan, Anita Acevedo, Rosanne Kho, Helen Knight.

Without Stephen Bowers and his astonishing cyber know-how this virtual neophyte could not have continued. He patiently kept me going—a *zillion* times—when my computer had a mind of its own and only he knew what to do. A huge thank you to Maryellen Zedlar with her big heart and amazing team and to Terri and the wonderfully helpful people at Avatar's.

Barbara & Gene Bullock-Wilson graciously let me use the photograph on the cover, taken by her father, that has been hanging on my kitchen wall and inspiring me for decades. Once I realized these interviews were becoming a book, it was the *only* cover I could imagine. Sandro Michahelles, Michelle Feileacan, Olivier Follmi, Heather Frandsen, Skip O'Donnell, Miranda Medina, Ina Von, Wazari Wazir, Mara Blom Schantz, Ana Stewart—their photographs say more than I can. Thank you for how you see. And to the anonymous photographer of the first photo in the book whom I haven't been able to track down—if you happen to see this book, please let me know!

Valerie Brewster and her remarkable patience and wizardry helped turn it all into that beautiful thing you're holding in your hands.

My wildest admiration for Kai Barry and Coeylen Barry who, with all young people, are the future and already way out ahead.

And always, my profound gratitude for all the wildernesses that have held me and sustained me, without fail, through some pretty stark and challenging times. The sanity of the wild.

Thank you all for this ongoing conversation.